Knowledge Management and Organizational Learning

Volume 8

Series Editors
Ettore Bolisani, Padova, Italy
Meliha Handzic, Sarajevo, Bosnia and Herzegovina

This series is introduced by the International Association for Knowledge Management (www.IAKM.net) with an aim to offer advanced peer-reviewed reference books to researchers, practitioners and students in the field of knowledge management in organizations. Both discussions of new theories and advances in the field, as well as reviews of the state-of-the art will be featured regularly. Particularly, the books will be open to these contributions: Reviews of the state-of-the art (i.e. syntheses of recent studies on a topic, classifications and discussions of theories, approaches and methods, etc.) that can both serve as a reference and allow opening new horizons Discussions on new theories and methods of scientific research in organisational knowledge management Critical reviews of empirical evidence and empirical validations of theories Contributions that build a bridge between the various disciplines and fields that converge towards knowledge management (i.e.: computer science, cognitive sciences, economics, other management fields, etc.) and propose the development of a common background of notions, concepts and scientific methods Surveys of new practical methods that can inspire practitioners and researchers in their applications of knowledge management methods in companies and public services.

More information about this series at http://www.springer.com/series/11850

Monica Fedeli • Laura L. Bierema
Editors

Connecting Adult Learning and Knowledge Management

Strategies for Learning and Change in Higher Education and Organizations

Editors
Monica Fedeli
University of Padua
Padua, Italy

Laura L. Bierema
University of Georgia
Athens, GA, USA

ISSN 2199-8663   ISSN 2199-8671   (electronic)
Knowledge Management and Organizational Learning
ISBN 978-3-030-29874-6   ISBN 978-3-030-29872-2   (eBook)
https://doi.org/10.1007/978-3-030-29872-2

© Springer Nature Switzerland AG 2019
This work is subject to copyright. All rights are reserved by the Publisher, whether the whole or part of the material is concerned, specifically the rights of translation, reprinting, reuse of illustrations, recitation, broadcasting, reproduction on microfilms or in any other physical way, and transmission or information storage and retrieval, electronic adaptation, computer software, or by similar or dissimilar methodology now known or hereafter developed.
The use of general descriptive names, registered names, trademarks, service marks, etc. in this publication does not imply, even in the absence of a specific statement, that such names are exempt from the relevant protective laws and regulations and therefore free for general use.
The publisher, the authors, and the editors are safe to assume that the advice and information in this book are believed to be true and accurate at the date of publication. Neither the publisher nor the authors or the editors give a warranty, expressed or implied, with respect to the material contained herein or for any errors or omissions that may have been made. The publisher remains neutral with regard to jurisdictional claims in published maps and institutional affiliations.

This Springer imprint is published by the registered company Springer Nature Switzerland AG.
The registered company address is: Gewerbestrasse 11, 6330 Cham, Switzerland

Marketing Text
This multidisciplinary book is the first attempt at connecting adult learning and knowledge management in theory and practice. This volume equips faculty, learners, and professionals of organizational development with new strategies and resources to develop active and effective pedagogy for preparing learners and practitioners to manage knowledge in organizations and higher education. This book collects contributions and case studies from a diverse set of authors worldwide and provides a theoretical and practical outline of new strategies and methods for facilitating adult teaching and learning. It also provides a fresh reading of active learning methods, by adopting a knowledge management viewpoint that is applicable, whether helping students master content in university courses or helping organizations learn and change.
The book is divided into three parts: Part I—Adult teaching and learning methods and theories; Part II—Knowledge

management in education; and Part III— Case studies and best practices that consider classroom learning, higher education change, and organization development.

Acknowledgment

We want to thank Fulbright for helping us to create this book by providing a context for great collaboration and initiating a warm and lasting friendship between us!

Monica and Laura

Introduction

Learning is the process of acquiring knowledge through programmed instruction, experience, study, or trial and error. Knowledge is ideas and skills attained through learning. Learning and knowledge are *not* synonyms. They are complementary processes needed by both individuals and organizations so they can thrive. Learners and organizations do not necessarily meet their goals when learning occurs. Learning must translate into knowledge that is created and shared with others and applied to improve lives and organizations. Dependable knowledge is imperative for people and organizations to build mutual relationships, identify wise choices, make good decisions, and solve challenging problems. Providing outstanding learning opportunities is not enough. The task is to help learners and organizations translate and transform learning into new knowledge that informs private, public, and professional spheres of adulthood and organization life.

This volume explores and connects two main themes: adult learning and knowledge management related to people and organizational development. It is divided into three main parts. The first part focuses on adult learning and its applications in different contexts. The second part develops the concept of knowledge management and its practices. The last parts presents four case studies demonstrating how knowledge can be developed and applied through active learning and teaching strategies in higher education and in adult education. Contributions collected in this volume propose interpretative frameworks, innovative teaching practices, and original case studies centered on fusing *adult education, higher education, and knowledge management*, in ways that promote human and organizational development and support professional development.

As coeditors of this volume, we took on the task of setting the stage for exploration and discussion by authoring and coauthoring five chapters. The challenge we faced in curating this volume was to create an international, multidisciplinary group of scholars representing diverse disciplines spanning pedagogy, engineering, and economics. Authors were invited to contribute to the topics and intersections of adult learning and knowledge management and introduce readers to innovative practices and strategies for learning and change in multiple contexts.

Chapter "Adult Learning Theories and Practices," by Laura L. Bierema, defines and introduces a framework of adult learning that focuses on the educators, learners, processes, contexts, and methods that contribute to adult learning in formal education. Effective teaching is critical in an age where problems are difficult to solve and require deep learning and collaboration. Bierema continues her focus on formal learning in chapter "Incorporating Active Learning into Your Educational Repertoire" with her discussion of how educators can shift away from instructor-centered education and embrace pedagogical alternatives to make learning more engaging, participative, and enduring so as to better support knowledge creation. Active learning is defined with recommended activities to involve learners. Strategies for improving participation and learning are presented that are grounded in adult learning principles. In chapter "Linking Faculty to Organization Development and Change: Teaching4Learning@Unipd," Monica Fedeli considers improving teaching and learning through faculty development. She profiles the program *Teaching4Learning@Unipd* as a strategy for using faculty development to impact organization development and create a higher education culture that promotes optional learning. She offers strategic actions and practices to promote change and research linked to faculty and organization development. Chapter "Student–Teacher Relationships: The Elephant in the Classroom" features Edward W. Taylor on the importance of teacher–student relationships. He explores the complexities that confound and confront student–teacher relationships and what is known empirically about their impact on learning and introduces key theoretical frameworks and core constructs used to make sense of these relationships, including the connection between knowledge management in the classroom and teacher–student relationships. Chapter "Linking Active Learning and Capstone Projects in Higher Education," by Tullio Vardanega and Monica Fedeli, presents multi-year experience of running a capstone project in a bachelor's degree program in computer science, at the University of Padua, Italy, designed and implemented using interactive learning methods. This study supports the fact that active learning strategies create a very productive context for better teaching and learning.

The last two chapters of the first section aim to speculate on strategies related to organizational development. Chapter "Teaching for Globalization: Implications for Knowledge Management in Organizations," by Maria Cseh, Oliver S. Crocco, and Chilanay Safarli, focuses on globalization in teaching and working and how systems should consider how adults with various national and ethnic backgrounds learn and share knowledge. The authors argue that learning and knowledge management can be enhanced by incorporating both the professional and technical knowledge in organizations and the diversity of thought and worldviews held among employees. They discuss the perspectives of global systems thinking and global mindset and how to cultivate this global system in teaching for globalization. Chapter "Knowledge Management for Organizational Success: Valuing Diversity and Inclusion Across Stakeholders, Structures, and Sectors," the final chapter of the first section, by Tomika Greer and Toby Egan, offers knowledge management as a core source of energy for any organization, arguing it is a critical element for organizational survival in our increasingly dynamic world. The authors promote the use of communities of practice as a tool to leverage human diversity and structural diversity to optimize knowledge management and improve organizational outcomes in a variety of organizational contexts. This chapter connects the first and the second part of this volume linking adult learning, communities of practice, and knowledge management.

Part II of the book begins with chapter "Knowledge Management: Theories and Practices" by John S. Edwards on knowledge management and its history over the last 30 years. The author reviews theories and practices that have developed under that name placing emphasis on the links between knowledge management and learning and on the area known as personal knowledge management. He discusses knowledge management practices using the three aspects of people, process, and technology. In chapter "Using Social Networks and Communities of Practice to Promote Staff Collaboration in Higher Education," Niall Corcoran and Aidan Duane address the use of community-based knowledge management techniques, such as using communities of practice to manage knowledge, particularly when coupled with enterprise social networks to create online communities. The lack of community of higher education institutions has led to a breakdown of collaboration and knowledge sharing among staff. A number of strategies for practice and specific tactical approaches for organizations to use are presented. Chapter "Knowledge Management for Adult and Higher Education: Mapping the Recent Literature," by Ettore Bolisani, is the last chapter of the second part and presents a recent literature review on connecting knowledge management to adult and higher education. The author argues that knowledge management concepts, models, and practices may be beneficial to teachers, learners, and university managers. This chapter proposes a systematic analysis of the literature to shed light on the intersection between the fields of knowledge management and adult and higher education. The main research trends are detected and highlighted. The analysis shows that there are promising applications of knowledge management to higher education and university management.

The third and last part of this volume presents four case studies that aim to connect learning practices in higher education that develop knowledge management and knowledge sharing among staff, students, and university managers with the aim of fostering teaching and learning for change. Chapter "Sharing Active Learning Practices to Improve Teaching: Peer Observation of Active Teaching in a School of Engineering," by Stefano Ghidoni, Monica Fedeli, and Massimiliano Barolo, presents the successful faculty development program *Teaching4Learning@Unipd* and how it fosters collaboration among instructors. Paralleling these activities, the school of engineering developed a "peer observation of active teaching" (POAT) process which was conceptualized, designed, and tested in a small group and finally proposed to the entire community of engineering instructors through a call for volunteers. The chapter presents how the POAT process was developed and put into practice and discusses some lessons learned after one year of experimentation. Chapter "Comparative Studies, the Experience of COMPALL Winter School," by Monika Staab and Regina Egetenmeyer, focuses on comparative studies presenting the project Erasmus+ Strategic Partnership "Comparative Studies in Adult

Education and Lifelong Learning—COMPALL" which developed a joint module in study programs related to adult education and lifelong learning. Through its innovative teaching and study program, which is based on blended learning mobility, COMPALL became a forum for knowledge sharing and creation. Over three years, seven European universities designed innovative learning and teaching strategies that foster the exchange of knowledge, cultural understanding, and knowledge creation by conducting comparative research. Chapter "Fostering Knowledge Sharing Via Technology: A Case Study of Collaborative Learning Using *Padlet*," by Daniela Frison and Concetta Tino, describes a collaborative learning experience in higher education carried out through the use of the additional collaborative tool *Padlet.* The authors present the design process of an online activity based on the use of Padlet, an online whiteboard that offers space for multiple participants to collaborate in real time. Students' feedback about the Padlet experience has been collected and analyzed. The last chapter, "The Peer Observation: "Mentore" Project at University of Palermo," by Marcella Cannarozzo, Pierluigi Gallo, Alida Lo Coco, Bartolomeo Megna, Pasquale Musso, and Onofrio Scialdone, shares a faculty development project of the University of Palermo called "MENTORE" ("Modifying and ENhancing Teaching through peer Observation and Reflections with Experts"). The objectives of the project are to help teachers improve their teaching, through the help of two mentors; to experiment new approaches in pilot courses to extend, if useful, to other ones; and to change the traditional model of academic teaching based on one single teacher with the class to go toward a model where there is a group of teachers working together in search of improvements. This chapter describes the aforementioned peer observation practice adopted at the University of Palermo and focuses on the role of mentors describing their activities during the peer observation process.

This international, multidisciplinary book represents a first attempt at connecting the fields of adult learning and knowledge management in theory and practice, collecting chapters from diverse authors, and highlighting the different perspectives of research and practices to equip professionals, instructors, academic managers, and learners with new strategies to teach and learn and innovative resources to prepare managers to create and manage knowledge in organizations and in higher education. We are pleased to offer this volume that connects adult learning and knowledge management and hope it inspires readers to improve lives and organizations.

University of Padua, Padua, Italy   Monica Fedeli
University of Georgia, Athens, GA,   Laura L. Bierema
USA

Contents

Part I Adult Teaching and Learning Methods and Theories

Adult Learning Theories and Practices 3
Laura L. Bierema

Incorporating Active Learning into Your Educational Repertoire 27
Laura L. Bierema

**Linking Faculty to Organization Development and Change:
Teaching4Learning@Unipd** 51
Monica Fedeli

Student–Teacher Relationships: The Elephant in the Classroom 69
Edward W. Taylor

**Linking Active Learning and Capstone Projects in Higher
Education** 85
Tullio Vardanega and Monica Fedeli

**Teaching for Globalization: Implications for Knowledge Management
in Organizations** 105
Maria Cseh, Oliver S. Crocco, and Chilanay Safarli

**Knowledge Management for Organizational Success: Valuing Diversity
and Inclusion Across Stakeholders, Structures, and Sectors** 119
Tomika W. Greer and Toby M. Egan

Part II Knowledge Management in Education

Knowledge Management: Theories and Practices 139
John S. Edwards

**Using Social Networks and Communities of Practice to Promote
Staff Collaboration in Higher Education** 157
Niall Corcoran and Aidan Duane

xiii

Knowledge Management for Adult and Higher Education: Mapping the Recent Literature 175
Ettore Bolisani

Part III Case Studies and Best Practices That Consider Classroom Learning, Higher Education Change, and Organization Development

Sharing Active Learning Practices to Improve Teaching: Peer Observation of Active Teaching in a School of Engineering 199
Stefano Ghidoni, Monica Fedeli, and Massimiliano Barolo

Comparative Studies, the Experience of COMPALL Winter School 215
Monika Staab and Regina Egetenmeyer

Fostering Knowledge Sharing Via Technology: A Case Study of Collaborative Learning Using *Padlet* 227
Daniela Frison and Concetta Tino

The Peer Observation: "Mentore" Project at University of Palermo 237
Marcella Cannarozzo, Pierluigi Gallo, Alida Lo Coco, Bartolomeo Megna, Pasquale Musso, and Onofrio Scialdone

About the Editors

Monica Fedeli is Associate Professor at the University of Padova. Her past academic experience includes adjunct professorships at the Michigan State University (USA), California University Berkeley School of Education (USA), and at Julius Maximilians University of Wurzburg (Germany).

She designs and delivers programs focused on organizational development and change, workplace learning, faculty development, teaching and learning methods in adult education, and gender equity. She has published more than 100 articles in a variety of national and international journals and in a variety of book series and has authored, coauthored, or edited four books including *Coinvolgere per Apprendere: Metodi e Tecniche per la Formazione*. She is a 2020 Fulbright Research Scholar at the University of Georgia, USA.

Laura L. Bierema is a Professor of Adult Learning, Leadership & Organization Development at the University of Georgia (USA). She designs and delivers programs focused on learning, leadership, and change in corporations, nonprofit, healthcare, government, and higher education. Her research interests include workplace learning, career development, women's leadership, organization development, executive coaching, and critical human resource development. She has published over 60 articles that have appeared in both research and professional publications and has authored, coauthored, or edited 6 books including *Adult Learning: Linking Theory and Practice*. Prof. Bierema is the winner of two "book-of-the-year" awards in 2015 and most recently was a 2018 US Fulbright Research Scholar at the University of Padova, Italy.

Part I
Adult Teaching and Learning Methods and Theories

Adult Learning Theories and Practices

Laura L. Bierema

Abstract The purpose of this chapter is to introduce the theory and practice of adult learning. The chapter defines adult learning and introduces a framework of adult learning (Bierema, *Strategic approaches towards curriculum development for adult learners in the global community,* pp. 7–33, 2008; Merriam & Bierema, *Adult learning: Bridging theory and practice,* 2014) that focuses on the educators, learners, processes, contexts, and methods that make up adult learning. Effective teaching is critical in an age where problems are difficult to solve and require deep learning and collaboration. Creating powerful formal instruction is easier and more impactful with an understanding of adult learning theory and how to translate it into meaningful practice to enhance learning.

Speaking a new language, navigating an unknown city, dealing with illness, listening to a friend's concern, dialoguing about a complex issue, making a self-discovery, attending a lecture, and uncovering an answer: these are ways adults learn. Learning is like breathing—you need it to live, and without it you die. Adults are learning constantly, whether engaged in formal instruction, such as attending a class, or experiencing informal learning, such as observing the power dynamics between colleagues at work.

The purpose of this chapter is to introduce the theory and practice of adult learning. The chapter defines adult learning and introduces a framework of adult learning (Bierema, 2008; Merriam & Bierema, 2014) that focuses on the educators, learners, processes, contexts, and methods that make up adult learning.

L. L. Bierema (✉)
University of Georgia, Athens, GA, USA
e-mail: bierema@uga.edu

© Springer Nature Switzerland AG 2019
M. Fedeli, L. L. Bierema (eds.), *Connecting Adult Learning and Knowledge Management*, Knowledge Management and Organizational Learning 8,
https://doi.org/10.1007/978-3-030-29872-2_1

1 Defining Adult Learning

Adult learning might be the most overlooked learning process across the lifespan. We tend to focus on the learning of children as they advance through primary and secondary school and later learning associated with vocational or higher education as young adults prepare for the workforce. Yet, adults are learning throughout their lives as they take new jobs, manage relationships, make mistakes, change careers, relocate cities, travel abroad, experience grief, attempt new challenges, and so forth. In fact, adulthood is not so much age-based as it is responsibility-based. You might know people who are chronologically adult, although they behave like children. Other people might carry sobering responsibilities at a young age and thus be considered more "adult" than an older person and be described as "wise beyond her years." By adult learning, we mean learning engaged in by individuals who have adult-type responsibilities in life such as caring for dependents, managing a household, holding a job, and being an engaged citizen. The following sections focus on key characteristics of adult learning to help further define the phenomenon.

1.1 Adult Learning Is Distinguishable from Children's Learning

Adult learning is distinguishable from children's learning in at least three ways: (1) reflective capacity, (2) experience, and (3) critical thinking. *Reflective capacity* is an adult's ability to hold contrary thoughts and examine them simultaneously: for example, reviewing the platform of opposing political parties and while assessing the merits of each. Also known as reflection or inquiry, this process of thinking engages the learner in not simply questioning assumptions behind our ideas "I'm an environmentalist—what does that mean I believe in?" but also assessing the quality of your learning, also known as metalearning: "How open am I to other views on environmental issues?" or "What assumptions do I hold that underlie my beliefs?" Next, adults have a rich repertoire of *experiences* that have taught them lessons and helped them develop values and assumptions about the world. For example: career experience helps adults build expertise in their profession and contribute to their organization in a valuable way. This same experience, however, can also make adults inflexible to consider alternative ways to do their work or accept "out-of-the-box" thinking on problems they are trying to solve. Thus, experience can be a double-edged sword in that it enables adults to use their prior learning to do their work but also prohibits them from accepting ideas or assumptions that are contrary to their experience. Finally, adult learning is distinctive due to adult's ability to engage in *critical thinking*. Critical thinking involves the ability to recognize and test assumptions, beliefs, and actions. It is also the capacity to assume a position or change is based on evidence, show open-mindedness, seek to understand problems and their complexities, show sensitivity to the knowledge and feeling of others, and use credible sources (Merriam & Bierema, 2014, p. 223).

A popular model of adult learning was developed by Knowles (1970) who is sometimes referred to as "the father of adult learning." Knowles popularized the notion of andragogy—literally the art of teaching men [sic], although he advanced the idea as the art of teaching adults. Andragogy was a contrast to traditional teacher-dependent, subject-centered instruction where the learner was viewed as an empty vessel to fill with knowledge. Knowles advanced ideas that the learner is self-directed and internally motivated to seek learning when it is relevant and timely to their life and work and that their experience serves as a rich resource for learning. The principles of andragogy are useful for making educational experiences learner-friendly, although the model has been critiqued for not translating well across cultures and ignoring the processes of learning (Rachal, 2002; Sandlin, 2005).

1.2 Learning Helps Adults Cope with Change

Change is often an impetus for learning in adulthood, and few changes can be mastered without learning and few lessons can be lasting without change. Change can be either planned (you plan to go to graduate school or change jobs) or it can be unplanned (you get fired, a relationship ends, or you have an unexpected failure). Whether planned or unplanned, change creates identity crises and may force adults to question who they are, what they want, and whom they can really trust. Change may also spur reflection on what they are giving back to others. One of the oldest and best-known models of change was Lewin's (1947) model of unfreezing–moving–refreezing. Essentially, change cannot happen until there is a thaw—an *unfreezing* or shift of mind, circumstances, or relationships. *Movement* represents the transformation to a new way of thinking or being, and finally *refreezing* involves the measures adults take to ensure the change's permanence. For example, let's say you do not achieve a hoped-for promotion and receive feedback that you lack the ideal leadership skills and interpersonal savvy (unfreezing), so you decide to hire an executive coach and attempt to be a stronger, more compassionate leader (moving) and finally create accountability measures and evaluation checks to ensure the new leadership and interpersonal behaviors stick (refreezing).

1.3 Adult Learning Is Life-Centered

Few adults are motivated to sign up for a parenting class, unless they are planning to welcome a new child into their lives. In the previous example, the aspiring promotion seeker was not motivated to seek help with leadership and interpersonal skills until they became aware the issues were holding them back in their career. These examples underscore that adults are not usually motivated to learn something unless it is relevant to their life or work. Think about your own learning in the past year. Was it relevant to concerns related to work or life? Probably few of us would sign up for organic chemistry courses once established in our careers, but we might enthusiastically take beer making or baking classes. Adult learners tend to crave learning that helps them manage life roles and responsibilities more effectively. In other words, they are problem-centered. Children's learning tends to be content-centered (doing math), whereas adults seek learning to solve problems (doing taxes). Additionally, adult learning is usually sought when the time is appropriate. For instance, I have a colleague who moved to the UK and lived there for years using public transportation and not possessing a driver's license until she needed the flexibility of having her own car to transport her cats to specialized veterinary care. Suddenly hiring a driving teacher and signing up for the test were both relevant and timely in her life.

1.4 Experience Is a Key Learning Asset

Mina Thomas Antrim (1902) once observed, "Experience is a good teacher, but she sends terrific bills" (p. 99). As mentioned earlier, sometimes adults' experience creates a barrier to learning when adults are suspect of new ways of thinking or doing that don't align with previous success. Although that is true, experience is usually a rich resource for learning between adults. A key task for educators is to help learners integrate the new learning with current knowledge, evaluate new ideas against current knowledge, and identify ways the new knowledge overlaps with current knowledge. Excellent learning facilitators create opportunities for adults to share and compare experiences.

1.5 Teaching Should Be Both Learner- and Learning-Centered

Often adult education texts focus on ways to make learners comfortable and honor their experience and knowledge—learner-centered. These are very important features of effective adult learning where respect for individuals and sensitivity to their needs are paramount. Yet, adults learn best when they are respectfully challenged to engage in critical thinking or do things they are afraid to try—learning-centered. Great adult educators find the sweet spot of high respect and high challenge— learning- *and* learner-centered (Bilimoria & Wheeler, 1995). Educators move the spotlight away from themselves as the knowledge source and shift it to the learners, fitting with the adult learning adage to strive to be the "guide on the side" not the "sage on the stage."

1.6 Adult Learners Tend to Be Risk-Averse

Adults may be cautious in learning settings, particularly when they do not feel safe. They tend to seek preservation of self-esteem and maintenance of self-efficacy. This means that adults fear making mistakes and looking "stupid" in front of their peers. Instructors can be sensitive to this fear by avoiding "cold calling" learners to give answers and participate. Inviting engagement is a better way to build rapport with learners and help them feel comfortable participating actively with other learners. Learners will feel more at ease when thought and attention have been given to developing a supportive learning community among learners where it is safe to share and make mistakes.

1.7 Learning Should Be Active and Self-Directed

Most of us can readily recall mind-numbing, boring lectures that have been endured throughout our educational experience. Yet, as much relied upon and loved as the lecture is by faculty, there are more effective ways of ensuring that learning is impactful and lasting. Engaging learners in active learning such as discussions, practice, or teaching others has been shown to be superior to passive learning activities such as lecture, reading, or demonstration. The majority of learning adults engage in is self-directed, that is, the learner plans, controls, adjusts, and evaluates the learning themselves (Hiemstra, 1994). For example, imagine you were seeking to improve your golf game. You might read books, watch videos, take a lesson, observe friends, and get tips as you play. As the learner, you have designed and implemented the learning plan. There is an entire chapter in this book dedicated to active learning where you can learn key strategies and design principles for making learning more engaging and lasting.

1.8 Learning Is Potentially Transformational

Learning and change are intertwined and sometimes learning can change the essence of a person. This type of learning is not adding to the repertoire of skills or knowledge learners build but rather shifts how a person sees themselves in the world (Taylor, 2008). For instance, a woman professional may not be conscious of gendered power relations in her organization until she begins to notice that no one pays attention to her ideas until they are repeated by a man. Suddenly she begins to notice how women are marginalized in the organization and becomes more interested in feminism. Transformative learning is grounded in change and change-producing learning. It does not change the information we know, but rather it changes how we see ourselves. Transformative learning can be gradual or sudden. It was gradual in the case of the woman professional whose ideas were ignored and would be sudden in the event of a tragedy, crisis, or major life transition. Transformative learning can be a desirable outcome of education, although it is not easily designed for or predictable. Transformative learning is also impacted by feelings, relationships, context, and culture.

1.9 Experience as a Learner Shapes How Teachers Teach

People tend to teach like they have been taught and can be resistant to shifting teaching methodology. Perhaps that is why the lecture is overused as an educational method, because it has been a dominant teaching tool throughout history. Alternatives to the lecture are presented in chapter "Incorporating Active Learning into Your Educational Repertoire" of this textbook. Effective educators are willing to experiment and try different approaches to teaching their content. This might mean developing interactive lectures or active learning that engages learners in reflection, group process, critical thinking, and applied learning. Instructors also tend to over-rely on teaching methods they prefer personally, which means they are missing opportunities to reach all learners who may prefer to learn in different ways. To be more effective as educators, instructors need to strive for greater balance of different pedagogies and instructional methods as are discussed in this chapter and chapter "Incorporating Active Learning into Your Educational Repertoire".

This section has defined adult learning and key characteristics of adult learners. The next section provides a framework that provides a historical and theoretical overview of adult learning. Practical strategies for facilitating effective adult learning are also presented.

2 A Framework of Adult Learning

Adult learning theory has a rich history dating to the early twentieth century. Using a framework helps understand the development of the field and various facets of adult learning (Bierema, 2008; Merriam & Bierema, 2014). The framework consists of the educator, learner, process, context, and method. It melds key issues and ideas together to value the processes of adult learning and teaching and bridge theory and practice. The framework considers educators and how their values and presence impact the learning process. It also reveres learners and strives to understand their motivations, challenges, and goals. The framework also addresses the process of learning—how learning happens and how to best foster it among diverse learners.

Next, the framework acknowledges the context or location of learning and how power dynamics impact individuals, groups, and systems of learning. Finally, the framework integrates the educator, the learner, the process, and the context in planning educational programs that facilitate optimal learning for diverse learners.

2.1 The Educator: The Who

Much of adult learning literature focuses on learners and developing pedagogy that resonates with their goals and needs. The other players who have a major impact on the design and delivery of formal education are the *educators* themselves, who tend to be ignored in discussions of teaching and learning. Yet, educators have a significant impact on formal learning and their self-awareness, mindset, and well-being directly affect the quality of instruction.

Self-Awareness Educators are at their best when they have deep self-understanding and are engaged in continual self-exploration. Part of self-exploration is understanding what drives you as an educator. Figuring this out can take some time. A helpful process used in executive coaching is the self-guided process from Corbett and Chloupek (2019) to find what they called your "Why It Matters." For example, my why it matters is "to challenge." You can see that driver in how I teach, advise, and push learners outside their comfort zones. Yet, some students are not up to continual challenge, and everyone has different learning edges. Diverse learners need to be challenged in varied ways and not all have the same tolerance to be pushed by activities and assignments. This means knowing myself and my learners to best serve them. Self-awareness was beautifully captured by Parker Palmer in his 1998 book, *The Courage to Teach*:

> Teaching, like any truly human activity, emerges from one's inwardness, for better or worse. As I teach, I project the condition of my soul onto my students, my subject, and our way of being together. The entanglements I experience in the classroom are often no more or less than the convolutions of my inner life. Viewed from this angle, teaching holds a mirror to the soul. If I am willing to look in that mirror and not run from what I see, I have a chance to gain self-knowledge—and knowing myself is a crucial to good teaching as knowing my students and my subject.
>
> In fact, knowing my students and my subject depends heavily on self-knowledge. When I do not know myself, I cannot know who my students are. I will see them through a glass darkly, in the shadows of my unexamined life—and when I cannot see them clearly, I cannot teach them well. When I do not know myself, I cannot know my subject—not at the deepest levels of embodied, personal meaning. I will know it only abstractly, from a distance, a congeries of concepts as far removed from the world as I am from personal truth.
>
> The work required to "know thyself" is neither selfish nor narcissistic. Whatever self-knowledge we attain as teachers will serve our students and our scholarship well. Good teaching requires self-knowledge: It is a secret hidden in plain sight. (pp. 2–3)

Knowing thyself also means you can state your teaching philosophy and understand where it comes from. Effective educators consider how their philosophy and style affect their teaching. Merriam and Brockett (1997) explained that "A philosophy of education is a conceptual framework embodying certain values and principles that renders the education process meaningful" (p. 28). Elias and Merriam (1995) wrote an entire book focused on educational philosophy and discerned:

> The educator is generally more interested in skills than in principles, in means than in ends, in details than in the whole picture. The philosophy of adult education does not equip a person with knowledge about what to teach, how to teach, or how to organize a program. It is more concerned with the why of education and with the logical analysis of the various elements of the educational process. (p. x, Italics in original)

Elias and Merriam (1995) maintained that understanding educational philosophy distinguished professional educators from paraprofessionals and novice teachers.

Educators interested in exploring individual teaching philosophy should refer to Zinn's (1991) PAEI, "Philosophy of Adult Education Inventory" <https://www.labr.net/apps/paei/>. The PAEI measures philosophical teaching inclinations. *Liberal* is traditional liberal arts education or education for the sake of acquiring knowledge. *Progressive* is pragmatic learning, aimed at providing learners with skills to prevail in the workforce. *Behaviorist* focuses on learning that yields observable behaviors. *Humanistic* sees the potential in all learners and strives to help them realize their full potential. Finally, *radical* teaching philosophy aims to change society by addressing oppression and marginalization and challenging the status quo. Another option for exploring teaching orientation is Pratt's (1998) TPI, "Teaching Perspectives Inventory" <http://www.teachingperspectives.com/tpi/>, developed from his research on over 250 adult educators in Canada, Singapore, Hong Kong, and the USA. The inventory measures five different orientations to teaching including *transmission* of content that is accurate and efficient, *apprenticeship* or helping learners experience authentic tasks as they learn, *developmental* in the sense that the instructor adapts the instruction to learner needs and capabilities, *nurturing* in that learners are provided with a safe environment and enough challenge to achieve the learning goal and maintain positive self-esteem, and *social reform* that teaches learners to challenge the status quo and advocate for the disenfranchised in society.

Mindset Educator mindset incorporates resiliency, flexibility, and openness. *Resiliency*, or "the capacity to rebound or bounce back from adversity, conflict, failure, or even positive events, progress and increased responsibility" (Luthans, 2002, p. 702), is being advocated as a key leadership competency (Smith, 2017). Resiliency has also been described as the ability to recover from challenging issues in order to survive, and possessing sustainability, or the positive determination to continue working toward goals (Zautra, 2008). Resiliency can be bolstered for both educators and their learners by being reflective and gaining clarity about values and purpose in life, tuning into emotions of self and others, building community (especially important in the classroom), being present in the moment rather than allowing attention to be usurped by distractions such as smart phones, and learning from feedback. Smith (2017) conducted semi-structured interviews with eight senior leaders and concluded that resilience was viewed as operating differently in relation to the past, the present, and the future and was described as a resource or fuel that provides both the capabilities and capacity to sustain their role as leaders. Resiliency has great efficacy for educators as their capacity and capability to not only cope with challenging contexts and difficult problems but also to thrive, learn, and develop others in the process.

Effective educators also demonstrate *flexibility* and do not teach the same topic the same way over and over again. Educators who are continually seeking new knowledge and revising their curricula have the flexibility and curiosity and willingness to change. Good educators also demonstrate *openness* to new ideas and difference. They are also advocating for diversity, equity, and inclusion in their classrooms. Ongoing reflexivity helps educators stay grounded and aware of how their values and skills play out in practice.

Well-Being Educators have a responsibility to be fit: physically, spiritually, intellectually, and emotionally. Educator fitness is multidimensional with expectations to be up-to-date in their content area, be powerfully present in the learning interaction, and influence the tone and culture of the learning community. "All educators are learners first. Being an educator is an honor and responsibility, and striving to continually improve as educators is a lifelong learning endeavor" (Merriam & Bierema, 2014, p. 251). Part of educator fitness is engaging in reflective practice to scrutinize teaching practice and make modifications to continually improve as a teacher. Schon (1983) advocated both reflection *on* practice (musing on what worked during a previous instructional session) and reflection *in* practice (assessing what is working or not in the moment and making tweaks).

Educators are only part of the equation. They need learners in order to practice their craft. The next section of the framework focuses on learners and how our understandings of them have evolved throughout history.

2.2 Learner: The Who

The *learner* is the individual we usually think about when planning educational programs, and as the earlier part of this chapter detailed what we know about adult learners, this section will supplement that information briefly with a historical overview of how our understandings of adult learning have evolved. Adult learning has been systematically studied since the 1920s, yet, there is no single explanation or theory of adult learning. Merriam (2001) metaphorically described the knowledge base of adult learning as a mosaic. The earliest research on adult learning was whether or not adults could learn (Thorndike, Bregman, Tilton & Woodyard, 1928). The professional field of adult education was founded in 1926 (Merriam & Brocket, 1997/2011). Early research was from a psychological, behavioral perspective and concentrated on memory and cognition.

Houle's (1961) work examined motivations of learners and concluded that adults have one of three goals when they participate in formal learning programs: (1) to fulfill a goal, such as a credential or promotion; (2) to enjoy the social benefits of learning with others; or (3) to learn for the sake of learning. Characteristics of adult learners were first systematically studied in 1965 by Johnstone and Rivera, and the findings have remained consistent across the decades (Merriam, Caffarella, & Baumgartner, 2006). For example, adult participants in formal education tend to be white, middle class, employed, younger, better educated, and seeking employment-related learning as compared to nonparticipants. Other highly subscribed programs by adults include English as a second language (ESL), adult basic education (ABE), general education development (GED), credential programs, apprenticeship programs, continuing professional education, and personal development courses. The majority of participation reported was work-related courses or training, and that trend has remained constant over the decades.

Knowles (1970) popularized the concept of andragogy (the art of teaching adults with learner-centered, life-driven instruction) as an antidote to pedagogy (the teacher-centered, subject-driven instruction typical of children's education). He also introduced self-directed learning as a preferred mode of adult learning, whereby adults control their own learning processes and plan, implement, and evaluate their own learning (Knowles, 1955). The Self-Directed Learning Readiness Scale (SDLRS) <http://www.lpasdlrs.com/> was developed by Guglielmino in 1978 to assess the degree of self-direction adults exhibited toward planning and controlling their own learning. Interest in and conferences on self-directed learning continue to this day.

The 1980s saw the development of learning style models and instruments that attempted to describe how adults learned from experience, for example, Kolb's learning cycle (1984) is one of the better-known experiential learning style models (explained in the next section) for which he developed the Kolb learning style inventory (LSI). Others developed their own versions such as Jarvis (1987), Tennant and Pogson (1995), and Fenwick (2003).

Adult learning in the 1990s continued exploration of memory, cognition, learner characteristics, and participation. The Education Participation Scale (EPS) was developed by Boshier in 1991 to measure adults' motivation to participate. Robinson (1995) suggested five purposes for adult learning: (1) personal growth and development, (2) personal and social improvement, (3) organizational effectiveness, (4) cultivation of the intellect, and (5) social transformation. During the 1990s, Mezirow's (1991) theory of transformative learning gained traction, and the field took a critical turn, using critical theory to examine issues of marginalization and access in education and to explore how intersectionality impacted learning (Tisdell, 1995). During this time the first text on women's learning emerged (Hayes & Flannery, 2000), and Cervero and Wilson (1994) applied critical principles to planning education programs. This period also saw the rise of human resource development programs as some academic programs sought to help graduates apply adult learning principles and change theory to address organization issues (Pace, 1991).

Since 2000, issues related to access, intersectionality, and critical adult education have continued to prevail. As the world becomes more global and complex, calls for more adaptive learning have been made to help adults make good decisions and solve problems with incomplete information, conflicting agendas, and no clear right answers. Nicolaides (2015) called this state "liquid modernity" (p. 1), referring to the fluidity of life where highly interconnected and interdependent professionals struggle to keep pace with relentless change and unpredictable outcomes and the ambiguity they create. Learners must learn to cope with this ambiguity by "...being flexible, adaptable, and constantly ready and willing to change tactics; to abandon commitments and loyalties without regret; and to act in a moment, as failure to act brings greater insecurity—such demands place adults 'in over their heads'" (Nicolaides, 2015, p. 2).

Adult learning has been important throughout modern history and will continue to play a key role in the lives of adults as they learn at work, at home, and in the community. The next section delves into how adults actually learn.

2.3 Process: The How

Now that we have discussed the who—key players in formal adult learning being learners and educators, let's consider how learning occurs. The *process* of learning is what transpires in the learner's head, heart, body, and soul that leads to new knowledge, behavior change, or perspective transformation. Change, as already discussed, is a major learning catalyst and learning can help adults cope. Merriam (2008) observed adult learning as multidimensional in her closing remarks of her edited book updating adult learning theory for the twenty-first century:

> For a good part of the twentieth century, adult learning was understood as a cognitive process, one in which the mind took in facts and information, converting it all to knowledge, which then could be observed as subsequent behavior change. Although there is still research going on in memory and information processing, especially as a function of age, currently learning is construed as a much broader activity involving the body, the emotions, and the spirit as well as the mind. (p. 54)

A key thread that runs through the process of adult learning is that adults are engaged in a continuous cycle of *experience and reflection*, and these activities are present in all of the different explanations of how adults learn. Adults are bombarded with activities in the private, public, and professional realms of their lives that demand engagement, reflection, and meaning-making. An adult's life experiences create learning and serve as resources for learning.

Experience Dewey (1938) was highly influential in how experience impacted learning. He saw learning as lifelong where learners applied and adapted knowledge to novel situations. For example, engineering students might have learned how to design a bridge for a warm climate and are now tasked with designing one for a cold climate. They can take their knowledge of what worked in the warm climate and link their learning to adjustments that have to be made in cold climates. Lindeman (1961), an early adult educator, built on Dewey's understandings and emphasized "experience is the adult learner's living textbook" (p. 7), and Knowles' (1980) introduction of andragogy also put experience front and center for our understanding of the process.

Models of experiential learning were developed beginning in the 1980s with the Kolb experiential learning cycle (1984). Kolb defined learning as "the process whereby knowledge is created through the transformation of experience" (p. 38). Kolb proposed that learners go through four stages of learning to include concrete experience, reflective observation, abstract conceptualization, and active experimentation. According to Kolb, effective learners need to master each of these abilities, so if you were attempting to learn how to drive, you might view a film about driving basics (concrete experience), reflect on the responsibility of driving (reflective observation), and imagine what you would do if certain driving challenges occurred such as a flat tire, engine malfunction, or inclement weather (abstract conceptualization) and finally you would practice driving (active experimentation). Kolb developed an instrument called the learning style inventory (LSI) where you can assess your learning preferences. Other experiential models are reviewed in Merriam and Bierema (2014).

Fenwick (2003) considered experiential learning from five different theoretical paradigms. The first is *constructivist*, or the making of meaning through engaging and reflecting on experience. For example, a professor might begin reflecting on their experience with teaching and what approaches might work best. Fenwick's second perspective, *situative*, assumed that learning occurs as the person lives through a situation, in which case the professor might begin paying more attention to their classes and other colleagues they have an opportunity to observe to assess when students are most engaged. The third perspective is *psychoanalytic*, or the process of tuning into unconscious desires and fears. For instance, the professor might deny that there is anything wrong with their teaching since acknowledging one conflicts with their self-image as a master teacher. Fenwick's fourth perspective is *critical cultural* where dominant norms are questioned. Here, the professor might begin to wonder why all faculty are set on lecturing and defensive of it as the only way they can teach. The fifth perspective is grounded in complexity theory and focused on the *relationships* connecting humans and nonhumans (material objects, mediating tools, environments, ideas). The professor might decide to form a group of interested faculty who want to explore innovative teaching. The faculty group is a system unto itself with a shared goal of learning new pedagogies and potentially improving their teaching, but each member brings their own experiences from their teaching, discipline, and department to the learning process where they interact and evolve.

Reflection Reflective practice is thinking about what we are doing either in the moment or following it. For example, the professor who starts to assess their teaching might begin to think through their class session in terms of what worked or did not work well. This is known as reflection-on-action (Schon, 1983). The professor might also reflect while they are teaching and perhaps decide that their lecture is losing attention and to interject a discussion question. This is known as reflection-on-action as it is happening in the moment in the midst of experience.

Reflection can also be focused on what Argyris and Schon (1974) called espoused theory (what I say I believe) versus theory-in-use (what I actually do). A professor might declare that they lead interactive lectures (what they say), but in reality, they deliver boring, passive lectures (what they do). Reflective practice examines the gap between what people say they believe and what they actually do. The contrast can be a space for learning and behavior or thought change. Critical reflection has been advanced as not just reflecting on experience but also identifying the assumptions underlying thought and action (Brookfield, 1991; Mezirow, 2000). This would entail the professor identifying what assumptions guide their teaching such as "I am the expert," "there is no other way to teach this material except by lecturing," or "I am a master teacher" and considering their validity and implications for learners.

The process of learning happens in multiple ways that are connected by reflection and experience. Adult learning processes will be discussed in terms of narrative, spirituality, embodiment, transformative, and brain along with strategies for tapping into these approaches.

Narrative Constructing stories is a process used by adults to make meaning, thereby developing a sense of self and identity. Narrative serves two purposes: (1) cultivating learning through stories and (2) conceptualizing the learning process itself (Clarke & Rossiter, 2008). The stories adults tell are complex, and in some they may be the hero and other times the victim. Through narrative, adults construct meaning from experience. For example, I began my career working in a human resources fast-track program in the automotive industry. My personal narrative at the time was "women have equal opportunity, and I'm going to prove it." My heroic stance on where my career was headed was soon conflicted: As a woman, I kept bumping up against patriarchal culture, unspoken rules, and unfair treatment. I advanced quickly enough and soon found myself as the lone woman executive on a team of men, some of whom were considerably older than me. Clarke and Rossiter noted that narrative needs an audience and that it is bound up in culture and social relations. One day, the CEO came to visit. It was a tense visit since our division was performing poorly. As my colleagues and I sat around a large conference table with the CEO and his entourage, he began berating my boss, the division president, about several problems in the business, including the lack of college degrees held among frontline supervisors in the manufacturing plants. Finally, as the conversation went on and the tension escalated, the president became more and more exasperated and finally pointed at me and exclaimed, "Laura here is a great example of our people getting education. She is working on her doctorate!" There was a pause, and then the CEO looked at me and said, "What's it in? Home economics?" That moment was wholly mortifying, and it grated against the narrative I had been constructing about my prospects in this company and in corporate life as a woman executive. Home economics is a wonderful profession, although you will not find many home economists making cars. Suddenly, I became marginalized in the narrative of my career, and remaining on my path became more and more difficult to reconcile with my emerging feminist identity. As painful as that moment was and memory remains, it has helped me define my identity, make a career shift from corporate to academic life, and create scholarship concerned with organization justice, women's leadership, and critical human resource development.

Clarke and Rossiter (2008) observed that we learn through *hearing* stories because they create understanding and speak to the cognitive, emotional, spiritual, and imaginative aspects of our being. We also learn through *telling* stories where the teller becomes the actor and is able to connect understanding of a concept to the experience. In my case, I was finally able to connect the overt sexism of corporate life to my own experience and story. Educators can help learners develop their own stories to help them make abstract concepts real—this is why it is so valuable to invite learners to share experiences in classroom settings. A third way of learning through stories is *recognizing* them. Clarke and Rossiter explained:

> It presumes that learners begin to understand the fundamental narrative character of experience. As they gain understanding, they also begin to understand that they themselves are narratively constituted and narratively positioned; this applies to themselves personally, as well as to groups, societies, and cultures. One example would be Americans recognizing they are positioned within a particular cultural narrative, one that privileges the individual over the community and emphasizes rights more than responsibilities; by recognizing this narrative situatedness, American learners could critique this larger narrative, question underlying assumptions and inherent power relationships, and identify whose interests are served and whose are exploited by this narrative. (pp. 65–66)

Narrative learning is an extension of experiential and reflective learning in that it helps learners contemplate prior experience while also critically evaluate the social conditions, power relations, and privileged or marginalized dynamics at play. Clarke and Rossiter (2008) also suggested that learners strive to "story" their learning to make sense of it and complete the gaps in understanding—essentially learning to make sense of the experience. Bringing narrative learning into practice in higher education or organization educational programs can be done by having learners journal, tell each other stories, write autobiographical life stories, or develop case studies related to the topic.

Spirituality

> Spirituality in learning relates to its role in an *individual's* creation of ultimate meaning, usually in relationship to a higher sense of self or what is referred to as "God," "Divine Spirit," "Lifeforce," or "Great Mystery"... spirituality is about an individual's personal experience or journey toward wholeness, whereas religion is about an organized community of faith. (Tisdell, 2008, p. 28)

Spirituality helps adults make meaning, understand the self, and connect with the world as they learn and often is an internal process that may occur through prayer, meditation, or other inner activities. Learners may also experience spirituality in how they interact with the external world. Tisdell (2003) identified four types of spiritual learning in her study of how spirituality informed the lives and practices of thirty-one culturally diverse adult educators. The first related to the *universality of human experience* across culture such as childbirth, close brushes with death, witnessing a death, and other experiences that gave learners a new sense of purpose. The second focused on reports of *memorable nighttime dreams* and *daytime synchronicities* that provided hope or affirmation in times of challenge, difficulty, or joy. The third type of spiritual learning occurred in *nature* where learners developed an appreciation for spiritual centering and affirmed a sense of connection to the world. Tisdell noted that learners participating in some type of spiritual practice such as prayer or meditation were able to learn to attend to the spiritual in their daily lives. The final spiritual experience Tisdell found in her research was related to *identity development*, particularly among women and people of color. She reported that several of her women participants discussed how they developed a more positive gender identity as they deconstructed patriarchal and religious experiences and reclaimed their spirituality through a more woman-positive spirituality lens. Tisdell (2008) explained:

> The spiritual part of those experiences was when they reclaimed aspects of the sacred in their own cultural or gender story, or found new power in reframing some of the cultural symbols, mythic stories, music, or metaphors that were part of their earlier life experience. (pp. 31–32)

Deep spiritual learning is relatively rare, yet, spiritual learning is important to the development of identity as people construct knowledge through their experiences throughout the lifespan (Tisdell, 2008). Ways to integrate spirituality into learning might be to invite reflection on special moments in learners' lives related to the topic, perhaps relating to the types of spiritual learning identified by Tisdell (2003) (universality of human experience, memorable dreams or synchronous experiences, or centering). Spiritual learning can also be fostered through journal writing, critical reflection, inquiry, dialogue, and narrative.

Embodiment Embodiment, or learning through the body, is also known as embodied or somatic learning (Freiler, 2008). Freiler reported that the Moken village sea gypsies who survived the 2004 tsunami that devastated the coast of Thailand had a cultural way of knowing that was connected with the environment allowing them to somatically detect tsunami warnings and get to safety, when other cultural groups did not notice the impending danger and perished. Embodied learning is a sense or force that your body knows you are angry, excited, or in harm's way more rapidly than your brain does. Embodied learning is the process of constructing meaning through bodily experiences that involve physicality, sensing, and engaging bodily and with the world (Freiler). "Embodiment and embodied learning generally refer to a broader, more holistic view of constructing knowledge that engages the body as a site of learning, usually in connection with other domains of knowing (for example, spiritual, affective, symbolic, cultural, rational)" (Freiler, 2008, p. 39). Freiler offered the following definition of embodied learning as:

> A way to construct knowledge through direct engagement in bodily experiences and inhabiting one's body through a felt sense of being-in-the-world. It also involves a sense of connectedness and interdependence through the essence of lived experiencing within one's complete humanness, both body and mind, in perceiving, interacting, and engaging with the surrounding world. Simply stated, embodied learning involves being attentive to the body and its experiences as a way of knowing. (p. 40)

Embodied learning can be used to help learners be more aware of safety in occupations where they might be at risk, such as mining that poses site dangers where workers need to tune into sights, sounds, or smells that might signal danger or social work that poses domestic dangers as social workers enter homes and must be aware of family dynamics, the condition of the home, and so forth. Athletes are also highly attuned to and sensitive of their teammates. Embodied learning might take place in a classroom and drawing attention to the body through breathing exercises, guided imagery, relaxation exercises, or yoga.

Transformation Think of a time when you shifted a strongly held belief or way of being and there was no going back. Realizing I was working in a sexist corporate culture made continued employment there untenable. Mezirow (1978) explained a learning process that shifted interpretations of adults' worlds irreversibly—transformative learning theory. This theory elucidated what happens when adults change or transform their perspective. For example, I had a transformative learning experience in the "home ec" story shared above when I could no longer reconcile my self-image of a corporate executive with the sexist, patriarchal culture that did not value women with education. The experience forced me to change my frame of reference—"structures of assumptions and expectations that frame an individual's tacit points of view and influence their thinking, beliefs, and actions" (Taylor, 2008, p. 5). Perspective can be transformed gradually—perhaps your political or religious beliefs slowly shifted as you became exposed to other ways of thinking, or critiques of your beliefs—or suddenly as the result of a crisis, natural disaster, health scare, or death of a loved one (Taylor, 2008).

Transformative learning is difficult to predict or create. Fostering conditions conducive to transformative learning include creating opportunities for critical reflection, dialoguing on difficult problems among learners, examining feelings and emotions, reflecting on experience, challenging learners' assumptions, and critiquing prevailing social arrangements and dynamics of privilege and marginalization (Taylor, 2008).

The Brain Our ability to understand the human brain is growing, and understanding brain function can help educators improve their ability to engage learners and enhance learning. "The brain changes as it learns" (Taylor & Lamoreaux, 2008, p. 49). Although most human cells in the body are regenerated, humans are born with all of their brain cells (neurons) and learning changes how neurons connect to each other. These changes allow humans to adjust their responses to the external environment (Taylor & Lamoreaux, 2008). Although a full description of the anatomy of the brain is beyond the scope of this chapter (see Center for Educational Research and Innovation, 2008, or Taylor & Lamoreaux for more information), learning occurs when neurons are exposed to new signals from the world, and signals between neurons change and make increasingly complex connections throughout the brain. The more frequent the signaling and connecting between neurons, the stronger the firing becomes, and vice versa. Memory becomes the weak or strong encoding of these connections. The brain attempts to connect new information to previously stored information. This is why memorization is only a short-term strategy, since memorization itself does not create new connections between neurons (Taylor & Lamoreaux) and it won't create lasting learning among students.

There are key characteristics of the brain. Plasticity is the brain's robust ability to change existing neural networks in response to environmental demands (Center for Educational Research and Innovation, 2008). This involves the strengthening, weakening, or eliminating of neuronal connections. The degree of brain modification depends on the type of learning. For example, infants' learning of language is profoundly different than learning to write and use grammar later in life. Brain plasticity is lifelong, although aging may affect brain dexterity (Taylor & Lamoreaux, 2008). Taylor and Lamoreaux observed that meaning-making happens at the cellular level and entails developing neural patterns that are easily accessible when needed. Some adults have better capacity to make meaning and thus may be more able to deal with the complexities faced in their lives (Taylor & Lamoreaux, 2008).

The quality of learning environments also impacts brain plasticity. Maximizing physical and intellectual well-being depends on having healthy social interactions. Additionally, adequate nutrition, exercise, and sleep are important for optimal learning. Mindful of this, I almost always bring chocolate to class, much to students' appreciation! Emotional states also matter, and stress is a useful learning tool only when it stimulates cognition and learning. Once it reaches the tipping point, learning diminishes. On the other hand, aha moments stimulate the pleasure centers of the brain and make learning exciting.

What is the best way to teach, mindful of the brain? Taylor and Lamoreaux (2008) observed that Kolb's (1984) learning cycle (concrete experience, reflective observation, abstract conceptualization, and active experimentation) matches how signals travel in the brain (sensory input to neural connections to integrative motor output). Thus, adult learners filter current and previous *experience* in ways that can create misinterpretations, and educators need to help them make conscious connections between the two. Helping learners compare experiences is also important in making connections between new and old information. Taylor and Lamoreaux explained:

> Listening to lectures and reading texts are valuable learning experiences, but the learners likely to derive the most benefit are those who can also draw on related prior experience.... This suggests that offering concrete examples, analogies, and experiential activities, thus helping learners create meaningful connection, is—from the brain's perspective—a more effective approach to teaching and learning than focusing primarily on how we, as educators and experts, understand the issue. (p. 54)

Fostering *reflection* helps the brain connect old and new events and developing more complex neural networks, in effect reframing past experiences in the context of new ones (Taylor & Lamoreaux, 2008). Activities useful here are journaling and self-assessment. *Abstraction* or how learners make sense of things involves solving problems, making decisions, and determining plans in ways that help learners use neural connections to complete tasks and assignments. Constructivist, meaning-making approaches work most effectively in these cases where learners are challenged to adaptive problem-solving—grappling with problems that do not have easy or right answers. Next, adult learners need to *test* the new meanings created between neurons that can help them clarify meaning and correct errors. This does not mean administering exams but rather helping learners identify and correct flawed thinking.

Assignments that task learners with synthesizing concepts learned across a semester, working with other learners, experiencing real-life applications, or dialoguing with the self and others are most effective for facilitating meaning-making at this phase (Taylor & Lamoreaux, 2008).

So far, we have explored learning theories describing educators, learners, and learning processes. These variables do not happen in a vacuum and are largely affected by the settings in which they occur. The next section considers the environment of learning and how it shapes learning and can be shaped by educators and participants to better serve learning needs.

2.4 Context: The Where

The place of learning, whether it be a physical classroom or the cultural vibe learners feel among classmates, is shaped by the world around it. Learning is significantly influenced by *context*—"the social system that affects the thinking and actions of people within a particular social situation such as a classroom, school, organization, community, or nation. . . .[that] incorporates culture, privilege, and power" (Merriam & Bierema, 2014, p. 241). Think about the context where you live, study, or work. Who are the members? What are the dynamics? What is the culture? The world today is shifting and learners must be equipped to function in that context. Diversity is increasing globally, and learners and educators also need to be able to proactively respond to difference and the ways it is affected by culture, privilege, and power.

Learning in a VUCA World VUCA—shorthand for volatile, uncertain, complex, and ambiguous—is a term that has been adopted broadly to describe the current and future state of the world as we grapple with the megatrends of globalization, technology, individualization, demographic change, digitization, political uncertainty, economic instability, and environmental crisis, where a state of VUCA is the new normal (van der Steege, 2017). The VUCA state generates "wicked problems," defined by Rittel and Webber (1973) as stubborn and the result of open social systems when theory is inadequate for accurate forecasting, our current knowledge is insufficient to the task, and pluralities in politics make achieving unified aims impossible. Wicked problems are challenges such as global warming, climate change, poverty, hunger, and incurable disease.

VUCA context places learners and educators in a chaotic world, where they have to lead through the muck when the way isn't clear and collaborate across disciplines to solve ambiguous, wicked problems. Nicolaides (2015) defined ambiguity as "an encounter with an appearance of reality that is at first unrecognizable, oblique, simultaneously evoking fear of "no-cognition" and the potential hope for multiple meanings irresolvable by reference to context alone" (p. 1). This time of "liquid modernity" (Nicolaides, 2015) echoes Vaill's (1996) metaphor of "permanent white water" representing the constant churn and turbulence typical of contemporary life. Vaill advocated embracing "learning as a way of being" as key to navigating the choppy waters of organization life. Kegan (1994) suggested that we are "in over our heads" in our efforts to meet the mental demands of life and work. Clearly the challenges of learning in work context are roiling and changing. Yorks and Nicolaides (2013) advocated that educators should help adults build capacity to make sense of the demands placed on them within complex contexts that move from dependence to independence to interdependence, with the assumption that professionals recognize how they are in relationship to others and their learning in complex contexts.

Culture, Privilege, and Power *"Culture* is a set of shared, yet often unarticulated assumptions that permeate thought and action" (Merriam & Bierema, 2014, p. 241, italics added). Culture influences its members, whether they be learners or teachers. Some cultures might eschew being learner-centered or exploring interactive learning. Others might embrace it. *Privilege* is unearned power based on gender, race, ability, class, sexuality, or another visible or invisible social position or positionality. All cultures have privileged and marginalized members and their status can change, depending on the environment. *"Power* is the ability to influence others to bring about change" (Merriam & Bierema, 2014, p. 241). Power is exercised through relationships such as learner–learner, learner–instructor, or instructor–instructor. When we have power in relationships, that gives us privilege. So, the learner who has respect of peer colleagues may enjoy power in the group to influence student roles and voice. That same learner might be marginalized in their workplace due to sexism or racism. A professor might wield a lot of power (privilege) in their classroom yet be bullied (marginalized) by faculty peers.

Acknowledging context in learning and education means accepting that we live framed by socially constructed positions, wanted or not. The human brain creates categorizations that translate into power relations. A person's success within a given context depends on her interaction with other individuals in the context. For instance, a student woman of color might find her comments are ignored unless repeated by another student who is white or male. Instructors might call on white male participants more often and view them more favorably when assigning grades.

Educators have a responsibility to be aware of these issues and work to make their classroom settings places that value diversity, equity, and inclusion, where learners can safely voice their ideas, share, and question assumptions. This means paying attention to culture, privilege, and power and setting expectations around participation and respect. It involves ensuring that the textbooks represent diverse voices and perspectives and that the examples and visual imagery are inclusive. One way of doing this is to examine your own positionality as an educator and consider how your gender, race, ableness, sexuality, class, and so forth shape your role as an educator. This is difficult work, as Merriam and Caffarella once observed "not everyone wants to admit that the issues of race, ethnicity, gender, and sexual orientation have or should have any educational relevance". Attending to learning context matters, because it impacts learners' lives.

2.5 The Method: The What

This section has put forth a framework to understand adult learning theory that considers the educator, learner, process, and context. The final aspect of the framework is the method, or what design bridges these ideas into robust learning programs that incorporate the who, how, and where of learning? How does delivery honor these aspects of the framework? Effective design and facilitation of learning bridges theory and practice in adult education. It also considers the stakeholders—educator and learner—as well as the learning processes and context. Design is the point to create relevant, timely, and engaging learning experiences for diverse learners, and delivery is the real-time implementation of practices to honor learners as beings and help them reflect on experience and new information. There is no single formula for creating powerful programs that will optimize learning for all learners. Yet, as discussed throughout this book, there are several things that educators can do to ensure that learners have opportunities to actively build knowledge. A full discussion of designing for active adult learning is presented in chapter "Incorporating Active Learning into Your Educational Repertoire". Table 1 raises questions educators can ask themselves to assess how well they are engaging the framework of adult learning and bridge theory into robust practice of facilitating learning.

Learning is the breath of life—it creates challenge, knowledge, and capacity to fully engage in the private, public, and professional spheres of adulthood. Teaching is a large responsibility and to do it well requires educators to know themselves and their learners. It also necessitates an understanding of adult learning theory and how to translate it into meaningful practice for learners. This chapter has defined adult learning and presented a framework to understand and apply adult learning theory.

Table 1 Bringing the adult learning framework together in educational design and delivery

The method of bringing the adult learning framework together	
Educator	• How am I showing up? • How resilient, flexible, and open am I? • What is my teaching philosophy? Have I written it down? Shared it with learners? • What is my teaching orientation? How does it help and hurt my teaching? • How balanced and centered am I? What can I do better?
Learner	• What are the characteristics of the learner(s)? • What motivates them to learn? • How is course content relevant to learners' lives?
Process	• How can I honor learners' experience? • How can I foster reflection and critical reflection? • How well do learner's espoused theories match their theories in use? • How can I incorporate learning that speaks to the narrative, spirituality, embodiment, or transformative experiences of learners? • How can I create learning that aligns with learner's brain function?
Context	• How can I create a safe yet challenging learning environment? • How can learners claim their voices? • What positionalities are at play in the classroom? How do learners experience me? Themselves? Each other?

Bringing these elements into educational design and delivery will help educators create powerful, relevant, and culturally sensitive learning experiences. Preparing learners to thrive in a VUCA context is an ongoing challenge and learning process for educators.

References

Antrim, M. T. (1902). *Naked truths and veiled allusions*. Philadelphia: Henry Altemus Company.

Argyris, C., & Schon, D. A. (1974). *Theory in practice: Increasing professional effectiveness*. San Francisco, CA: Jossey-Bass.

Bierema, L. L. (2008). Principles of instructional design and adult learners. In V. Wang (Ed.), *Strategic approaches towards curriculum development for adult learners in the global community* (pp. 7–33). Malabar, FL: Krieger.

Bilimoria, D., & Wheeler, J. V. (1995). Learning-centered education: A guide to resources and implementation. *Journal of Management Education, 19*(3), 409–428.

Brookfield, S. D. (1991). Using critical incidents to explore learners' assumptions. In J. Mezirow & Associates (Eds.), *Fostering critical reflection in adulthood* (pp. 177–193). San Francisco: Jossey-Bass.

Center for Educational Research and Innovation. (2008). *Understanding the brain: The birth of a learning science*. Paris: Organisation for Economic Cooperation and Development.

Cervero, R. M., & Wilson, A. L. (1994). The politics of responsibility: A theory of program planning practice for adult education. *Adult Education Quarterly, 45*(1), 249–268.

Clarke, M. C., & Rossiter, M. (2008). Narrative learning in adulthood. *New Directions for Adult & Continuing Education, 2008*(119), 61–70. https://doi.org/10.1002/ace.306.

Corbett, B., & Chloupek, J. (2019). *Why it matters: The Sherpa guide to what you are looking for*. Cincinnati, OH: Sasha Corporation.

Dewey, J. (1938). *Experiential education*. New York: Collier.

Elias, J. L., & Merriam, S. B. (1995). *Philosophical foundations of adult education* (2nd ed.). Malabar, FL: Krieger.

Fenwick, T. (2003). *Learning through experience: Troubling orthodoxies and intersecting questions*. Malabar, FL: Krieger.

Freiler, T. J. (2008). Learning through the body. *New Directions for Adult & Continuing Education, 119*, 37–47. https://doi.org/10.1002/ace.304.

Guglielmino, L. M. (1978). Development of the self-directed learning readiness scale. *Dissertation Abstracts International, 38*(11-A), 6467.

Hayes, E., & Flannery, D. D. (2000). *Women as learners: The significance of gender in adult learning. The Jossey-Bass higher and adult education series*. San Francisco, CA: Jossey-Bass.

Hiemstra, R. (1994). Self-directed learning. In W. J. Rothwell & K. J. Sensenig (Eds.), *The sourcebook for self-directed learning* (pp. 9–20). Amherst, MA: HRD.

Houle, C. O. (1961). *The inquiring mind*. Madison, WI: University of Wisconsin Press.

Jarvis, P. (1987). *Adult learning in the social context* (1st ed.). London: Croom Helm.

Johnstone, J. W. C., & Rivera, R. J. (1965). *Volunteers for learning: A study of the educational pursuits of adults*. Hawthorne, NY: Aldine de Gruyter.

Kegan, R. (1994). *In over our heads: The mental demands of modern life*. Cambridge, MA: Harvard University Press.

Knowles, M. S. (1955). *Informal adult education: A guide for administrators, leaders, and teachers*. New York: Association Press.

Knowles, M. (1970). *The modern practice of adult education: Andragogy versus pedagogy*. New York: Association Press.

Knowles, M. S. (1980). *The modern practice of adult education: From pedagogy to andragogy.* Cambridge: The Adult Education Company.

Kolb, D. A. (1984). *Experiential learning: Experience as the source of learning and development* (1st ed.). Englewood Cliffs, NJ: Prentice Hall.

Lewin, K. (1947). Frontiers in group dynamics: Concept, method and reality in social science; social equilibria and social change. *Human Relations, 1,* 5–41. Retrieved from http://search.ebscohost.com.proxy-remote.galib.uga.edu/login.aspx?direct=true&db=fgh&AN=MRB-CDAS0040458&site=eds-live.

Lindeman, E. C. (1926/1961). *The meaning of adult education in the United States.* New York: Harvest House.

Luthans, F. (2002). The need for and meaning of positive organizational behavior. *Journal of Organizational Behavior: The International Journal of Industrial, Occupational and Organizational Psychology and Behavior, 23*(6), 695–706.

Merriam, S. B. (2001). Andragogy and self-directed learning: Pillars of adult learning theory. *New Directions for Adult and Continuing Education, 89,* 3–14.

Merriam, S. B. (2008). Adult learning theory for the twenty-first century. *New Directions for Adult & Continuing Education, 2008*(119), 93–98. https://doi.org/10.1002/ace.309.

Merriam, S. B., & Bierema, L. L. (2014). *Adult learning: Bridging theory and practice.* San Francisco: Jossey-Bass.

Merriam, S. B., & Brockett, R. G. (1997/2011). *The profession and practice of adult education: An introduction.* San Francisco: Jossey-Bass.

Merriam, S. B., Caffarella, R. S., & Baumgartner, L. M. (2006). *Learning in adulthood: A comprehensive guide.* San Francisco, CA: Jossey-Bass.

Mezirow, J. (1978). Perspective transformation. *Adult Education, 28,* 100–110.

Mezirow, J. (1991). *Transformative dimensions of adult learning.* San Francisco: Jossey-Bass.

Mezirow, J., & Associates. (2000). *Learning as transformation: Critical perspectives on a theory in process.* San Francisco: Jossey-Bass.

Nicolaides, A. (2015). Generative learning: Adults learning within ambiguity. *Adult Education Quarterly, 65,* 1–17.

Pace, R. W. (1991). *Human resource development: The field. The Prentice Hall series on human resource development.* Englewood Cliffs, NJ: Prentice Hall.

Palmer, P. J. (1998). *The courage to teach: Exploring the inner landscape of a teacher's life.* San Francisco: Jossey-Bass.

Pratt, D. D. (1998). *Five perspectives on teaching in adult and higher education.* Melbourne, FL: Krieger.

Rachal, J. R. (2002). Andragogy's detectives: A critique of the present and a proposal for the future. *Adult Education Quarterly, 52*(3), 210–227.

Rittel, H. W. J., & Webber, M. M. (1973). Dilemmas in a general theory of planning. *Policy Sciences, 4*(2), 155–169.

Robinson, R. D. (1995). *An introduction to helping adults learn and change* (Rev. ed.). West Bend, WI: Omnibook.

Sandlin, J. A. (2005). Andragogy and its discontents: An analysis of andragogy from three critical perspectives. *PAACE Journal of Lifelong Learning, 14*(1), 25–42.

Schon, D. A. (1983). *The reflective practitioner: How professionals think in action.* New York: Basic Books.

Smith, C. L. (2017). Coaching for leadership resilience: An integrated approach. *International Coaching Psychology Review, 12*(1), 6–23.

Taylor, E. W. (2008). Transformative learning theory. *New Directions for Adult & Continuing Education, 2008*(119), 5–15. https://doi.org/10.1002/ace.301.

Taylor, K., & Lamoreaux, A. (2008). Teaching with the brain in mind. *New Directions for Adult & Continuing Education, 2008*(119), 49–59. https://doi.org/10.1002/ace.305.

Tennant, M., & Pogson, P. (1995). *Learning and change in the adult years.* San Francisco: Jossey-Bass.

Thorndike, E. L., Bregman, E. O., Tilton, J., & Woodyard, E. (1928). *Adult learning*. New York: Macmillan.

Tisdell, E. (1995). *Creating inclusive adult learning environments: Insights from multicultural education and feminist pedagogy. Information series No. 361*. Columbus, OH: ERIC Clearing House on Adult, Career, and Vocational Education.

Tisdell, E. (2003). *Exploring spirituality and culture in adult and higher education*. San Francisco: Jossey-Bass.

Tisdell, E. J. (2008). Spirituality and adult learning. *New Directions for Adult & Continuing Education, 119*, 27–36. https://doi.org/10.1002/ace.303.

Vaill, P. B. (1996). *Learning as a way of being: Strategies for survival in a world of permanent white water*. San Francisco: Jossey-Bass.

van der Steege, M. (2017). Introduction. In M. Van Der Steege, R. Elkington, & J. Glick-Smith (Eds.), *Visionary leadership in a turbulent world: Thriving in the new VUCA context*. Bringley: Emerald.

Yorks, L., & Nicolaides, A. (2013). Toward and integral approach for evolving mindsets for generative learning and timely action in the midst of ambiguity. *Teachers College Record, 115*, 1–26.

Zautra, A., Hall, J., & Murray, K. (2008). Resilience: A new integrative approach to health and mental health research. *Health Psychology Review, 2*(1), 41–64.

Zinn, L. M. (1991). Identifying your philosophical orientation. In M. W. Galbraith (Ed.), *Adult learning methods* (pp. 39–77). Malabar, FL: Krieger.

Incorporating Active Learning into Your Educational Repertoire

Laura L. Bierema

Abstract This chapter examines the problems with instructor-centered education and offers pedagogical alternatives to make learning more engaging, participative, and enduring. The chapter begins with a critique of the traditional lecture method and offers interactive lecture as an alternative strategy. Next, active learning is defined with recommended activities to involve learners. Strategies for improving participation and learning are presented that are grounded in adult learning principles. Finally, strategies for designing active learning are provided to help instructors begin shifting their educational programs to more participative, effective learning sessions.

1 Anyone, Anyone?

The 1986 US hit teen comedy film, "Ferris Bueller's Day Off," written, co-produced, and directed by John Hughes and co-produced by Tom Jacobson, featured the antics of star Matthew Broderick as Ferris Bueller, a high-school slacker who skips school, with hilarious, disastrous consequences. One of the most famous scenes was actor-teacher Ben Stein's monotonous lecture about the Smoot-Hawley Tariff Act where he drones on to the class asking questions, followed by a quick, "Anyone, anyone?" pleading for student participation, before swiftly moving on to the next point, only to repeat the process over and over again. It is painful to watch the actor pleading "Anyone, anyone?" as students dozed, drooled on their desks, chewed gum, and goofed off during the lecture. Stein was quite proud of his acting moment to perfectly portray a boring professor. Perhaps you have been that instructor, asking "Anyone, anyone?" to a silent room filled with glazed-over eyes?

Electronic supplementary material The online version of this chapter (https://doi.org/10.1007/978-3-030-29872-2_2) contains supplementary material, which is available to authorized users.

L. L. Bierema (✉)
University of Georgia, Athens, GA, USA
e-mail: bierema@uga.edu

© Springer Nature Switzerland AG 2019
M. Fedeli, L. L. Bierema (eds.), *Connecting Adult Learning and Knowledge Management*, Knowledge Management and Organizational Learning 8,
https://doi.org/10.1007/978-3-030-29872-2_2

The purpose of this chapter is to introduce active learning as a concept and practice for educators seeking to make their teaching more engaging and students' learning more experiential and enduring. Although lecture may be a crutch or even preferred mode of teaching for many, the hard truth is there are more effective ways to promote learning. Yet, creating powerful, active learning is easier said than done:

> We have all seen—and alas, been an integral part of—some audience that was trying to endure the last half hour of an unendurable speech. Everybody was shifting his [sic] position, crossing one leg over the other or back again, moving the fingers, playing with watch-charms or chains, yawning, twitching, folding programs, wiping eye-glasses, twisting moustaches. Those were all fatigue signs. (Gulick, 1908, p. 96)

Never were truer words spoken by Luther H. Gulick in his 1908 book, *Mind & Work*. Others have noted the mind-numbing, sleep-inducing experience of passive learning. An old adage, often credited to W. H. Auden, described a professor as "A person who talks in other people's sleep" (Mendelson, 2013). These historical references lament the oldest instructional method: the dreaded lecture.

The lecture, also known as a speech, sermon, talk, address, oration, panel, symposium, forum, and so on, is perhaps the oldest form of instruction known to humankind, likely invented shortly after people learned to talk. Lecture was used by the ancient Greeks, Roman educators, and the great universities of the Middle Ages. Lecture has even survived the invention of the printing press and social media. As much as lecture has been heralded by teachers and damned by learners, it remains one of the most widely used instructional modes in existence.

The lecture has been defined as "an instructional technique through which an agent presents an oral discourse on a particular subject" (Verner & Dickenson, 1967, p. 85). Others have been more critical observing:

> A single instructor lectures and lectures and lectures fairly large groups of business and professional people, who sit for long hours in an audiovisual twilight, making never-to-be-read notes at rows of narrow tables covered with green baize and appointed with fat binders and sweating pitchers of ice water. (Nowlen, 1988 in Cervero, 1992, p. 91)

Most of us have memories of lectures. They might be positive, or less so. The challenge with lectures is that they are often passive and give learners little opportunity to compare or share experience—a hallmark of adult learning (Merriam & Bierema, 2013). Recall the memorable lectures of your educational experience. Were they particularly good or bad? What do you remember? What made the lecture notable? How do you use lecture in your own practice? How would students rate yours (be honest!)?

When learning is effective, particularly lecture, what happens? Usually learners are engaged. They are thinking, reflecting, comparing, and talking with others. Effective instruction engages learners and invites their interaction—with the subject, with other learners, and with the instructor. These sessions involve the audience as active participants and may even create subgroups that work on small tasks. The best lectures are essentially a collection of small lectures that present information in short doses, usually 10–15 min maximum, and then invite learners to react and interact with activities. Strong lecturers engage in ongoing assessment of their learning community to ensure learning. Have yours?

Incorporating Active Learning into Your Educational Repertoire   29

As already mentioned, this chapter introduces active learning as an antidote to passive, boring lectures. This chapter will contrast traditional and interactive lecturing, define active learning, and provide strategies and techniques for you to integrate active learning into your own practice, including lectures.

2 The Traditional Lecture

Consider lectures you have experienced. How many times have you been bored by a lecture? Given a boring lecture? Experienced an interactive, interesting lecture? Given an interactive, interesting lecture? Chances are you might benefit from learning more about engaging teaching if you answered yes to even one of these questions. Consider for a moment: How do you know if students are learning or if they misunderstand key points? Lectures can be problematic due to their passive nature and failure to assess learning.

I am not advocating that you quit lecturing all together and critique others who choose to lecture in their teaching practice. What I am advocating is that you take a critical look at your lectures, understand their limitations, and consider how you can maximize learning whether using a traditional lecture format or more contemporary interactive approaches. Traditional lectures typically involve the instructor talking while the students listen. Interruptions are rare, and learners begin to lose interest after approximately 10–15 min. Finally, the instructor's ability to assess student comprehension and ability to apply learning is minimal (Eison, 2010). Donald Swinehart (in Dickson, 1980) astutely noted: "The lecture is that procedure whereby the material in the notes of the professor is transferred to the notes of the students without passing through the mind of either" (p. 211).

A standard teaching adage in adult education is that there are two approaches to teaching. You can either be the "sage on the stage," as in a traditional lecturer as described above, or the "guide on the side," where you take a more facilitative approach to helping learners actively and experientially learn their way through the topic and construct their own meaning as they go.

Historically, lecture has involved the following characteristics: The knowledgeable instructor talks at length about the topic. Learners respond by raising hands and waiting to be called on by the instructor. Generally, student-to-student talk is discouraged, and instead, they listen and take notes independently. This pedagogy is also known as direct instruction because the focus is on the instructor who stands in front of a passive class and presents the information with little interaction. Based on this instructor-centric format, few opportunities exist to correct misunderstandings of the content, because learners have no chance to process their understanding or compare notes with their classmates. Finally, with the traditional lecture format, student absenteeism is often high (Eison, 2010).

There are good reasons to choose lecture as a pedagogy. Lectures are time-efficient and cost-effective and allow equal access to the instructor's expertise, not to mention fair in the sense that everyone is hearing the same information—*if* they are paying attention. Lectures also provide an opportunity for speakers to showcase their expertise. The disadvantages of lecture include that they are ineffective at meeting individual learning needs, holding attention, promoting active learning, assessing understanding and comprehension, avoiding monotony, or being effective for learning.

Penner (1984) synthesized 30 years of lecture research in the 1980s and concluded that the average student's attention span was 10–20 min and that concentration faded after about 10–20 min. Another study conducted a meta-analysis of "Audience Reaction to Commencement Addresses and Similar Speeches." According to the findings, at any point during lecture-type presentations, approximately only 18% paid attention at any given time, listening in 45-s increments, and less than 1% retained anything after 6 months (Reilly, 1992, p. 696). Medina (2009) argued that if keeping someone's attention in a lecture were a business, the failure rate would be 80%. According to Rimer (2009), lectures are going the way of the blackboard. Rimer covered Massachusetts Institute of Technology's (MIT) shift away from lecture noting:

> The physics department has replaced the traditional large introductory lecture with smaller classes that emphasize hands-on, interactive, collaborative learning. Last fall, after years of experimentation and debate and resistance from students, who initially petitioned against it, the department made the change permanent. Already, attendance is up and the failure rate has dropped by more than 50 percent. (n.p.)

The evidence is not favorable for traditional lecturing. Although lectures certainly have their place as an educational method, they are not always the best pedagogical choice. Shifting to a more active learning format allows instructors to experiment and learners to more fully engage with content.

3 Active Learning

Active learning can be understood literally—it is the process of engaging learners with the topic and each other where they are talking, doing, and creating, together. Active learning is also known as guided instruction—a constructivist process grounded in the belief that learners learn best through interactions with the world and other learners that allow them to create and cocreate meaning about the topic. This section defines and provides strategies for active learning. Active learning is important since it is not possible to transmit knowledge to learners simply by telling them what they need to know. Active learning challenges learners' thinking and engages them in applied activities to test their knowledge:

> Active learning is an umbrella term for learning and teaching methods which put the students in charge of their own learning: through *meaningful* activities, they *think about* and *apply* what they are learning. It is a deliberate contrast against passive learning (italics added for emphasis). (University of Leicester, n.d.)

Active learning is a process that shifts the focus from the instructor as central to the student as central. Concern is focused on the *process* of learning, not just the *content*. Active learning encourages learners to think about and apply the content in ways that enhance learning. Active learning has several markers: Learners do most of the work, use their brains, are on the move, and do most of the talking. Learning is fast-paced and engaging. Some people might blanch at the idea, "learners do most of the work." That does not mean the instructor throws out a discussion question and sits in a corner. What it means is that the instructor has prepared in advance so that when learners are in class, they are the ones talking and engaging, with the instructor guiding and advising as needed, rather than droning on in a passive lecture.

Before launching into a discussion of how to make your teaching more engaging and active, you might want to take Lang's (2016) advice from his book, *Small Teaching*. Lang was not an advocate of whole-scale dumping of your curriculum and starting over with an entirely new teaching approach. Instead, Lang advocated making small changes that have a big impact such as adding small modifications to course design, changing how you communicate with students, or shifting how you give feedback. Lang also recommended adding brief 5–10-min classroom or online learning activities that provide quick opportunities for engagement, introducing, or concluding topics. Five minutes is not much time to take an adequate lesson and make it memorable. Lang also advised using one-time interventions in a course where you might do a longer interactive event once or twice a semester but not build your entire course around new activities. The next section focuses on interactive lecturing and alternatives to lecture.

3.1 Interactive Lecturing

Interactive lecturing is an excellent process for creating more engaged, active learning experiences for learners in face-to-face or online classes. Interactive lecturing is considered an active learning method, one grounded in a constructivist philosophy of designing pedagogy that fully engages learners in the process and helps them create meaning. To alleviate the audio bombardment of lecturing, master trainer Bob Pike recommended that participants be given a chance every 8 min to internalize what they have been hearing before it's simply supplanted with the next wave of information (Pike, 2003 in Silberman, 2006, p. 3). This might mean giving short opportunities to discuss the issue, write, or take a quiz. Additionally, interactive lectures should be visually pleasing. Silberman (2006) underscored that 80–90% of all information absorbed by the brain is visual. Accordingly, adding visuals to a lesson resulted in a 14–38% improvement in retention. Additionally, vocabulary mastery can be improved up to 200% with the addition of visuals, and the time required to present a concept decreases up to 40% when visuals are used (Silberman, 2006, p. 3).

Lecturing has its limitations, as outlined earlier in this chapter. What are the alternatives for instructors who wish to improve their teaching? The good news is that they don't have to stop lecturing entirely. One effective option is to create an interactive lecture. Another is to integrate active learning experiences into the class period, which will be discussed in the next section.

Sometimes lecturing is necessary and can be more effective when learners are engaged. Interactive lecture is when "Students interact with the instructor in two-way communication, asking questions and engaging in discussion" (Abeysekera, 2008, p. 192), or "A social event where the lecturer can enhance (student) participation" (Morell, 2004, p. 326). Interactive lecturing has been shown effective, for example: Afrasiabifar and Asadolah (2019) studied a shift from traditional lecture to interactive lecture with nursing students and found statistically significant differences between groups in mean test scores and satisfaction with their learning experience. The interactive lectures also promoted more sharing of feedback and active participation. Downs and Wilson (2015) reported positive effects of shifting to active learning in biology courses at a South African university. Further, when students work together to solve real-world problems, engagement, attention, and knowledge retention increase dramatically (Bishop & Verleger, 2013; Strayer, 2012). Finally, other advantages of interactive lecture include as follows: Students enrolled in active learning courses ($N = 2084$) outperformed students in traditional courses by two standard deviations (Hake, 1998). Students reported more learning from active learning activities versus lecture only. Nursing students who experienced active learning activities scored significantly higher on a standardized assessment test than students who only received lectures (Everly, 2013).

Interactive lecture has several characteristics (Eison, 2010): The instructor pauses the lecture periodically for structured activities such as small group discussion, writing exercises, or non-consequential quizzes. The instructor is also monitoring the learners' energy and attention and introduces activities when interest wanes and assesses learner comprehension as the class period unfolds. Interactive lecturers create expectations that learners will respond to their questions, rather than fall into the "Anybody, anybody?" routine described at the beginning of this chapter. Interactive lecturers bolster participation by encouraging student-to-student conversation, assigning interactive work, providing opportunities to correct misunderstandings, and using interactive technology such as clickers, cards, or web-based activities. Finally, interactive lectures have high rates of attendance (Eison, 2010). What are some ways to make lectures interactive?

Giving a Practical Demonstration Demonstrations have been used in education since ancient times and are likely as old as the lecture. A demonstration involves conveying ideas, principles, or processes using visual prompts such as a flip chart, poster, presentation, or following specific steps. Instead of just telling students about the lesson, you are showing them how to do it. Cooking shows, for example, are popular demonstrations for teaching cooks the techniques of measuring, sautéing, or baking. Demonstrations usually produce a finished product such as showing how to use a database or computer program, filling out a form, conducting an experiment, or performing a procedure. When conducting a demonstration, you should make sure it is relevant to the subject, collect the necessary supplies, list the steps to be followed, rehearse how you will describe each step, and assemble any visual aids you will be using.

Posing Questions Asking good questions is a key aspect of learning (Chin & Osborne, 2008) and can be powerful during a lesson, and the ability to critically question and argue is viewed as core to developing scientific literacy (UNESCO, 2005). Questions not only help students learn but also guide educators' assessment of learners' thinking and understanding. Yet learners rarely ask questions (Almeida & Teixeira-Dias, 2012). Questions can serve multiple purposes such as to pique interest, assess prior knowledge, challenge world views, stimulate recall or prior knowledge, focus on key theories or ideas, extend thinking, promote reflection and critical thinking, and assess learning.

One challenge when posing questions is to give ample "wait time" or periods of silence following a question posed by the instructor (Rowe, 1972, 1987). Rowe, who originated the term, found that the average pause after a teacher asked a question was 1.5 s—not long enough for learners to formulate a question. Interestingly, she found that even doubling that time to 3 s improved responses. Allotting 3+ s resulted in a higher proportion of correct answers, higher student participation, and improved test scores. Stahl (1990, 1994) evolved the concept to "think time" as allotting a period of uninterrupted silence for information processing tasks, feeling assessment, oral responses, and action. Irving and Garling (n.d.) recently observed:

> It is necessary to give students some time to think about the questions and formulate a response. Even though it can feel like you have been waiting forever for an answer, or even just some small sign that they heard you, in reality it was probably less than one second. On average, teachers only wait 0.7 and 1.4 seconds after asking a question (Stahl, 1994). Try counting to at least three in your mind (one mis-sis-sip-pi, two mis-sis-sip-pi, etc.) before repeating the question or rewording it. Nobody wants to turn into the economics teacher in *Ferris Bueller's Day Off.* (n.p.)

More complicated questions require even longer "think time" for learners to formulate a meaningful reply. I have found counting slowly to 10 almost always results in good questions from learners. And, if there are none after counting to 10, that is a good indicator that learners are ready to move on to the next point.

When posing questions, it is also important to avoid asking closed questions that can be answered with a "yes" or "no" such as "Do you agree with this model?" A better question is an open question that requires a response such as: "What about this topic is still unclear or confusing to you?" or "What aspects of this theory do you agree/disagree with?" or "What else would you like to know about the topic?" Open questions help learners review what was presented and participate by asking questions. You can also use these questions to promote small group discussions, discussed below.

Using Learner Polling Technology has made using "clickers" in the classroom possible with strokes on a keyboard or smartphone, and Freeman, Blayney, and Ginns (2006) found that the anonymity increased student response rates. You can use polling to track attendance, assess learning, administer quizzes, determine stances on emotionally or politically charged issues, solicit feedback, manage question-and-answer periods, or play games. Free or reasonably priced apps are available to help you customize your classroom and engage learners in your lectures. Technology is not even required to poll learners. You can simply do it by inviting a show of hands: "How many of you have heard of this principle?" or "How many of you have experienced this phenomenon?" or "How many of you agree/disagree with this view?" You can also give learners cards to hold up that show degrees of agreement: green = agree, yellow = not sure, and red = disagree. You can also engage in polling on foot by putting answers or ideas in the corners or on the walls of the room and asking learners to stand by what they agree with or represents their ideas. I did this once with quotes on leadership. Learners had to stand by the quote that best represented their philosophy and discuss why among the class.

Promoting Small Group Discussions Small group activities are possible even in large lecture classes. Many learners will be timid about speaking up in front of the entire class, so creating safer ways for them to engage with each other is a good strategy. You can facilitate in semester-long classes. For shorter-term educational programs, you can assign different groups during the session. I have achieved this by putting different color dots on folders or notecards and passing them out and asking learners to find others who have matching dot colors. You can also use playing cards, candy, birth months, and so on. The list is endless. The only grouping that works poorly in my experience is counting off. It takes time, people forget their number, and chaos ensues as you try to move people into groups.

You can assign all groups the same question or different questions dealing with different issues, as is appropriate for the lesson. After small group discussion, it works well to bring everyone back together and entertain key insights, controversies, and questions. Another strategy is to have students pair with just one other person before moving them into larger group discussion. This small "warm-up" conversation will prime the conversation with the larger, more challenging group. When you assign activities, particularly small group discussion, you will need to actively monitor the groups and intervene when there are questions or confusion about the process and remind the learners about the time limit for the activity. Brookfield and Preskill (2012) have written a comprehensive guide to using discussion as a pedagogy, and their book is an excellent resource.

Quick Strategies for Bolstering Participation in an Interactive Lecture If, per Lang's *Small Teaching* advice (Lang, 2016), you prefer to begin with small steps as you shift to interactive lectures, you might adopt one or more of the following quick and easy activities to bring more life to lectures.

Focused Listing Focused listing is giving participants the chance to do some brainstorming. If you have time, you can ask learners to discuss their answers with a partner or raise them with the class at large. Here are examples of questions that you can put on a slide or handout or simply ask:

1. On your notes, create a list of terms or ideas related to. . .
2. List 5 things you know about. . .
3. List 3 things that are unclear about. . .

Generate Real-Life Examples This strategy involves asking students to identify real-world instances of a concept or category. For example, if you are studying climate change, you might ask students to identify recent natural catastrophes in the news such as hurricanes, rising water levels, drought, or flooding. Once you begin generating examples, these provide great springboards for conversation among pairs or small groups.

Finish the Sentence This activity involves presenting a topic for learners to consider and then asking them to finish a sentence that will prompt paired, small group, or full class discussion. Consider, for example, the debate about vaccinations. You might ask students to finish the following sentences:

An alternative way of thinking about this would be _____.
A point I agree/disagree with is _____.

A variation of this activity is to use it to introduce or conclude a topic. For example, when you are introducing a topic you might ask:

My challenge with [topic] is _____.
My excitement about [topic] is _____.

When you conclude an interactive lecture, you might try one or more of these sentences for learners to complete:

I didn't know that _____.
The thing about [topic] that isn't clear is _____.
Next, I will try _____.
This experience has made me think _____.

Think-Pair-Share This format is popular because it is easy to remember the steps of (1) *think* about a topic, (2) *pair* with another person to discuss your thinking, and (3) *share* your insights, conclusions, or questions. After the pairs have finished their conversation, you can invite unresolved questions, issues, and other points to debrief the activity and to synthesize reflections.

As you can see, there are many options for making your lectures more engaging and interactive. The bottom line is that interactive lecturing is a best practice when time, budgets, or the topic lends itself to lecturing. Even the largest lectures can do interactive activities that help break up the monotony of listening to one person speak beyond the point that anyone is still listening. Links to examples of interactive lecturing are provided at the end of this chapter.

3.2 Engaging Learners Through Active Learning

Perhaps you are ready to shift away from lecture as your primary pedagogy and would like to try active learning techniques or guided instruction. That does not mean you never lecture, or that you have to radically shift your teaching repertoire.

Active learning was defined earlier in this chapter as engaging learners with the topic and each other where they are talking, doing, and creating, together.

Michael (2006) reviewed pedagogical research across the sciences to find the best evidence available and found "There IS evidence that active learning, student-centered approaches to teaching physiology work, and they work better than more passive approaches" (p. 165). Michael noted five conclusions about active learning from his research: (1) learning involves the active construction of meaning by the learner (p. 160); (2) learning facts ("what"—declarative knowledge) and learning to do something ("how"—procedural knowledge) are two different processes (p. 161); (3) some things that are learned are specific to the domain or context (subject matter or course) in which they were learned, whereas other things are more readily transferred to other domains (p. 161); (4) individuals are likely to learn more when they learn with others than when they learn alone (p. 161); and (5) meaningful learning is facilitated by articulating explanations, whether to one's self, peers, or teachers (p. 162).

In fact, although I have argued for abandoning the traditional lecture, some lecture might be necessary to reach your educational objectives. What you might consider is using the "lecturette"—a short, 10–15-min description of the concepts, followed by activities that engage learners. Shorter lectures align with the limited attention span of adult learners that has been reported at approximately 20 min (Bonwell & Eison, 1991). Johnstone and Percival (1976) studied learners in 90+ lectures with 12 different instructors. They found that learners took 3–5 min to settle at the beginning of a class session before they fully focused their attention on the instruction. Learners experienced their next attention lapse approximately 10–18 min later. Fatigue set in toward the end of a lecture where attention span was as little as 3–4 min. Cluskey, Elbeck, Hill, and Strupeck (2011) confirmed that Johnston and Percival's findings are consistent with Burns' (1985) conclusion that considering the limited attention span of 15–20 min for university students and the reality that university courses last approximately 50–75 min, faculty need to act to hold learners' interest. Attention spans are even shorter today (Cluskey et al., 2011; Moses, 2000), thanks to the highly sensory activities of television and more recently smartphones and tablets, the mere presence of which decreases cognitive capacity (Ward, Duke, Gneezy, & Bos, 2017; Wilmer, Sherman, & Chein, 2017).

Nouri and Shahid (2005) concluded that when faculty rely on a single pedagogy such as lecture with PowerPoint slides, they are viewed as neither effective teachers nor receptive to student concerns. Compensating for low attention spans means that classroom activities should be varied to avoid learner fatigue and loss of attention. This is where interactive lectures and active learning can shift the attention span and engagement of learners to significantly higher levels. An active format allows direct instruction to set up learners to effectively engage in active learning. Demonstration was already described above as an interactive lecture strategy and that method works equally well as an alternative to lecture. I have grouped these active learning alternatives according to the categories of reflective practice; information seeking, analysis, and synthesis; group inquiry; games and simulations; and arts-based. Note that these categories are somewhat artificial, as they may overlap. For example, reflective practice activities can be given to individuals or groups.

Reflective Practice Schön (1983) advocated that technical knowledge was not enough for practitioners to excel at their work, and he explored learning, change, and reflection and helped professionals tap into their behavioral and emotional selves. Schön encouraged both reflection in action (making meaning in the midst of an activity—"this isn't going well, how can I intervene?") and reflection on action (after the activity—"What could I have done differently?"). Activities that invite learners to individually and sometimes collectively examine past or current thoughts and actions of themselves or others are processes of reflection. It follows the adage: *The more reflective you are, the more effective you are.* Reflective practice asks learners to stop what they are doing and think about it. This may seem obvious, although people tend to get caught up in the doing or acting phases and often need reminders to stop and think. Reflective practice can be used both during class and between sessions. Reflection can be accomplished in myriad ways, such as journaling. The suggestions below are ideas for reflecting during a class session.

Reflective Pause This break occurs when the instructor builds in some time to reflect. The *Think-Pair-Share* model was discussed earlier and that method works well for a quick reflective activity. You might give learners something to *think* about silently, perhaps using writing. Next, you ask them to *pair* with one other learner and share their reflections. Finally, you invite *sharing* with the partner or class at large. This model is particularly helpful at building learner confidence toward taking more risks in sharing as they begin with the self, next with the other, and finally with the class.

Observation Observation can be a powerful instructional strategy that can occur both during and outside class. A typical observation might be to group the class into triads and ask persons 1 and 2 to engage in an activity such as a discussion about the topic or a role play. Person 3 observes and then shares observations after persons 1 and 2 complete the activity. You can also send learners outside the classroom to observe something relevant to the class and have them report back. For example, a public health class studying safety behaviors might observe people commuting on campus and count how many students are wearing bike helmets (or not wearing them).

Writing Tasks Asking learners to write about the topic under study is powerful because it gives them an opportunity in the moment to synthesize their learning. This type of activity can help learners summarize their thinking, organize their notes, and even assess their learning. A favorite tool is the *minute paper* (Cross & Angelo, 1988). This activity gives the students 1 min to write about the session. Questions might be: "What is the key insight you are taking away from today's class?" or "What do you need to better understand to master this topic?" The instructor can distribute and collect the index cards with answers or invite students to share their comments via an electronic method such as Padlet <https://padlet.com/>. Stead (2005) surveyed the evidence of the minute paper's efficacy concluding "The benefits for both students and teachers appear sizeable for such a modest amount of time and effort, and students generally perceive the one-minute paper favourably" (p. 118).

Mind or Concept Mapping A visual organization or representation of a thought process or idea is a mind or concept map. The map begins with a main idea such as "agriculture," and then other ideas branch from it to show relationships, such as "sustainability" or "pesticides." The maps can be drawn by hand or created using web-based programs to document ideas and how they connect to other ideas. Mapping allows students to both reflect on their understanding of a concept and construct knowledge about it as they make linkages. These maps are also valuable to have learners share and compare how they are understanding the topic. Mapping can be done in class, as homework, or online. The assignment can be given to individuals or groups. Daley and Torre (2010) conducted a literature review to assess 35 studies of concept maps and found that instructors use them in four ways: (1) to promote meaningful learning, (2) to serve as an additional resource for learning, (3) to enable instructors' feedback sharing with students, and (4) to assess learning and performance.

Information Seeking, Analysis, and Synthesis Rather than telling learners the key points, arguments, and connections with other ideas, an active learning strategy is to assign them the task of creating meaning about the topic, grounded in the constructivist philosophy that learners create meaning as they learn. These activities can be individual or collective and help learners deepen their understanding of the topic under study.

Information Search This information-seeking activity assigns individuals or groups different topics and asks them to search for information and share it with a small group or the class. For example, learners could identify top professionals in their field to understand their career path and preparation and compare notes. Learners might also seek out answers to questions about the course content. Another searching activity is to have learners conduct a library search or examine current events on a topic they are learning about.

Study Group Creating study groups where learners complete "homework" done collectively helps them learn from and teach each other during or outside class time. Examples include non-consequential quizzes or tests, creating chronologies or timelines, defining terms, analyzing text, and so forth. Study group activities cover content as efficiently as lecture while saving class time for other activities that require interaction or discussion if done outside class. Instructors can collect written work or quizzes to assess learning.

Debate A debate is a powerful learning method that involves learners taking a perspective, preparing arguments, presenting their position, and competing with another team that has taken the opposing view on the topic. The debate process:

> Requires students to work as individuals and as a team to research critical issues, prepare and present a logical argument, actively listen to various perspectives, differentiate between subjective and objective information, ask cogent questions, integrate relevant information, develop empathy, project confidence, cultivate poise, and formulate their own opinions based on evidence. (Darby, 2007, p. 78)

Usually the debate occurs before an audience, likely the other learners in the class. Participating in or observing a debate allows learner exposure to alternative perspectives on issues and can help the debaters develop communication, critical thinking, and argumentation skills. Darby concluded it was an effective pedagogy with her dental hygiene students because it gave them responsibility for learning and active involvement.

Application Exercise Individual participants or small groups practice applying the course content to real or hypothetical situations so they can improve their performance of the task. Campitelli and Gobet (2011) called this "deliberative practice" and explained, "Deliberate practice (DP) occurs when an individual intentionally repeats an activity in order to improve performance. The claim of the DP framework is that such behavior is *necessary* to achieve high levels of expert performance" (p. 280). For example, accounting students might have to create profit and loss statements or medical students might practice taking blood pressure on each other. These professionals must master these procedures to be effective in their fields. Applying the content or procedure is essential to developing competence on the key course objectives; it involves participants actively, helps transfer learning to real world, and allows assessment and feedback in the moment.

Group Inquiry Group inquiry is the process of small groups engaging in reflective practice about the concepts or issues under study. If you are skeptical about grouping students, consider the following ways the activity enhances learning by: anchoring new knowledge to existing knowledge, enhancing knowledge retention, helping recall due to contextual application, promoting intellectual and emotional connections to topic, offering peer guidance and immediate feedback, and facilitating synthesis and integration. Group learning also encourages attentive and respectful listening between learners; builds relevant skills in the areas of decision-making, problem-solving, and application; develops real-world collaborative and interpersonal skills; fosters diversity of perspectives; promotes tolerance for ambiguity or complexity; and helps cultivate empathy. Group learning can present challenges to the instructor in terms of balancing levels of participation whether it is student to student or student to instructor. It can also be difficult to monitor and assess learning; to create inclusive activities that are sensitive to race, gender, class, and other positionalities; and finally, to manage different knowledge levels among learners.

Case Study Case study involves introducing learners to actual or hypothetical circumstances related to course content where they attempt to solve or resolve the challenges of the situation. Current events can serve as excellent case studies that relate to the case content. Most fields have case studies featured in their publications (e.g., *Harvard Business Review* case studies appear in every issue) and association websites and sometimes are available as texts. Case studies can be open-ended or include conclusions. Case studies are beneficial because they demonstrate real-world application of course content and provide an exciting basis for discussion, exercises, or papers.

Jigsaw Activity The jigsaw (Aronson, 1975, 1978) is a collaborative learning technique. Just as in a jigsaw puzzle, each piece—each learner's part—is essential for the completion and full understanding of the final product. Continuing the jigsaw

Jigsaw Learning Activity Groupings (n=12 students total)		
Original Grouping	**Second Grouping**	**Original Grouping**
Each of the 4 groups has 3 members that will separate into new, larger groups with unique learning tasks.	The four groups move into 3 new, larger groups, and are given a teaching task that they will bring back to their original group.	The original groups reunite. Each member was in a different group (A, B, C) and shares their lesson with the original group. So, group number 1 paired with learning task A, B, or C, and so on.
Group 1: 1, 1 ,1	**Group A:** 1, 2, 3, 4	**Group 1:** 1A, 1B, 1C
Group 2: 2, 2, 2	**Group B:** 1, 2, 3, 4	**Group 2:** 2A, 2B, 2C
Group 3: 3, 3, 3	**Group C:** 1, 2, 3, 4	**Group 3:** 3A, 3B, 3C
Group 4: 4, 4, 4		**Group 4:** 4A, 4B,4C

Fig. 1 Jigsaw learning activity groupings

metaphor, this activity consists of putting a group together (original group), taking it apart (second group), and putting it back together again (original group) with a lesson imparted as a final product and completion of the puzzle (see Fig. 1). Here is how it works: You begin with groups of 3–4 members (group size depends on the topic being covered). Once these groups are established, they are divided up again and separated into new, larger groups. So, like a puzzle that started out put together, it is taken apart at the start.

The new groups are now given a specific learning task. For instance, if the topic were learning theory, each group would receive a learning theory to cover (e.g., andragogy, self-directed learning, transformational learning, experiential learning). The new or second groups now have the task of learning their topic and creating a teaching plan to bring back to their original group. Once the new groups have completed their lessons, the members return to their original group to deliver the lesson. The only access any member of the original group has to the other lessons is through each group member who has a unique contribution to make to group learning. The jigsaw is beneficial because it is interactive, egalitarian, effective, and efficient. The jigsaw process also encourages listening, engagement, and empathy by giving each member of the group an essential part to play in the academic activity. This collaborative activity helps build learning community and facilitates interaction among all learners and helps them value each other as contributors to their common task. This activity works best if the instructor prepares written materials to assist each group with their teaching tasks. This also ensures that key information is included in the lessons. This activity will be a bit chaotic—just like learning tends to be!

Games and Simulations Learners practice course concepts using simple to complex structure with rules such as a board game, quiz show, or simulated real-life situation. A simple Google search will yield several platforms on which to create a game that can be played using smartphones or tablets. Games or simulations represent a fun, creative way to introduce or review course content that can involve competition and/or cooperation. Kumar and Lightner (2007) found that corporate trainers were more inclined to use games in teaching than were university faculty and that learners generally responded favorably to learning games.

Learning Tournament A learning tournament may use a game or simulation format and small groups compete against each other, usually to see how many correct answers they can tally or who can complete steps of a process or procedure most accurately or fastest. A popular format is to play a form of a US game show called "Jeopardy" where students have to guess questions to answers that are flashed on a screen. Fisher (2019) reviewed 12 free customizable Jeopardy templates for instructional use, and additional resources are readily available via a Google search.

Role Play Learners assume roles of individuals or groups and act out planned or improvised scenarios. For example, students could role play how to and how not to do something (e.g., a procedure, interview, or social interaction). The amount of structure for the role play can vary, depending on purpose and educational objectives. Role plays are effective in teaching attitudes and interpersonal skills; plus, they provide practice on course objectives while enhancing transfer of learning to real world.

3.3 Arts-Based

Arts-based education embraces artistic skills as key tools to understand concepts, disciplines, and ideas and to foster creative thinking, collaboration, and critical thinking. Artistic activities apply to any field, not just the arts.

Moving from STEM to STEAM There has been advocacy to move from STEM (science, technology, engineering, and mathematics) to STEAM (science, technology, engineering, *art*, and mathematics) education. Arguments for making this shift to add arts emphasis are grounded in the need for learners to develop skills in creative thinking, collaboration, confidence building, critical thinking, and cultural awareness. Arts in education have been found to help nonscience majors understand the science underlying chemistry where separate sections of an introductory chemistry course was taught using a traditional instructor-centered lecture approach (control group) and the other section taught using hands-on activities performed by groups (experimental group) (Hemraj-Benny & Beckford, 2014). The study concluded that students who were exposed to the experimental group preferred a balance of activities and summary lecturing, appreciated the scientific works through hands-on activities, developed better self-confidence in using scientific facts, had less fear than the control group, and earned higher overall averages on their chemistry exams.

Visual Thinking Strategies Visual thinking strategies (VTS) are one example of how using the arts can help learners grapple with challenging problems. VTS helps learners cultivate an openness and capacity to share their own ideas while respecting the diverse perspectives of other learners. Recently, I attended a lecture using classical paintings to help us understand learning and gendered power relations.

The instructor showed pieces of art and then followed a VTS process by asking us to discuss what was happening in the social interactions depicted. The conversation was rich and varied—no one saw quite the same things in the artworks under discussion. VTS has a range of applications, for example, visual brainstorming where participants sketch their ideas and then describe them to each other. Having recently built a house, I often observed my architect and builder sketching out ideas or potential fixes to design challenges.

Börekçi's (2017) detailed findings of visual analyses conducted on 369 sketch ideas generated visual brainstorming sessions by a total of 25 participants, following the same design brief. The paper provides a blueprint for trying this activity in your own practice and concluded that there are a range of individual visual thinking styles in producing design solutions and that this type of activity yields rapid development of alternatives. The type of idea generator a learner is also impacts their participation. Individuals were overly sensitive to feedback from the group. The idea generation strategies of the participants were the most challenged with this process, whereas the most effective were able to use the group dynamics to help generate and communicate solutions.

Active learning has multiple benefits for learners. Even the smallest changes to your courses can yield big results. Keep in mind that learning is enhanced if people are asked to do the following with their peers: State the information in their own words, give examples, see connections with other ideas, and apply it to case situations (Silberman, 2006, p. 4). The next section offers some strategies for designing active learning into your own teaching.

4 Designing for Active Learning

Winston Churchill (1952) was known for saying, "I am always ready to learn although I do not always like being taught." What he was likely referring to was the drudgery that is sometimes considered learning when the learner must passively absorb wisdom from a teacher. Designing for active learning can help you create more meaningful, engaging experiences for learners so your learners are not experiencing Churchill's lament.

This section has offered evidence that active learning promotes improved learning over passive approaches. It also highlighted strategies for integrating active learning into your teaching whether in higher education courses, corporate seminars, or community workshops. How do you design for active learning? It is not something that should be left to chance. Active learning should be intentional and doing it well requires planning. To begin, you should identify a subject you regularly teach and select a 10–15-min segment of it to revise into an active learning session. One way to think about the segment is in the major pieces of beginning, middle, and end.

The Beginning The beginning is important, because this is where you pique the interest and motivation of the learners. This can be done in at least three ways. The first is to *hook the learner*—motivate them to participate with a topical story, provocative statement, rhetorical question, video, images, music, surprise, or some other interesting connection to the topic. Next, you should *state the goals* of the lesson by finishing this sentence: "As a result of our class period on _____ you should be able to _____." Finally, you should engage learners in *reflection* about the topic. Ask: What is their previous experience with the topic? What do they know about it? How do they feel about it? What would they like to know about it? During the beginning, I also like to give a brief exercise that serves as an ice breaker that accomplishes the previous activities (hook, goal, reflection) as well as gets learners engaging and talking with each other. Opening exercises also help to build community among the learners, assess the level of knowledge about the topic, and immediately engage learners in activity.

The Middle The middle section is the heart of the lesson—it incorporates the content and activity. Generally, active learning should include a moderate amount of content that allows for learners to spend time engaging with the information. A variety of learning approaches should be used that moderate activity from something that is low-activity, such as a demonstration, to a high-activity task such as discussing a case study in small groups. Lectures tend to focus primarily on cognitive information such as terms, concepts, or chronologies that must be memorized, at the expense of behavioral activities where students have to follow the steps of a process or procedure and learn by doing or affective activities where learners engage with topics that may be emotion-laden, controversial, or contested and have to manage feelings, conflicted values, and motivations. Active learning also plans for learners working with each other to share their expertise and experience as they grapple with real-life issues.

As you build the middle of your course, you should plan a brief introduction to the topic and an activity for learners that helps meet the intended learning goals. You can select one of the activities shared earlier in the chapter. For example, a psychology course might begin with a principle of group dynamics, and the activity might be a group decision simulation that would allow the learners to see how group dynamics play out in real life. The course section might repeat this process multiple times, depending on the length of the class period. More about planning the heart of the lesson is discussed in the next section.

The End To create a memorable ending, it is recommended that the class end with an activity. Reflective activities are especially powerful because they help learners summarize key points and consider what was meaningful about the lesson or how they might apply it. Some quick introspective activities might include having learners assess their key insights, recognize areas of confusion, connect the lesson to real life, determine applications of the lesson, identify new questions, or take a practice quiz. Ending in this way helps to ensure learning transfer—that the lessons learned will be applied or translated in real life. Some useful strategies for bolstering transfer included having learners write 1-minute papers on the topic, participate in non-consequential contests or games, write action plans, take pretests or quizzes, do homework, or work on team projects outside class. Note that activities requiring additional time can often start in class and be completed outside of class. This is also a good time to share a preview of what is coming in the next lesson.

4.1 Another Design Approach for Active Learning: The "POP"

Many years ago, when I was a faculty at a community college, my colleague, Dr. Linda Howdyshell, shared her rubric for planning meetings: the "POP" (*purpose, outcomes, and process*). The simple planning design resonated, and I have been tweaking the model for over 20 years. The POP can be used to plan just about anything, and I use it regularly to design curriculum, create training programs, and plan meetings. Let's break it down.

P = Purpose The first step to planning anything is to determine the overarching purpose of the event, in this case a classroom session. The easiest way to complete this step is to complete the following statement: "*The purpose of this lesson is to share and process information relative to _____.*" You should be able to succinctly state what you intend to do with the course session. If you cannot articulate the purpose, you have more work to do to ensure it is clear and will provide direction for your curricular design.

O = Outcomes Next, you complete the following statement: "*As a result of this lesson, you should be able to _____.*" Table 1 provides some examples. The outcomes should be active and starting them with a verb is recommended. They should also be specific and address one outcome at a time. Outcomes are useful for creating common expectations among all participants, providing a focus for instructional design, helping assess whether diverse approaches to the content are being taken, and establishing benchmarks for measuring outcomes. Once the outcomes are developed, everything you do in your course session, whether it is content or activity, should serve one or more of the outcomes. If content and activities do not serve the intended outcomes, they should not be included in the session.

P = Process The final step is to determine the best process or method for achieving the stated purpose and outcomes. This entails determining the content and activities from beginning to end and sequencing them in a coherent format for the class session. Selecting content is challenging because the temptation exists to include more that is ideal to cover in a course session. This is where balancing key content and activity is helpful. You should start by prioritizing content into three categories and focusing primarily on the first:

1. What participants must know.
2. What participants should know.
3. What participants could know.

Table 1 Outcome examples

Example	Your turn
1. Describe the main shortcomings of lecture as an instructional method	1. Outcome 1...
2. Plan an interactive learning session	2. Outcome 2...
3. Apply at least one active learning strategy to a class session	3. Outcome 3...

Incorporating Active Learning into Your Educational Repertoire

Table 2 Activity levels of instructional strategies

Low	Medium	High
Lecture	Reflective pause	Think-pair-share
Panel	Writing tasks	Case study
Symposium	Small group discussion	Debate
Demonstration	Reflective practice	Real-world trial and error
Polling	Listening group	Skill or procedure practice
Posing questions	Role playing	Jigsaw
Focused listing	Reflective practice	Games and simulations
Generate real-life examples	Observation	Learning tournament
Finish the sentence	Information search	Mind or concept mapping
	Storytelling	Application exercise
	Silence	Visual thinking strategies

Once your content is confirmed, planning your process provides a roadmap of your plan, including structured learning activities that correspond with the session learning purpose and outcomes. As you select activities to complement the content, keep in mind that you will want to vary the activity level from low to medium to high as depicted in Table 2.

Keep in mind the short attention spans of learners and intersperse content with activities. I aim to incorporate opening and closing activities which helps create a beginning hook and an ending closure for the session as discussed in the previous section. Mapping the process also allows you to identify what media, materials, and methods you will use so you can assess how varied the levels of involvement are and whether you are balancing content and active participation. You might also choose to build in activities that help you assess learning during the session such as a "1-minute paper" and/or evaluate the session at the end. I like to include some concluding activities that help learners focus on: (1) What are your key learnings from this session? (2) What is at least one thing you will try in your own practice?

A template of a POP is featured in Table 3 for your own adoption. There is space at the top for logistical information such as session title, date, time, place, attendees, and prework if needed (e.g., reading assignments). The process section has columns for time of day (e.g., 9:00 AM); allotted time (e.g., 0.15 min or 1.0 h); learning outcome(s); content, methods, and activities; and materials and media. The beauty of this document is it has all of the information you need for your educational session at a glance.

Active learning means giving learners exercises during or outside the session. Incorporating exercises creates powerful experiences for learners. A caution: a smooth exercise is a well-facilitated exercise. Table 4 features tips for ensuring your activities are well-managed.

Debriefing an exercise properly is also important to ensure learning transfer. To debrief, review the activity's purpose and evaluate performance against objectives. Ask the learners how they did to keep the energy and participation high. Invite participants to reflect on and share their insights. Reflect on how well the participants

Table 3 POP template

Session title	
Date	
Time	
Place	
Attendees	
Prework	(Activities or assignments you want done in advance of class)
Purpose	The purpose of this session is to share and process information related to...
Outcomes	As a result of this session, you should be able to: 1. 2. 3. ...

Process

Time of day	Allotted time	Learning outcome(s)	Content, methods, and activities	Materials and media

Table 4 Ten strategies for facilitating group exercises

Ten strategies for facilitating group exercises
1. Explain *why* the exercise is being done. Share objectives and benefits
2. Specify *what* participants are supposed to do. Visual backup is recommended. Demonstrate where needed
3. Indicate *who* will do what
4. Direct participants to *where* the activity will take place
5. Indicate *when* the activity will end
6. *Summarize* instructions (or ask a participant to do this)
7. *Observe*, monitor and adjust (to time and other unanticipated variables), and keep activity energized
8. Conduct *process* and *time checks* with groups
9. *Debrief* exercise for key points, feelings, insights, and learning
10. Establish *So what's* and summarize the highlights

learned from others and what was well done during the activity. Also identify opportunities for improvement. Finally, ask participants how they can apply the learning to their life and work.

You do not want your classes to end up like the economics course in the film, "Ferris Bueller's Day Off," with the professor taking an exciting subject and making it boring and then trying to engage the learners who have completely zoned out by pleading, "Anyone, anyone?" How do you avoid being that instructor? I have argued that active learning promotes more engaged and enduring learning, and shared strategies for shifting your teaching away from passive lectures to integrating small collaborative practices, presenting interactive lectures, or, if you are ready, completely shifting your teaching to a more active learning format. Facilitating learning is more powerful than telling learners what you know. Although your boring lectures will soon be forgotten by most students, learning experiences that engage and involve learners will stick with them for years to come.

The key to powerful teaching and learning is variety. Ever mindful of the short attention span of most learners, simply breaking up instruction every 10–15 min with a short activity and change of pace keeps learners attention. Alternating between activities that have low, medium, and high learner involvement also helps keep the pace lively. Taking time to design for interaction and activity is key and will help you be a more mindful, effective educator. Finally, observing colleagues' teaching is a powerful way of learning, as well as inviting them into your classroom to observe and share feedback. It is always possible to improve on a course and learn something new to help you be an even better teacher. My challenge to you is to try something new and see what happens.

This chapter has addressed problems with instructor-centered education and offered alternatives to make learning more engaging through interactive lecturing and active learning. Strategies for improving engagement and learning were shared. Finally, approaches for designing active learning were outlined. Following the ending strategy of inviting reflection, I ask you, as the reader, to consider: What are your key insights from this chapter? What is at least one thing you will try in your own practice? Keep Silberman's (1995) advice in mind as you design and facilitate active learning: "You can tell people what you know very fast. But, they will forget what you tell them even faster. People are more likely to understand what they figure out for themselves than what you figure out for them" (p. ix).

References

Abeysekera, I. (2008). Preferred learning methods: A comparison between international and domestic accounting students. *Accounting Education: An International Journal, 17*(2), 187–198.

Afrasiabifar, A., & Asadolah, M. (2019). Effectiveness of shifting traditional lecture to interactive lecture to teach nursing students. *Investigacion and Educacion En Enfermeria, 37*(1), e07. https://doi-org.proxy-remote.galib.uga.edu/10.17533/udea.iee.v37n1a07.

Almeida, P. A., & Teixeira-Dias, J. J. (2012). Aligning teaching, learning and assessment in a first-year chemistry course. *International Journal of Learning, 18*(4), 143–158.

Aronson, E. (1975). The jigsaw route to learning and liking. *Psychology Today, 8*, 43–59.

Aronson, E. (1978). *The jigsaw classroom*. Thousand Oaks, CA: Sage.

Bishop, J. L., & Verleger, M. A. (2013, June). The flipped classroom: A survey of the research. In *ASEE national conference proceedings, Atlanta, GA* (Vol. 30, No. 9, pp. 1–18).

Bonwell, C. C., & Eison, J. A. (1991). *Active learning: Creating excitement in the classroom*. ASHE-ERIC higher education report no. 1. Washington, DC: Georgetown University Press.

Börekçi, N. A. (2017). Visual thinking styles and idea generation strategies employed in visual brainstorming sessions. *Design and Technology Education, 22*(1), n1.

Brookfield, S. D., & Preskill, S. (2012). *Discussion as a way of teaching: Tools and techniques for democratic classrooms*. San Francisco, CA: Wiley.

Burns, R. A. (1985, May 22–25). *Information impact and factors affecting recall*. Paper presented at the 7th annual national conference on teaching excellence and conference of administrators, Austin, TX.

Campitelli, G., & Gobet, F. (2011). Deliberate practice: Necessary but not sufficient. *Current Directions in Psychological Science, 20*(5), 280–285.

Chin, C., & Osborne, J. (2008). Student's questions: A potential resource for teaching and learning science. *Studies in Science Education, 44*(1), 1–39.

Churchill, W. (1952, November 9). *The Observer*, n.p.

Cluskey, B., Elbeck, M., Hill, K. L., & Strupeck, D. (2011). How students learn: Improving teaching techniques for business discipline courses. *Journal of Instructional Pedagogies, 6*. Retrieved from http://search.ebscohost.com.proxy-remote.galib.uga.edu/login.aspx?direct=true&db=eric&AN=EJ1097028&site=eds-live.

Cross, K. P., & Angelo, T. A. (1988). *Classroom assessment techniques. A handbook for faculty*. San Francisco, CA: Jossey-Bass.

Daley, B. J., & Torre, D. M. (2010). Concept maps in medical education: An analytical literature review. *Medical Education, 44*(5), 440–448.

Darby, M. (2007). Debate: A teaching-learning strategy for developing competence in communication and critical thinking. *American Dental Hygienists' Association, 81*(4), 78–78.

Downs, C. T., & Wilson, A. L. (2015). Shifting to active learning: Assessment of a first-year biology course in South Africa. *International Journal of Teaching and Learning in Higher Education, 27*(2), 261–274.

Eison, J. (2010). Using active learning instructional strategies to create excitement and enhance learning. *Jurnal Pendidikantentang Strategi Pembelajaran Aktif (Active Learning) Books, 2*(1), 1–10.

Everly, M. C. (2013). Are students' impressions of improved learning through active learning methods reflected by improved test scores? *Nurse Education Today, 33*(2), 148–151.

Fisher, S. (2019, May 8). 12 free Jeopardy templates. *Lifewire*. Retrieved from https://www.lifewire.com/free-jeopardy-powerpoint-templates-1358186.

Freeman, M., Blayney, P., & Ginns, P. (2006). Anonymity and in class learning: The case for electronic response systems. *Australasian Journal of Educational Technology, 22*(4), 568.

Gulick, L. H. (1908). *Mind and work*. Page: Doubleday.

Hake, R. R. (1998). Interactive-engagement vs. traditional methods: A six-thousand student survey of mechanics test data for introductory physics courses. *American Journal of Physics, 66*(1), 64–74.

Hemraj-Benny, T., & Beckford, I. (2014). Cooperative and inquiry-based learning utilizing art-related topics: Teaching chemistry to community college nonscience majors. *Journal of Chemical Education, 91*(10), 1618–1622.

Irving, A., & Garling, B. (n.d.). Wait time. *Classroom*. Retrieved from https://questioninganddiscussionforteaching.wordpress.com/wait-time/.

Johnstone, A. H., & Percival, F. (1976). Attention breaks in lectures. *Education in Chemistry, 13*(2), 49–50.

Kumar, R., & Lightner, R. (2007). Games as an interactive classroom technique: Perceptions of corporate trainers, college instructors and students. *International Journal of Teaching and Learning in Higher Education, 19*(1), 53–63. Retrieved from http://search.ebscohost.com.proxy-remote.galib.uga.edu/login.aspx?direct=true&db=eric&AN=EJ901287&site=eds-live.

Lang, J. M. (2016). *Small teaching: Everyday lessons from the science of learning*. San Francisco, CA: Jossey-Bass.

Medina, J. (*2009*). *Brain rules: 12 principles for surviving and thriving at work, home and school*. Seattle, WA: Pear Press.

Mendelson, E. (2013). Who wrote Auden's definition of a professor? *The W. H. Auden Society*. Retrieved from http://audensociety.org/definition.html.

Merriam, S. B., & Bierema, L. L. (2013). *Adult learning: Linking theory and practice*. San Francisco, CA: Jossey-Bass.

Michael, J. (2006). Where's the evidence that active learning works? *Advances in Physiology Education, 30*(4), 159–167. Retrieved from http://search.ebscohost.com.proxy-remote.galib.uga.edu/login.aspx?direct=true&db=cmedm&AN=17108243&site=eds-live.

Morell, T. (2004). Interactive lecture discourse for university EFL students. *English for Specific Purposes, 23*(3), 325–338.

Moses, E. (2000). *The $100 billion allowance: Accessing the global teen market*. New York: John Wiley & Sons, Inc.

Nouri, H., & Shahid, A. (2005). The effect of PowerPoint presentation on student's learning and attitudes. *Global Perspectives on Accounting Education, 2*, 53–73.

Nowlen, P. (1988). Cited in Cervero, R. (1992). Professional Practice, learning, and continuing education: An integrated perspective. *International Journal of Lifelong Education, 11*(2), 91–101.

Penner, J. G. (1984). *Why many college teachers cannot lecture*. Springfield, IL: Thomas.

Reilly, R. F. (1992, September 1). The Erosion of Trust, a speech delivered to the Juniata College Annual Spring Awards Convocation, Huntington, Pennsylvania, April 20, 1992. In *Vital speeches of the day* (Vol. LVIII, No. 22).

Rimer, S. (2009, January 12). At M.I.T., large lectures are going the way of the blackboard. *New York Times*. Retrieved from https://www.nytimes.com/2009/01/13/us/13physics.html.

Rowe, M. B. (1972). *Wait-time and rewards as instructional variables, their influence in language, logic, and fate control*. Paper presented at the National Association for Research in Science Teaching, Chicago, IL. ED 061 103. ERIC Resource Center www.eric.ed.gov http://eric.ed.gov/?id=ED061103.

Rowe, M. B. (1987). Wait time: Slowing down may be a way of speeding up. *American Educator 11*(2), 38–43, 47. EJ 351 827.

Schön, D. A. (1983). *The reflective practitioner: How professionals think in action*. London: Temple Smith.

Silberman, M. (1995). *101 ways to make training active*. San Diego, CA: Pfeiffer.

Silberman, M. (2006). *Active training: A handbook of techniques, designs, case examples and tips*. San Francisco, CA: Wiley.

Stahl, R. J. (1990). *Using "think-time" behaviors to promote students' information processing, learning, and on-task participation. an instructional module*. Tempe, AZ: Arizona State University.

Stahl, R. J. (1994). *Using "think-time" and "wait-time" skillfully in the classroom*. ERIC Clearinghouse. Retrieved from https://files.eric.ed.gov/fulltext/ED370885.pdf.

Stead, D. R. (2005). A review of the one-minute paper. *Active Learning in Higher Education, 6*(2), 118–131.

Strayer, J. F. (2012). How learning in an inverted classroom influences cooperation, innovation, and task orientation. *Learn Environments Research, 15*, 171–193.

Swinehart, D. F. (1980). Swinehart's definition. In P. Dickson (Ed.), *The official explanations*. New York: Dell Publishing.

UNESCO. (2005). *Towards knowledge societies: UNESCO world report*. Paris: UNESCO.

University of Leicester. (n.d.). *Active learning*. Leicester Learning Institute. Retrieved from https://www2.le.ac.uk/offices/lli/developing-learning-and-teaching/enhance/strategies/active-learning

Verner, C., & Dickenson, G. (1967). The lecture: An analysis and review of research. *Adult Education, 17*(2), 85–100.

Ward, A. F., Duke, K., Gneezy, A., & Bos, M. W. (2017). Brain drain: The mere presence of one's own smartphone reduces available cognitive capacity. *Journal of the Association for Consumer Research, 2*(2), 140–154.

Wilmer, H. H., Sherman, L. E., & Chein, J. M. (2017). Smartphones and cognition: A review of research exploring the links between mobile technology habits and cognitive functioning. *Frontiers in Psychology, 8*, 605.

Linking Faculty to Organization Development and Change: Teaching4Learning@Unipd

Monica Fedeli

Abstract Faculty development is intricately connected with organization development and change. Most of the research on faculty development focuses on faculty teaching effectiveness and faculty personal and professional development. The instructor remains the only unit of analysis, with little attention given to the actions and strategies to develop the organization in order to foster excellent teaching while building strong communities of learning. Further, research on faculty development overlooks how to create a culture of innovation, fails to identify the impact of faculty development programs on the organization, and neglects the organizational implications of promoting teaching innovation.

The aim of this chapter is to demonstrate that faculty development, and in particular the program Teaching4Learning@Unipd, could not be realized without a strong institutional commitment to develop and change and to invest money and energy in the innovation process.

Faculty development in this sense can become a means and an opportunity to develop old and prestigious institutions like the University of Padova, involving all different actors at different levels of the organization: personally, and in group, through the building of faculty learning community (FLC) (Adams and Mix, AILACTE J 11:37–56; Cox, New Dir Teach Learn 97(97):5–23, 2004; Int J Acad Dev 1324(September):1–13, 2013; Stanley, Arts Educ Policy Rev 112 (2):71–78, 2011).

This chapter aims to address the following questions: What are the challenges of promoting faculty development at a big Italian university? How can faculty development impact organization development and change? Which strategic actions and practices most cffcctively promote change? What are future opportunities to develop research and practices linked to faculty and organization development?

M. Fedeli (✉)
University of Padova, Padova, Italy
e-mail: monica.fedeli@unipd.it

© Springer Nature Switzerland AG 2019
M. Fedeli, L. L. Bierema (eds.), *Connecting Adult Learning and Knowledge Management*, Knowledge Management and Organizational Learning 8,
https://doi.org/10.1007/978-3-030-29872-2_3

1 The Context and the Background

The University of Padova's (UNIPD) faculty development program, called Teaching4Learning@Unipd, started in January 2016 in response to findings from a nationally funded study called Employability & Competences (Fedeli, 2016; Fedeli, Frison, & Grion, 2017). The goal of the study and research project was to elicit students' voices and perspectives regarding teaching and learning contexts in five Italian universities. Student responses indicated that lecturing was the dominant instructional format, with limited student–faculty interaction during class discussions and group activities. A second emerging theme among the data was faculty's insufficient attention to or consistency regarding informal and formal feedback to students; further, peer and self-evaluation skills and activities were not promoted. Overall, student responses regarding their teaching and learning contexts highlighted the need to foster change in university teaching culture and practices, as well as the importance of involving students more interactively in this change process.

Findings also suggested that instructors of Italian higher education themselves lack awareness of and appreciation for more innovative, personalized, and learner-centered teaching approaches (Dirkx & Serbati, 2017). Furthermore, it is crucial to consider as Neal and Peed-Neal (2010) stated that the effort of innovating teaching practices needs to be "integrated into the cultural fabric of the institution." Historically, Italian higher education culture has de-emphasized attention to pedagogic practice in favor of research activities (Zara, 2017). In the context of a faculty member's career progression, Italian universities assign little importance to teaching performance. Student course evaluations are the only teaching-related documentation considered in the tenure review procedure. Unsurprisingly, lecturing remains the preponderant instructional format, with student–teacher interaction limited or disregarded.

The findings of the study were also consistent with the larger European higher education community where there is a recognized need to draw on both pedagogical and organizational frameworks to foster a more innovative, interactive teaching culture (European Commission, 2011). Other recommendations include regular feedback to students and informing curriculum design through collaborative dialogue inside and outside the university, across stakeholders like instructors, students, graduates, and actors in the labor market (European Commission, 2013).

Despite articulated interest in faculty development across the university, government, and international levels, as exemplified by these study findings, most training initiatives have thus far focused on individual teaching practices without sufficient attention to how the organization contexts can mutually inhibit and foster pedagogical change. This dilemma elicits questions concerning faculty development, such as: How does the institutional context influence the development of innovative practices among faculty? How can innovative teaching and learning practices be defined, shaped, and implemented both inside and outside the university classroom? How is the confluence of institutional and national culture instantiated in Italian universities like UNIPD, and what challenges does it pose for faculty development program promotion and buy-in?

In addressing these questions, this chapter will examine the relationships between faculty development and organizational development and change to navigate these challenges. This relationship also provides insight into the Teaching4Learning@Unipd program's design framework, which is rooted in the understanding that intensive, innovative, long-term faculty development involves faculty and the academic organization which has to demonstrate a strong institutional commitment and readiness to change.

2 Teaching4Learning@Unipd: History, Framework, and Impact

Teaching4Learning@Unipd started in early 2016, and it represented the first step for UNIPD to foster innovative teaching in response to the aforementioned national survey results and European recommendations (European Commission, 2011, 2013). Specifically, it encouraged faculty to experiment and discover new teaching strategies; involved students and promoted their active participation in educational activities; de-privatized teaching; and progressively increased the number of faculty learning communities by building on relationships with interested colleagues. It was initiated by faculty who self-selected to participate and who had significant inclination to improve their approach to teaching and learning.

Each department involved implemented a faculty development program based on the needs of its instructors. The goal was to introduce interactive teaching practices reflecting a model or "an Italian way" for faculty development based on contemporary research of effective practices for student teaching and learning. In addition, as this program was implemented, it became apparent that equal attention had to be given to organizational change alongside training individual faculty innovative practices. This meant putting teaching and learning at the center of reflective discussions and creating a culture for change.

Since 2016, 450 faculty have participated in the faculty development program. A consequence of this experience has been significant anecdotal responses expressed by faculty about the training. A constant among these responses has been that most faculty found the training impactful. As one faculty member stated: "the training was very useful, we should have spent more time at UNIPD in teaching and in training faculty" (Faculty A, July 2018). Similarly, another faculty member stated: "It is sad that after twenty years of teaching, only now we are asked to innovate and devote time to our teaching activities, I really hope that young colleagues can do it better, having the possibility to attend this training" (Faculty B, July 2018). These comments and others reflect the need for UNIPD to spend more time fostering faculty's professional development. They also reflect a desire by faculty members to improve their teaching; even many faculty have spent their careers without ever receiving formal training. Furthermore, UNIPD is implementing a faculty development program for new faculty at the beginning of their career. However, despite their articulated enthusiasm for the program, there was also general sense from the faculty that these new teaching practices were going to be difficult to implement, particularly concerning the institutional emphasis on covering content, which privileges a passive transmission teaching model and formal examinations. The challenge of supporting faculty in this process involves identifying related implications of fostering innovative teaching and learning and the role the organization/institutional culture plays in the development process.

3 Cultural Implications and Faculty Development

Most research focuses on teaching effectiveness of faculty and their personal and professional development, where the instructor is the primary unit of analysis, with little attention given to organization within the university and its role in building a culture of innovation (Adams & Mix, 2014; Swanwick, 2008). Faculty development should be "an institution-wide pursuit with the intent of professionalizing the educational activities of clinical teachers, enhancing educational infrastructure, and building educational capacity for the future" (Swanwick, 2008, p. 339). Faculty development can have an important impact on the curriculum, on career development, but also on and in concert with the organization, can promote cultural change, and improve the performance of both students and faculty.

The Teaching4Learning@Unipd program design affirms the need to instantiate faculty development at both the practice and institutional levels. As such, its faculty development framework is informed by constructivist learning and teaching theories. It also situates faculty development, particularly its emphasis on transforming teaching practice, in relation to organizational development and change. The following sections outline the key theoretical frameworks and constructs underpinning faculty development and link faculty development with organization change. The chapter concludes by discussing the mutually constitutive roles of faculty and organizational development, whereby faculty development promotes organizational change, in turn, supports faculty development.

4 Faculty Development: How Faculty Learn to Teach

Scholarship concerning faculty development has predominantly been grounded in constructivist social learning theories and adult learning theories. What these two domains of theory share is an assumption "that (human) knowledge is acquired through a process of active construction" (Fox, 2001, p. 24) in relation to others. Along with a constructivist framework, situated learning theory offers insight into how a novice learner becomes more expert (Lave & Wenger, 1991). From this perspective, faculty build new knowledge and understanding through gradual participation in an academic community (e.g., teacher study groups; faculty learning communities) committed to innovative teaching and learning (Cornelius-White, 2007; Hagenauer & Volet, 2014). These theories also bring the significance of learning contexts to the fore, especially the importance of creating more authentic learning environments within the classroom.

Conceptually, a "community of practice" construct (Lave & Wenger, 1991) offers a rich framework for understanding the process of faculty change, especially in terms of fostering faculty development within an authentic and collaborative context. Wenger (1998) defined a community of practice as "a unique combination of three fundamental elements: a domain of knowledge, which defines a set of issues, a community of people who care about this domain and the shared practice that they are developing to be effective in their domain" (p. 15). A community of practice stance views learning as a fundamentally social phenomenon. This resonates with the complexity of university culture, in which each academic department reflects its own practices, norms, and conventions regarding teaching and learning. Communities of practice, like faculty development, emerge out of necessity to accomplish tasks and promote growth within, across, and outside of organizations.

A community of practice approach also offers insight into how those new to the academy learn about teaching—both effective and ineffective practices—informally, especially through direct experience with students and peer faculty. These contexts promote nuanced and complex faculty development when taken up through the communities of practice lens. Faculty learn directly from students in the learning community of a classroom, and they learn from both structured and unstructured discussion within their peer community (such as in the office, at formal meetings, and so forth). Recognizing the significance that a community of practice has in shaping practice among new and more experienced faculty, establishes a rationale for creating purposeful communities of practice with the intent to foster innovative teaching and learning.

5 Faculty Development as a Community of Practice

Communities and groups are often the focus of organizational development interventions, based on the value that adults are continually learning, developing, and changing throughout their lives (Merriam & Bierema, 2014). One of the most powerful interventions of organization change in universities is to create purposeful communities of practice among faculty that collaboratively exchange teaching approaches and support each other within the workplace context. Identified often as a faculty learning community (FLC) which is designed to improve teaching, promote scholarship, and build collaboration among peers, with an emphasis on sharing and practicing teaching and learning activities within small groups (Adams & Mix, 2014; Cox, 2004, 2013; Stanley, 2011). Terminology for faculty communities of practice varies in the literature, differentiated by a variety of factors like institutional type and purpose, such as the following: faculty learning communities (Cox, 2004; Daly, 2011; Nugent et al., 2008; Schlitz et al., 2009); learning communities (MacKenzie et al., 2010; Sherer, Shea, & Kristensen, 2003); critical friendship groups (Adams & Mix, 2014); faculty study groups (Wildman, Hable, Preston, & Magliaro, 2000); collaborative teacher study groups (Stanley, 2011); research learning community (Holmes & Kozlowski, 2014); peer mentoring (Angelique, Kyle, & Taylor, 2002; Darwin & Palmer, 2009); and teacher groups (Heinrich, 2014).

The following characteristics are relatively consistent across these variations of faculty learning communities—FLCs: they are generally small groups of faculty volunteers (8–15) who establish a symmetrical relationship among participants and collaboratively plan meeting agendas. Group norms in the FLCs are often interdisciplinary and group members are diverse in rank. FLCs meet regularly over sustained period of time during the academic year. The process is seen as "members moving towards a de-privatization of teaching" through an open sharing of their practice alongside recognizing the "social, emotional, and personal nature of sharing such work" (Adams & Mix, 2014, p. 41). Structurally, they can range from independent organic entities that emerge in response to a particular issue, self-manage, and dissolve over time to institutionally established and organized, with outside persons involved as facilitators and leaders. As Stanley (2011) observed, "with or without external leadership, the most successful study groups contain collaborative elements: goals are shared, and groups are organized around the aim of codifying and improving the local knowledge that is most important to their particular members" (p. 72). They operate from the assumption that such groups are essential for change because they provide the ideal setting for faculty to "reinvent themselves as educators" in concert with their peers, "experimenting, reflecting, discussing, and assessing" their conceptions and approaches to teaching and learning (Sturko & Gregson, 2008, p. 36). The attention to community of practice and their importance has increased over the last several decades. This form of collaboration combined with the complexity of the organizational context encourages universities to devote efforts to their creation and support (Anderson, 2016). Also, successful organizational interventions, such as community of practices, are aligned with the organization's mission in order to support people to commit to the goal of improving practice.

This collaborative orientation is theoretically informed by the tenets of human inquiry (Dewey, 1916), in which the purpose of education and learning is to instill the ability and the desire for change in experience. It is also based on the concept of collaborative learning that helps faculty and students to work together interdependently in an increasingly collaborative world (Bruffee, 1987). Finally, this orientation is also supported by the concept of communities of practice (Sherer et al., 2003; Wenger, McDermott, & Snyder, 2002). The collaboration evolves from the development of a learning community. The "community structure creates a social fabric for learning with the development of trust and energy to encourage risk-taking, to share the specific knowledge and products that the community develops" (Cox, 2013, p. 19).

At present, the major research findings, although tentative at best, emerge from a variety of case studies where faculty development programs have been implemented and evaluated. They have been discussed in the literature as having "multiple benefits for faculty members including increased feelings of support within the university setting, increasing the sense of professional identity, higher rates of achieving tenure, as well as increased skill and knowledge base" (Holmes & Kozlowski, 2014, p. 36). Furthermore, the purposeful communities of practice provide mentoring opportunities for early career faculty to connect with senior faculty. As a result, faculty often become more open-minded and have a greater appreciation for ambiguity; some may become more civic-minded (Cox, 2004), and many leave with greater competence and confidence concerning teaching skills (Adams & Mix, 2014; Daly, 2011). Daly (2011) concluded from his research that faculty learning communities (FLCs) provide the following benefits:

> Opportunities for faculty members to self-organize and direct their own developmental activities (autonomy). The needs assessment processes and the research associated with the campus-wide change projects-built competence in the areas of pedagogical and curricular reform. And the connections among the seminar members—built through trust and extended conversations over the course of an entire semester and supported with release time from other responsibilities—established a sense of relatedness and commitment to long-term collective goals for teaching improvement. (p. 11)

Informed by these theoretical and practice frameworks, the faculty development program at UNIPD encouraged the linkage of faculty development to FLCs in order to deepen the relationships among peers and the sharing of practices, as well as to encourage people to reflectively assess their needs for improvement and how to acquire new skills.

Despite the power of purposeful communities of practice in fostering faculty development, they are limited without a recognition of the larger organization context and how it inhibits and fosters the impact of these learning communities on promoting innovative change. In response, the next section provides an overview of organization development and organizational change, along with its role in promoting faculty development at the University of Padova.

6 Organizational Development

Organizational development (OD) contributes significantly to the architecture of Teaching4Learning@Unipd and role it plays in fostering innovative teaching and learning. That said, the scholarship encompasses many conceptual and operational definitions. We suggest a foundational definition: "Organizational development is an effort, planned, organization wide and managed from the top, to increase the organization effectiveness and health through planned interventions in the organization's processes, using behavioral sciences knowledge" (Beckhard, 1969, p. 9). More specifically, it involves planning informed action and interventions that improve the organization and people in terms of competence and knowledge. Along the same lines, Anderson (2016) highlighted the change process as specifically linking to personal and organization development: "Organizational development is the process of increasing organization effectiveness and facilitating personal and organizational change through the use of interventions driven by social and behavioral sciences and knowledge" (p. 3). Through this lens, faculty development can be seen as an OD process, because it promotes the growth of the organization, it reflects a series of interventions driven by knowledge management, and it is based on the need for a changed culture of teaching and learning throughout the higher education institution.

Another fundamental concept of OD is that it is an interdisciplinary field that draws on different contributions from business to organizational psychology and human resources management to communication, sociology, and education (Anderson, 2016; Burke, 2011). This aspect is crucial in recognizing the complex nature of a university's organizational structure, especially in Italy. UNIPD exemplifies this complexity; established in 1222, its teaching and learning traditions are conservative and deeply rooted. As discussed earlier, its academic culture affirms a strong hierarchical relationship between faculty and students, reflective of both Italian higher education ideology and its larger society. This includes faculty emphasizing course content as true or privileged knowledge versus students' experience, standpoints, and contributions, which are generally considered less import or relevant knowledge. UNIPD's scale amplifies its complexity: it is one of the largest universities in Italy, with 68,000 students, about 3000 instructors, and 32 academic departments, all of which feature their own different approaches to teaching, change, and interest in pedagogical innovation beyond the traditional didactic paradigm. From an organizational standpoint, each department also has a long history of limited interactions among other departments; they function like isolated silos, even if they share a disciplinary mission and/or student.

Organizational change is the explicit purpose of most OD work (Anderson, 2016). These OD practices shift from individual to group as they increase effectiveness, which in university contexts means building from a single instructor to groups of faculty to, ultimately, the whole university organization. This also means that such change has to be rooted in the culture of the organization, including its mission and its unique rules. It also needs to engage faculty values and beliefs about teaching and learning as central involved to the change process. To facilitate purposeful change, OD frameworks include a range of tools, techniques, and processes that prepare the organization for change, plan strategic courses of action, managing the change process, and adapting it over time for the most effective outcomes. While it is a complex and often a nonlinear process, research elucidates how it is possible to distinguish, and even manage, different levels and times of change (Anderson, 2016; Bierema, 2014). Relatedly, change can be planned or unplanned, it can be a continuous process or just a "one-shot" initiative, and it can be addressed to different groups—individually, collectively, or broadened to the whole organization.

7 The Relationship Between Faculty Development and Organizational Change

The faculty development process aims to change the organization at different levels, including the personal, the group (such as FLCs and academic departments), and the organization. At UNIPD, some of the instructors who take part in the training are also occupying multiple roles across different levels (e.g., short-term assistant professor, tenure-track assistant, associate, and full professors; school coordinators and deans) within the organization, although very few are departmental deans. This diversity in faculty participation created the need for various levels of interventions, some of which are planned and predictable, while others are unpredictable due to competing factors in different departments. For example, there are instructors in some departments who took the responsibility as leaders and involved other colleagues in the training. In other departments, the deans or the schools' coordinators promoted and took part in the training; this kind of participation transmitted a stronger message regarding the importance of the teaching and learning innovation. Finally, there are some scientific concentrations, like the STEM fields (science, technology, engineering, and mathematics) that are more interested and feel a stronger need to change—more so than other fields, such as the social sciences and humanities.

Uncertainly is, perhaps, a hallmark of our faculty development program. The university is engaged in an enterprise with consequences that are quite unknown in Italy and most European universities, as they lack the history, tradition, and current model of faculty development. Our response to this uncertainty is to offer faculty, at this point, solid training on topics associated with innovative teaching, supported by external and internal experts (Tosi & Pilati, 2008). This training is also a part of a more comprehensive development plan for instructors who collaboratively experiment and discover new teaching strategies that encourage active student participation and open their classrooms to their colleagues more. This approach frames change as a continuous process, rather than as the result of a specific project. This perspective also emphasizes the active roles that the faculty members take up in terms of making decisions, facilitating the change process, affirming the importance of collaborative relationships, and, ultimately, shaping the organization.

There are several factors to consider for change to successfully occur, such as communication, interpersonal relationships, task reorganization, the introduction of new methods and new technologies, and the replacement of people. This approach assumes that change can be realized optimally when members—in our case faculty, institutional administrators, and stakeholders—work together to define new approaches to teaching and learning.

8 Organizational Change

By its nature, change rarely begins from a response of the entire system; instead, it more often originates from a specific organizational element, such as structure, strategy, or organizational culture (Burke, 2010). Considering the ways in which organizational change manifests itself, it is possible to distinguish two main types—planned change and emerging change. Planned change is the most recognized in the literature, documented in the context of Lewin's theory (1951), upon which other authors have built. According to this conceptual strand of literature, change consists in passing from one determined condition to another through predefined phases: unfreeze, change, and freeze (Bamford & Forrester, 2003; Livne-Tarandach & Bartunek, 2009). This approach involves analyzing and understanding change by destabilizing the balance and creating motivation for change. The second phase, called "transformation" or more simply "change," consists in the actual fulfillment of the change itself. In other words, the system (i.e., the organization) moves in new directions, using different modes of operation and technologies (Burke, 2010). Finally, "refreezing" has as its objective the stabilization and, therefore, the reinforcement of the new status quo (Burke, 2010; Burnes, 2004). This is necessary, according to Lewin (1951), to guarantee the long duration of the change, thus avoiding that the behaviors just learned are subsequently replaced by the old ones. In order for this to happen, the coherence of new behaviors with the personality of the individual is fundamental. On the organizational level, on the other hand, this phase involves changes in rules, procedures, and culture.

Both types of organizational change can be analyzed by considering three primary levels: the individual, the group, and the system (Anderson, 2016; Bierema, 2014). At UNIPD, these three levels would be the instructors, the community of faculty as a means to promote change in the departments and hopefully among the departments, and the institution with its own rules and its mission and vision. In fact, with reference to each level, the impact of change varies. For example, the actions of a single instructor, who is normally acting in isolation, represent a weak impact in the process of teaching innovation. Furthermore, we are aware of the fact that we have to put more effort in involving students in systematic ways and sharing with them organizational interventions for promoting change. Our next goal will be to create mixed community of students and instructors together. Stronger can be the influence of the faculty and students learning community and students' communities within a single department and, if supported by the director, the impact is likely to be even greater. Finally, if the request for change is coming from several stakeholder levels, including the organizational level, the potential for change is likely even more significant.

However, some scholars see this definition of the different levels as limited (Burke, 2010), particularly since organizations are complex and the three levels are interrelated. Despite that limitation, this classification may be useful for identifying the starting point of a change at each of the three levels and, consequently, how to plan and manage this process. In general, it is important to highlight that, in order for change to have an impact on the whole organization, regardless of the organizational level from which it begins, it is necessary to define a global direction. In this case, the upper administration of UNIPD has moved beyond relying solely on faculty voluntary participation in T4L to a stronger approach by instituting compulsory training for all new faculty (2 years or less).

To better make sense of the abovementioned theories of organizational change, it is helpful to reduce them to two main approaches. The first is the planned approach to organizational development which means that organizational members are conscious and intentional about the change that they want to make. This approach, although popular, has received significant criticism (Bamford & Forrester, 2003; Todnem By, 2005). First, this approach emphasizes a small and incremental change and, therefore, cannot be adopted in situations in which rapid and transformative changes are necessary. Second, according to the planned approach, organizations perform their activities in a constant environment and can decide to move from one stable condition to another. These hypotheses have been questioned by authors who argue that the environment is currently evolving rapidly, and change is an open process. This means that it should be monitored and modified when necessary and provide for the participation of all the actors involved. Third, planned change does not consider situations in which a more guided approach is needed. In a crisis situation, for example, we need to implement change quickly and without involving all the actors. Finally, a further criticism of this approach is that not always all the actors involved commit themselves to change toward a particular direction and without disagreeing, even on important issues. These approaches and theories are consistent with a systems theory perspective like Lewin's (1951).

On the other hand, there is a second approach which reflects emerging paradigms of organization change rooted in social constructivism. This approach considers organization as a concept developed out of its own actions and language. This perspective is more focused on seeing the study of the organization as the study of the processes related to organizational development and connected with individuals and groups who are living in the context. It offers an alternate perspective, including the consideration of different contexts and of the organization as socially constructed. This approach is more indicative of the institutional change process at UNIPD. This perspective deals "with what we experience in organization as we make sense of our activities and the actions of others" (Anderson, 2016, p. 87). This approach respects the diversity of experiences and the ambiguity of the different meanings. The roles of people are negotiated and not predetermined. This perspective seems to be the one which gives a more dynamic approach to the development process in organization. In this sense, it seems to be more adequate to the higher education context at UNIPD. This means that decisions are made on the basis of both facts and unfolding activities, and they take different factors and meanings into consideration. In the UNIPD case, for example, promoting faculty development for innovative teaching can be considered an interpretative process that characterizes the life of the university and a way to develop the institution.

A central factor in this approach is that individual and organization respond differently to the changes. This implies that the change is not only from a top-down direction but also from a bottom-up. Faculty voices are considered important for change; as Olson and Eoyang (2001) asserted, "the role of the change agent is to use and understanding of evolving patterns to effect the self-organization path, to observe how the system responds and to design next intervention" (p. 16). This approach best captures Teaching4Learning@Unipd, recognizing the need to continuously involve faculty in the change process as actors and to listen to their voices in order to promote change. They have power and know better how to impact their department, which can be more effective than just promoting change from the top administration.

9 Discussion: The Role of Faculty Development in Promoting Organizational Change

Recognizing the role of faculty development in promoting change, the following discussion highlights areas that emerge in the change and innovation process in relationship to the three units of analysis: the individual, the community of practice (FLC), and the organization.

Scaffolding participation began at the individual level by first analyzing the needs of faculty concerning teaching and learning. Faculty were seen as the promoters of change in the university. The starting phase at UNIPD was small and incremental involving a group of 30 volunteer instructors who had a desire of knowing more how to innovate teaching in a more participatory way. It was a unique initiative co-financed by the School of Engineering. Its coordinator, together with a group of instructors, attempted to pioneer new innovative practices within their departments. Despite their efforts, initiatives like this often tend to promote few changes institutionally and are likely to remain isolated events when lacking interest and support from the top administration. However, at UNIPD this departmental action together with recent efforts from the Ministry of University and Reserach of introducing a new accreditation system for the state universities helped place a new emphasis on teaching and learning in the classroom (Decreto Ministeriale, 2016). Furthermore, some contexts at the national and broader European level also highlighted the importance of rewards and certification for faculty teaching. In response to this, UNIPD started to offer in-house certification for tenured faculty who voluntarily participate in training. This context isn't consistent in all Italian universities.

These efforts and others helped the program to receive greater interest, along with faculty support and enthusiasm for involving other people and giving voice to the movement for change. At the same time, the impetus and policy orientation toward change, stemming from the Italian and European recommendation, created a positive atmosphere for change. For example, in less than 2 years 225 instructors have been trained, with more than 200 faculty committed to participate for the next academic year 2018–2019.

Looking at this process through an organizational development lens, however, the change has also been very slow and incremental even though the program has institutional support. It went through an initial period of strong doubts and fear regarding finding a way to continue. For example, in approaching this most recent academic year, 2018–2019, there was a large change due to the fact that the university provided one million euro to be shared among departments for projects related to teaching innovation. This provision provided the support for the development of several faculty programs in different departments. This was a clear sign of approval by the upper administration, and people become more confident in promoting training and involving themselves in the process. In considering this changing landscape of faculty development, it was also interesting to observe the different ways in which people became involved in the program, as well as how they started to question their perspective about teaching and change. At this stage, our unit of analysis remained predominantly the individual instructor, specifically his or her own choice to innovate his or her practice.

At the beginning, the resistance and change were and remained at a very private and personal level. Each instructor who came to the training reflected on the implications for his or her practices, with some trying some new techniques in class (Fedeli & Taylor, 2016) and observing the related implications. These small changes in teaching and adopting some new techniques are very much related to the individual change and less to the organizational change, even if they can motivate people to promote change creating an engaging dimension for change and generating new insights. As noted before, this perspective prioritizes how "members experience organization as social environments, in today's knowledge intensive organizations" (Anderson, 2016, p. 87).

10   Engaging Informal Networks Through Communities of Practice

Since the beginning, the aim of Teaching4Learning@Unipd faculty development program was to develop two different and connected dimensions: the active teaching strategies and methods and the creation of a community of practice among faculty as a means to promote changes. At UNIPD, the community of practice that arises in an informal way becomes an output of the training and was considered a way to foster innovation in the classroom and outside in the department and among departments.

One of the most important factors was the birth of informal networking as the result of the workshops. This included voices of the instructors both within departments and outside, sharing of practices and resources (Wenger et al., 2002), but also a lot of "corridor voices" that disseminated the good results of the training and created a sort of movement for innovation in teaching. Some spontaneous communities of practice arose in the departments involved.

The community of practice approach helps to remove barriers for change and to build authentic relationships that make change possible through the connections, networking, and consolidation of new and possible organizational strategies, seeing the change as a continuous process rather than a specific project (Anderson, 2016). This is related to our second question, which wants to explore ways to promote change not only for the single faculty but also for the department and the organization in large. This is a way to incorporate notions of organization development and change in the faculty development, choosing an approach that is related to the social construction perspective.

11 Merging Predictable and Unpredictable Organizational Change and Knowledge Management

The process of faculty and organization development at UNIPD offers several distinct inputs for changes, as we stated before, at individual, at group and community of practices, and at organizational level. Some of the strategies were planned; other arose along the way and came out from conversations among colleagues, from the sharing of information, and from interpretations of new insights that the change process caused.

Both predictable and unpredictable changes are linked in the faculty development initiatives and policies. As affirmed, the change at the beginning of 2016 was slow and planned as well through regular meetings to discuss the impact of the training. The emerging change also had an unplanned and unpredictable aspect, which derived from the relationships of various factors, internal and external, within the organization (Myers, Hulks, & Wiggins, 2012; Todnem By, 2005). This approach rejects the belief that systems can be completely controlled. This view sees the organization as ever-changing based on emerging patterns of self-organization created by interactions of those agents acting as part of it (Olson & Eoyang, 2001).

Coming back to predictable and unpredictable changes, it is apparent that faculty members are going through a transformation in terms of values and beliefs related to teaching and learning (Taylor, 2007, 2016).

Again, the two-level top-down and bottom-up are involved in the change and in the development process (Holbeche, 2006; Hosking & McNamee, 2006). For example, at the top the Vice Rector of Teaching at UNIPD provided significant funds to each department to promote their own innovative teaching learning. From the local or faculty level, some of faculty who participated in the program have become inspired to organize additional training opportunities unique to the discipline in which they work. This approach also aims to anchor new approaches to teaching within the traditional culture of the institution, motivating the need for further change along with innovating the policy and the roles of the actors involved in the process. This is how UNIPD incorporated notions of organizational development and change in its faculty development process. Faculty and organizational development are seen as managerial processes of knowledge management related to interventions with human and intangible resources. These processes involve different approaches and a variety of people, communities, and managers at multiple levels of the organization. Learning organization shares similar characteristics, where the improvement is based on knowledge and its development. The knowledge processes we normally face in order to promote faculty and organizational development are based on knowledge acquisition, knowledge sharing, knowledge distribution, knowledge transformation, knowledge storing, and knowledge using (Bolisani & Bratianu, 2018). These are concepts that are related to learning and how people learn and process the knowledge in learning organizations.

University faculty are knowledge operators who not only increase the level of the knowledge among students, but as well organization of the university and their peers thanks to their continuous involvement in learning related to their professional development as instructors and as knowledge managers. The relationship between faculty, organizational development, and knowledge management within a learning organization fosters knowledge processes on how and why knowledge is implemented to support people and organizations.

12   Lessons Learned and Implications for Next Steps

In closing this discussion, it is important to reflect on future actions based on what has been learned from this initial experience of fostering faculty development. Three significant actions have been identified as a result of this program. First, it is an effort to document the impact of faculty development program on student satisfaction, grades, attendance, and level of preparation and instructors' teaching and use of new techniques. This effort will take time and also involve a collection of variety of data from different perspectives (students, faculty, administration). Also, the findings need to be systematically informed and analyzed by related research data to give consistency and credibility to the future actions.

Second, to move beyond the incremental efforts that have taken place so far, a large-scale plan and intervention for faculty development at UNIPD is needed. As Anderson (2016) stated: "Three characteristics of contemporary large-scale interventions are: (1) the involvement of a variety of participants, (2) greater timeline of the intervention and (3) a change of the consultant's role" (p. 298). In this case, a necessary intervention would be to reinvent the faculty role where there is a greater expectation of faculty for service and development of the teaching innovation. Also, this second action needs to be explored at the administrative level where successful teachers could be rewarded, not just research, in terms of career and professional development.

The third critical future action for promoting change should involve de-privatizing teaching. More specifically, this means requiring faculty to open their classrooms to their peers, sharing teaching practices and knowledge also through peer observation and participation in faculty learning communities. Peer observation has been associated with improved practice and greater involvement among faculty about innovative teaching (Gosling, 2014; Jensen & Aiyegbayo, 2011; Kahut, Burnap, & Yon, 2007; McGrath & Monsen, 2015). Some of our faculty learning communities have started this process of faculty observation and have found the experience to be quite beneficial to their practice. More time needs to be invested in this process and to involve more faculty, leading to greater sharing and enriching perspectives.

Finally, sharing models for and studies of faculty development programs with peer universities, both nationally and internationally, helps promote change within the broader field of faculty development and at participating universities. The University of Padova is one of the few Italian members of the European University Association, which facilitates cross-country collaboration among academic program managers and develops European policies and recommendations and guidelines and influences decision makers at European, national, and regional levels. Furthermore, it aims to strengthen the governance, leadership, and management of institutions through the creation of networking, mutual learning, exchange of experience, and the transfer of best practice (EUA, 2018). The intent of UNIPD is to contribute to the realization of research for ensuring the quality and relevance of learning and teaching across the countries and being part of the thematic working group focused on teaching innovation continuous professional development. The program Teaching4Learning@Unipd will likely play an active part in the European faculty development community, with a shared goal of advancing dynamic communities of practice in which innovative teaching and learning can thrive. Finally, the relationship between faculty, organizational development, and knowledge management can be further explored in terms of sharing research with scholars of both fields: higher education and adult education and management. This is a cross-disciplinary field that deserves more attention and connections to promote a plurality of interventions for change.

References

Adams, S. R., & Mix, E. K. (2014). Taking the lead in faculty development: Teacher educators changing the culture of university faculty development through collaboration. *AILACTE Journal, 11*, 37–56.

Anderson, D. L. (2016). *Organization development. The process of leading organizational change.* Thousand Oaks, CA: SAGE.

Angelique, H., Kyle, K., & Taylor, E. W. (2002). Mentors and muses: New strategies for academic success. *Innovative Higher Education, 26*(3), 195–210.

Bamford, D., & Forrester, P. (2003). Managing planned and emergent change within an operations management environment. *International Journal of Operations and Production Management, 23*(5), 546–564.

Beckhard, R. (1969). *Organization development: Strategies and models.* Reading, MA: Adison-Wesley.

Bierema, L. (2014). *Organization development: An action research approach.* San Diego, CA: Bridgepoint Education.

Bolisani, E., & Bratianu, C. (2018). *Emergent knowledge strategies. Strategic thinking in knowledge management.* Swiss: Springer International.

Bruffee, K. A. (1987). The art of collaborative learning. *Change, 19*(2), 42–47.

Burke, W. W. (2010). *Il cambiamento organizzativo: Teoria e pratica.* Milano: FrancoAngeli.

Burke, W. W. (2011). A perspective on the field of organization development and change: The Zeigarnik effect. *Journal of Applied Behavioral Sciences, 47*(2), 143–147.

Burnes, B. (2004). Kurt Lewin and the planned approach to change: A re-appraisal. *Journal of Management Studies, 41*(6), 977–1002.

Cornelius-White, J. (2007). Learner-centered teacher-student relationships are effective: A meta-analysis. *Review of Educational Research, 77*(1), 113–143.

Cox, M. D. (2004). Introduction to faculty learning communities. *New Directions for Teaching and Learning, 97*, 5–23.

Cox, M. D. (2013). The impact of communities of practice in support of early-career academics. *International Journal for Academic Development, 1324*(September), 1–13.

Daly, C. J. (2011). Faculty learning communities: Addressing the professional development needs of faculty and the learning needs of students. *Currents in Teaching and Learning, 4*(1), 3–16.

Darwin, A., & Palmer, E. (2009). Mentoring circles in higher education. *Higher Education Research and Development, 28*(2), 125–136.

Dewey, J. (1916). *Democracy and education: An introduction to the philosophy of education.* New York: Macmillan.

Dirkx, J., & Serbati, A. (2017). Promoting faculty professional development: Strategies for individual and collective reflection towards institutional change. In E. Felisatti & A. Serbati (Eds.), *Preparare alla professionalità docente e innovare la didattica universitaria* (pp. 21–38). Milano: Franco Angeli.

European Commission. (2011). *Supporting growth and jobs—An agenda for the modernisation of Europe's higher education systems.* Retrieved from http://ec.europa.eu/education/library/pol icy/modernisation_en.pdf

European Commission. (2013). *Report to the European Commission on improving the quality of teaching and learning in Europe's higher education institutions.* Luxembourg: Publications Office of the European Union.

European University Association. (2018). *A positive learning and teaching climate through the continuous development of teaching competences.* Retrieved from https://eua.eu/resources/ expert-voices/71:a-positive-learning-and-teaching-climate-through-the-continuous-development-of-teaching-competences.html

Fedeli, M. (2016). Coinvolgere gli studenti nelle pratiche didattiche: potere, dialogo e partecipazione. In M. Fedeli, V. Grion, & D. Frison (Eds.), *Coinvolgere per apprendere. Metodi e tecniche partecipative per la formazione* (pp. 113–142). Lecce: Pensa Multimedia.

Fedeli, M., Frison, D., & Grion, V. (2017). Fostering learner-centered teaching in higher education. In V. Boffo, M. Fedeli, F. Lo Presti, C. Melacarne, & M. Vianello (Eds.), *Teaching and learning for employability. New strategies in higher education* (pp. 89–115). Milan: Pearson Italia.

Fedeli, M., & Taylor, E. W. (2016). Exploring the impact of a teacher study group in an Italian university. *Formazione & Insegnamento, XIV*(3), 2279–7505.

Fox, R. (2001). Constructivism examined. *Oxford Review of Education, 27*(1), 23–35.

Gosling, D. (2014). Collaborative peer-supported review of teaching. In J. Sachs & M. Parsell (Eds.), *Peer review of learning and teaching in higher education* (Professional learning and development in schools and higher education) (Vol. 9). Dordrecht: Springer, Science+Business Media.

Hagenauer, G., & Volet, S. E. (2014). Student relationship at university: An important yet under-researched field. *Oxford Review of Education, 40*(3), 370–388.

Heinrich, E. (2014). Toward using relevant collegial contexts for academic development. *Active Learning in Higher Education, 15*(3), 215–230.

Holbeche, L. (2006). *Understanding change: Theory, implementation and success.* Amsterdam: Elsevier.

Holmes, C. M., & Kozlowski, K. A. (2014). Faculty experiences in a research learning community. *Journal of Faculty Development, 28*(2), 35–42.

Hosking, D. M., & McNamee, S. (Eds.). (2006). *The social construction of organization.* Herndon, VA: Copenhagen Business School Press.

Jensen, K., & Aiyegbayo, O. (2011). *Peer observation of teaching: Exploring the experiences of academic staff at the University of Huddersfield.* Working paper. Huddersfield: University of Huddersfield.

Kahut, G. F., Burnap, C., & Yon, M. G. (2007). Peer observation of teaching: Perception of the observer and the observed. *College Teaching, 55*(1), 19–25.

Lave, J., & Wenger, E. (1991). *Situated learning: Legitimate peripheral participation.* New York: Cambridge University Press.

Lewin, K. (1951). *Field theory in social science.* New York: Harper.

Livne-Tarandach, R., & Bartunek, J. M. (2009). A new horizon for organizational change and development scholarship: Connecting planned and emergent change. In R. W. Woodman, W. A. Pasmore, & A. B. Rami Shani (Eds.), *Research in organizational change and development* (Vol. 17, pp. 1–35). Bingley: Emerald Group.

MacKenzie, J., Bell, S., Bohan, J., Brown, A., Burke, J., Cogdell, B., & Tierney, A. (2010). From anxiety to empowerment: A learning community of university teachers. *Teaching in Higher Education, 15*(3), 273–285.

McGrath, D., & Monsen, S. (2015, March 27). *Peer observation of teaching.* A discussion paper prepared for the peer observation of teaching colloquium. Institute for Teaching and Learning Innovation.

Merriam, S. B., & Bierema, L. L. (2014). *Adult learning: Linking theory and practice.* San Francisco, CA: Jossey-Bass.

Ministero dell'Istruzione della Ricerca e dell'Università. (2016). *Autovalutazione valutazione, accreditamento iniziale e periodico delle sedi e dei corsi di studio universitari.* Decreto Ministeriale 978 del 12 dicembre 2016. Retrieved from http://attiministeriali.miur.it/anno-2016/dicembre/dm-12122016.aspx

Myers, P., Hulks, S., & Wiggins, L. (2012). *Organizational change: Perspectives on theory and practice.* New York: Oxford University Press.

Neal, F., & Peed-Neal, I. (2010). Promoting your program and grounding it in the institution. In K. J. Gillespie, D. L. Robertson, & Associates (Eds.), *A guide to faculty development* (2nd ed., pp. 99–115). San Francisco, CA: Jossey-Bass.

Nugent, J. S., Reardon, R. M., Smith, F. G., Rhodes, J. A., Zander, M. J., & Carter, T. J. (2008). Exploring faculty learning communities: Building connections among teaching, learning, and technology. *International Journal of Teaching and Learning in Higher Education, 20*(1), 51–58.

Olson, E. E., & Eoyang, G. H. (2001). *Facilitating organization change: Lessons from complexity science.* San Francisco, CA: Jossey-Bass/Pfeiffer.

Schlitz, S. A., Connor, M. O., Pang, Y., Stryker, D., Markell, S., Krupp, E., & Redfern, A. K. (2009). Developing a culture of assessment through a faculty learning community: A case study. *International Journal of Teaching and Learning in Higher Education, 21*(1), 133–147.

Sherer, P., Shea, T., & Kristensen, E. (2003). Online communities of practice: A catalyst for faculty development. *Innovative Higher Education, 27*(3), 183–194.

Stanley, A. M. (2011). Professional development within collaborative teacher study groups: Pitfalls and promises. *Arts Education Policy Review, 112*(2), 71–78.

Sturko, P. A., & Gregson, J. A. (2008). Learning and collaboration in professional development for career and technical education teachers: A qualitative multi-case study. *Journal of Industrial Teacher Education, 45*(3), 5.

Swanwick, T. (2008). See one, do one, then what? Faculty development in postgraduate medical education. *Postgraduate Medical Journal, 84*(993), 339–343.

Taylor, E. W. (2007). An update of transformative learning theory: A critical review of the empirical research (1999–2005). *International Journal of Lifelong Education, 26*(2), 173–191.

Taylor, W. R. (2016). Fostering transformative learning. In M. Fedeli, V. Grion, & D. Frison (Eds.), *Coinvolgere per apprendere. Metodi e tecniche partecipative per la formazione* (pp. 113–142). Lecce: Pensa Multimedia.

Todnem By, R. (2005). Organisational change management: A critical review. *Journal of Change Management, 5*(4), 369–380.

Tosi, L. H., & Pilati, M. (2008). *Comportamento organizzativo. Attori, relazioni, organizzazione, management.* Milano: EGEA.

Wenger, E. (1998). *Communities of practice: Learning meaning and identity.* New York: Cambridge University Press.

Wenger, E., McDermott, R. A., & Snyder, W. (2002). *Cultivating communities of practice: A guide to managing knowledge.* Boston, MA: Harvard Business School Press.

Wildman, T. M., Hable, M. P., Preston, M. M., & Magliaro, S. G. (2000). Faculty study groups: Solving "good problems" through study, reflection, and collaboration. *Innovative Higher Education, 24*(4), 247–263.

Zara, V. (2017). Prefazione. In E. Felisatti & A. Serbati (Eds.), *Preparare alla professionalità docente e innovare la didattica universitaria* (pp. 9–10). Milano: Franco Angeli.

Student–Teacher Relationships: The Elephant in the Classroom

Edward W. Taylor

Abstract Teaching is a deeply subjective and relational activity; although often assumed to rest exclusively on effective instrumental practices, teaching's success resides predominantly in the ability of the teacher to foster and engage reciprocating authentic connections with students. The import of teacher–student relationships is the central focus of this chapter. It explores the complexities that confound and confront student/teacher relationships and what is known empirically about its impact on learning and introduces key theoretical frameworks and core constructs used to make sense of this phenomenon. Discussed is the connection between knowledge management in the classroom and teacher–student relationships. The chapter ends with a discussion of strategies that can foster successful teacher–student relationships.

1 Introduction

A math instructor enters a large lecture hall to begin a class on Introductory Statistics. Looking throughout the room, there must be over 100 students scattered throughout, many sitting alone and a few others in groups of two or three. This course hasn't been an enjoyable one for the students or the instructor this year. The students have been particularly passive and reticent about being engaged. In general, except for a few, they also seem distant and anxious, projecting a sense of not understanding or caring about statistics and its relevancy to their everyday lives. Despite the lack of comprehension, few students ask questions and they seem ready at a moment's notice to flee from class once the clock strikes the appropriate hour.

The instructor is equally frustrated with this course, because of the lack of engagement and understanding demonstrated by the students. He remains fixed behind the lectern speaking in a fairly pedantic voice to the students as he flips through an endless number of power point slides. The slides are devoid of everyday

---

E. W. Taylor (✉)
Penn State University-Harrisburg, Middletown, PA, USA
e-mail: ewt1@psu.edu

© Springer Nature Switzerland AG 2019
M. Fedeli, L. L. Bierema (eds.), *Connecting Adult Learning and Knowledge Management*, Knowledge Management and Organizational Learning 8,
https://doi.org/10.1007/978-3-030-29872-2_4

examples of statistics and how they give meaning to students' daily lives. At different points of the lectures, he asks if the students have any questions, but he gets little to no response. Based on past experience, the results of the final exam for many students will be marginal at best, and quite a few will likely not pass. Students' continued poor performance on the test strengthens his belief that students today are not as bright or motivated as when he was a student.

Further frustrating this professor is his colleague's teaching experience in a second section on Introductory Statistics. The other day as he walked by her class, he could hear students laughing and actively engaging each other and the instructor. When he peeked through the open door of the lecture hall, he initially couldn't find the instructor. Then out of the corner of his eye, he found her walking around the hall, up and down the long steps between the rows of seats, looking over groups of student's shoulders giving them individual feedback on their work. All the students were sitting in small clusters of two or three talking with each other about a particular statistics problem she had placed on a PowerPoint. He watched for a while, losing track of time. His colleague was animated and passionate about the topic. When students responded to her questions or asked questions, she complimented them and often called them by their names. As the class ended the students didn't rush out; they mingled with each other as well as with the teacher, slowly exiting the classroom. After this initial observation, he was perplexed and a bit jealous that students in this class seem to be enjoying statistics. Despite his observation and reflection, he concluded that the students in her course were obviously brighter than his and once he had better students, hopefully next semester, his class would become more engaging and understanding as well.

Unfortunately for this instructor, he has overlooked or missed what is central to his colleague's success at teaching statistics. Teaching is a deeply subjective and relational activity; although often assumed to rest exclusively on effective instrumental practices, its success resides predominantly in the ability of the teacher to foster and engage reciprocating authentic connections with students (Cranton, 2006). "University teachers and students are always in relationship and, no matter how they experience it, this relationship matters" (Karpouza & Emvalotis, 2018, p. 1). As an area of research, student–teacher relationships, although explored deeply in public school settings, remain on the margins in the field of adult and higher education and even more so in the study of adult education (Ei & Bowen, 2016; Hagenauer & Volet, 2014). In many ways, relationships are like the elephant in the classroom, always omnipresent but few recognizing or appreciating their profound influence on the everyday life of classroom teaching. Relationships impact not only student learning but also the well-being of the teacher and are potentially transformative for both students and teachers as they engage with each other within an educational experience. From a knowledge management perspective, teacher–student relationships are foundational in understanding the construction of knowledge in the classroom. They form the means to establish the necessary conditions so students and faculty together with high degree of confidence can conclude that "the necessary and sufficient condition for knowing that something is the case are first that what one is said to know be true, secondly that one be sure of it, and thirdly that one should have the right to be sure" (Ayers, 2009, p. 13). Truth and its justification is continually constructed and deconstructed in the classroom. Management of truthful knowledge seeks transparency, trust, and authenticity from the instructor in relationship with students.

Recognizing the significance of student–teacher relationships is at the heart of this chapter. It will attempt to make sense of the complexities that confound and confront teacher–student relationships and what is known empirically about the related impact for both the teacher and the student and discuss theoretical frameworks that have been used to make sense of this phenomenon. In addition, the chapter will end with a discussion of relational pedagogy, an approach that can enhance relationship among teachers and students in the classroom.

2 Classroom Relationships: Complex

Before engaging in the complexity of student–teacher relationship, it is important to recognize that it is impossible for an instructor *to not have a relationship with his or her students*. Once an instructor walks in the door of the classroom on the day of the first class, a relationship—some manifestation thereof—has begun to form and will continue to evolve throughout the semester. There is not any way for instructors or students to *not* "relate" to each other. The question for instructors is what kind of relationship do they have, what kind of relationship would they like to have, and what kind of relationship is most effective for promoting learning and facilitating teaching in their classrooms?

The nature of student–teacher relationships is quite complex and varied, particularly since there are so many shifting variables (individual personalities of the students and faculty, positionality, expectations of the course, dynamics of the context, etc.) that come into play in the average university classroom. Looking at the instructor as a unique individual, there are a host of factors that can impact his or her relationship with students. For example, they include the degree of accessibility, approachability, confidence, creativity, preparedness, punctuality, and effectiveness as communicator and as a listener, just to mention a few (Keeley, Smith, & Buskist, 2006). A quality that has received particular attention is the instructor's expertise (Frymier & Houser, 2000) and credibility (Docan-Morgan, 2011), identifying it as having significant import in teacher–student relationship. Further complicating this endless list of characteristics is how individual students assess and perceive these qualities differently, further challenging the process of developing a connection between the student and teacher.

Although literature is limited, insight into some of these complexities is found in focusing on student–teacher interactions, particularly the quality and amount of interaction (Pascarella, 1980; Pascarella & Terenzini, 2005). "In general, the research reveals that the more contact between students and faculty, both inside and outside the classroom, enhances college students' development and learning outcomes." A recent study by Kim and Sax (2009) found a host of patterns exists among students based on gender, race, social class, or first-generation standing. They include, for example, that first-generation students and African American students are least likely to be assisted by faculty with their research and that "females, whites, upper-class students and non-first-generation students are more satisfied with their interaction with faculty, their male, non-White, lower-class and first-generation counterparts" (p. 252). Practically, this means that faculty need to pay particular attention to students in underrepresented groups, making a concerted effort to engage these students both in and outside the classroom, being more purposeful when discussing graduate education as well as reaching out to them for assistance with research projects.

Along with the import of recognizing marginalized groups in the classroom, another significant factor shaping relationships is recognizing the imbalance of power that exists between the instructor and the students (Ei & Bowen, 2016). Students' fate (passing or failing) rests in instructor's hand. Even though there are often institutional norms and policies to protect the students, the instructor wields a strong saber in deciding the life of students within the classroom on a daily basis. He or she establishes the mood and determines the degree of access to the content of the course and how the students will be assessed. This power differential challenges both student and teacher in freely entering into a consensual relationship. In addition to the asymmetrical power dynamics, students have some agency and can resist to some degree what the instructor imposes or expects of them, which can further complicate the development of positive relationships. Often referred to as student resistance, instructional dissent, or student misbehavior, all of which are indicative of "actions students take in the classroom when they become frustrated, upset or disengaged from what is happening there" (Seidel & Tanner, 2013, pp. 586, 587). Basically, resistance is in response to instructor "compliance-gaining" efforts, through a variety of means. They include actions such as failure to engage, inconsistent attendance, violation of normative behaviors, failure to prepare for class, and academic dishonesty. In collaboration with others, students can resist by being disrespectful, engaging in excessive sociability, and demonstrating visible contention. "Students choose particular resistance strategies when they believe their teacher owns the problem and selects different strategies when they hold themselves responsible for the problem" (Richmond, McCroskey, & Mottet 2006, p. 249). Student resistance further confounds both the students and instructor to engage in positive teaching and learning relationships.

Also, complicating the understanding of student–teacher relationships is the lack of institutional guidance for the teacher and student in providing understanding into the promotion of effective student–teacher relationships. This is often referred to as code of conduct for faculty of which part of its intent is to help clarify boundaries distinguishing what is appropriate and not appropriate in student–teacher relationships. Overall code of conduct policies have received limited attention, particularly on how they help educators form positive and successful relationships with students. Furthermore, "attempting to make relationships simple by legislation, rather than dealing with inevitable complexity, prepares students poorly for the work they must do" (Ryder & Hepworth, 1990, p. 127). Successfully managing working relationships for most students is central to their future careers. The classroom provides an ideal setting for teachers to model healthy working relationships and students to learn ways to work productively with their peers and the instructor. Legislating relationships obstructs the exploration by students into dual relationships (extracurricular student–instructor interactions) essential for professional development particularly within fields such as psychology and medicine (Ei & Bowen, 2016). An approach for instructors in the classroom, where little institutional guidance is provided, is for the teacher and student to collaboratively develop ground rules at the beginning of each course not only outlining behavioral expectations but also identifying ways students can effectively interact with faculty (e.g., office hours, after class, informal meetings, email, texting).

In addition to the lack of institution guidance for the instructor is the dearth of information available about the nuts and bolts of managing the everyday student–teacher relationship in classroom. This includes, for example, what do faculty and students, at the minimum, need to know about each other to develop successful student–teacher relationships? What should instructors share (emotionally, biographically) about themselves with students? How much opportunity should be given to students to share about themselves (emotionally, biographically) with their peers and the instructor? How informal can the teacher be in the classroom? How much understanding and care for a student rests on the responsibility of the instructor? Answering these questions and others is challenging and quite varied based on who the instructors seek for advice, the institutional norms, as well as the country location of the university. This vital information seems to be a part of a hidden curriculum of the university (e.g., Haidet & Stein, 2006). Although extremely relevant, it is not often written about or agreed upon among faculty and students. Instructors usually acquire some understanding of these questions often implicitly, through prior classroom experiences (as a student and teacher), former teachers they admired and respected, trial and error during classroom teaching, listening to experiences from fellow instructors, and possibly giving attention to formal and informal ways of student feedback.

3 Impact of Successful Student–Teacher Relationships

Teacher–student relationships are quite complex, and it is also conceptually difficult to pin down exactly what makes up a successful student–teacher relationship. Research has shown student–teacher relationships as a precondition for effective learning (Hagenauer & Volet, 2014: Quinlan, 2016). Furthermore, relationships are crucial for successful learning outcomes (Docan-Morgan & Manusov, 2009; Haidet & Stein, 2006), and the stronger the connection between the student and teacher, the greater the outcomes. Some scholars argue that "the relational variable accounts for roughly half the variance in teaching effectiveness" (Tiberius, Sinai, & Flak, 2002, p. 464). The students who have close relationships with instructors are found to be more confident and self-directed, in contrast to students who see their instructor as distanced and non-supportive (Creasey, Jarvis, & Knapcik, 2009). This is particularly significant for courses that have a reputation for being difficult, such as statistics, and other highly abstract courses.

Not only does the student benefit from successful relationships but also the instructor. Like most people, instructors have a need to relate to their students. "Relationships with students [are] the most important source of enjoyment and motivation" (Spilt, Koomen, & Thijs, 2011, p. 460). For many instructors, the quality of relationships will determine to a great extent whether they remain in the profession or the institution. Overall positive relationships are the key factor in retention and professional well-being. Contrarily, negative teacher–student relationships are often an indicator of stress and poor job satisfaction for instructors.

4 Theoretical Framework

Often when questions are raised about an issue that hasn't been adequately researched, theory provides a place for guidance. However, most of "the studies of TSR (teacher-student relationships) in higher education often lack a clear theoretical/conceptual" framework (Hagenauer & Volet, 2014, p. 371). Despite this shortcoming, there is a relational theory (from therapeutic settings) with several key constructs that help bring meaning to positive aspects of relationship and means to foster those relationships among students and instructors. Theoretically, the most recognized theory is relational cultural theory (RCT), initially referred to as self-in-relation theory, which is based on the assumption that growth in relationship to others is a sense of interdependence, as opposed to the traditional Western assumption of individual human autonomy and independence (Jordan, 2017; Miller, 1986). RCT is a theory about interconnectedness: that humans are wired to relate to others. Connection is seen as "the primary organizer and source of motivation in people's lives" (Jordan, Hartling, & Walker, 2004, p. 1), whereas isolation is seen as the primary source of human pain and suffering. Connection defined in relationship to RCT is seen as both mutually empowering and empathetic. Miller (1988) identified five positive outcomes (The Five Good Things) from connected relationships. They include (a) a "zest" or energy, where both parties feel empowered to act beyond the relationship; (b) a desire to engage more relationships with others because of this positive relationship; (c) an increased knowledge in oneself and the other person; (d) a motivation to take action within this growth-fostering relationship; and (e) a greater sense of self-worth. In addition, this theory, also encourages reflection on the context in which relationships evolve and the assumptions we have about power in relationships, so there is a continual effort for a power shared approach (e.g., collaborative decision making, team work) and less of a power over approach in relationships. Viewing teaching and learning from the perspective of RCT foregrounds teaching as a relational activity, providing a medium for students and teachers to question their assumptions about how authority figures relate to others and for educators to explore ways to reduce the hierarchical nature of teaching and begin to expand their interpersonal boundaries with students (Schwartz, 2013). Unfortunately, these (Good Things) are difficult to assess and lack a shared standard of what they mean and how they are practiced in the classroom.

5 Key Relational Constructs in the Classroom

A response to the lack of clarity found in relational cultural theory are three constructs that offer some insight into why relationships matter in the classroom and how to foster more positive student–teacher relationships. These constructs include mattering, immediacy, and emotions.

5.1 Mattering

Mattering helps provide a basis for instructors to foster Miller's (1986) five positive relational outcomes. Mattering is a feeling that "one is significant and is valued by others" (Strayhorn, 2016, p. 57). In other words, students "matter" from the perspective of the teacher. Mattering gives meaning to how people, in this case students and teachers, belong with others relationally. For people to feel they belong, they must feel that they matter and they are of interest and import, respected, and cared about. Earlier scholars believed that "the conviction that one matters to another person is linked to the feeling that (a) one is an object of his [her] attention; (b) that one is important to him[her]; and (c) that he[she] is dependent on us" (Rosenberg & McCullough, 1981, p. 163). Scholars in higher education have found that paying attention to mattering motivates students to participate, learn, and develop a sense of commitment to the course and the larger institution (Rosenberg & McCullough, 1981; Taylor & Turner, 2019). Looking at mattering within the particular context of teacher–student relationships, Schwartz (2013) referred to it more specifically as intellectual mattering, "that is when we tell students that their thinking, ideas and intellectual and academic work has impressed us, informed us, or inspired us, they notice and they may be influenced beyond simply feeling good that we have complimented their work" (p. 1). Mattering can help build confidence in students and help students begin to perceive themselves as scholar-practitioners.

5.2 Immediacy

A second construct is that of immediacy. Immediacy is the "perception of closeness" (Frymier & Houser, 2000, p. 209) communicated through both verbal and nonverbal behavior that has been shown to impact students' learning positively and increase their motivation to engage in the classroom (Titsworth, 2001). Examples of verbal immediacy include calling students by their names, asking students for their input and insight into course discussions, and asking about their lives in general. Nonverbally, it means engaging students by being in close proximity (moving around the room) to them, maintaining eye contact, and demonstrating a range in voice modulation. Research has shown that when students perceive their teachers to be more immediate, they tend to report more positive emotional experiences in the classroom (Titsworth & Mazer, 2010). A similar concept used in the literature is approachability, having many of the same characteristics as immediacy, but also explained in contrast to teachers who are considered unapproachable (e.g., bored, talks down to students, not prepared) (Hagenauer & Volet, 2014).

5.3 Emotions

A third construct, emotions, is at the very core of establishing relationships, although often neglected and overlooked in higher education classroom (Hagenauer, Gläser-Zikuda, & Volet, 2016). "Interactions with students are frequently emotionally laden and that student-teacher-interactions are the most prevalent sources of emotions" (p. 47). Emotions between students and instructor are inherently linked, both in expectation and in how they are evoked in the classroom. Emotions are argued to be the filter for how instructors teach and what teaching strategies are chosen, based in part on how these strategies will affect both student and teacher emotionally (Sutton & Wheatley, 2003). Also, there seems to be a direct relationship between the quality of emotional experience and interactions with students. The challenge for instructors is how emotions are communicated in classroom, particularly when it comes to fostering positive relationships. Although some scholars argue for neutrality in teaching and learning, the majority of the literature argues for authenticity, which encourages instructors to express emotions in a controlled manner (Cranton & Carusetta, 2004). Drawing on this concept of authenticity provides a basis for sharing emotions in the classroom. It requires being genuine with students, demonstrating consistency between actions and beliefs, seeking out relationships with students, and engaging in a reflexive practice (Cranton, 2006). These practices and others are discussed in more detail in the next section.

6 Relational Pedagogy as a Practice

In response to the essentiality of teacher–student relationships in the classroom, it is also important to identify strategies and teaching approaches that can help foster positive relationships among students and instructors. A framework for these strategies is relational pedagogy: an approach to teaching and learning is seen primarily as "a process of building relationships" (Sidorkin, 2002, p. 88). The students are seen as central by the instructor with an intended purpose to enter into a positive relationship and be open to change for both the teacher and the student (Hobson & Morrison-Saunders, 2013). The practice of relational pedagogy "takes seriously the personal needs and desires of students while situating these needs at the centre of the struggle for a more democratic higher education" (Murphy & Brown, 2012, p. 644). Through an exploration of related literature and direct experience at observing other instructors and reflecting on my own practice, discussed below are several teaching strategies that can help instructors develop more positive and engaging relationships with students in the classroom.

6.1 Engaging in a Critically Reflexive Practice

First and foremost is the need to continually engage in a critically reflexive practice. It "is a process of inquiry involving practitioners in trying to discover, and research, the assumptions that frame how they work" (Brookfield, 1998, p. 197). In relational pedagogy this involves both the instructors and the students taking time to reflect on how they are relating to each other. It means to identify their underlying assumptions about student–teacher relationships. For the instructor, critical reflection should be a natural response to everyday classroom critical incidences, for example, if there has been a conflict or problem in the classroom (e.g., behavior, student resistance, passive engagement) between the students and teachers. These events provide an ideal medium for exploring relationships and how and why both the teacher and students responded in the manner that they did and what does it reveal about their underlying assumptions about relationships in the classroom. Critical reflection can also be fostered in more structured ways, with planned activities. For example, it would be in the best interests of the instructor to self-evaluate himself or herself according to a Teacher's Behavior Checklist (Keeley et al., 2006) and reflect on why these particular behaviors were selected and others not. Also, students with the same list could be asked to identify the instructor's strengths and concerns and ways they could improve their relationship with students. This also could provide a means to discuss how students are relating to each other and to the instructor. Metaphorically engaging in critical reflection particularly focused on relationships is not hesitating to name and discuss the "elephant in the room" and challenges instructors and students to think more deeply about how they are relating to students.

6.2 Fostering a Learner-Centered Teaching

More often defined operationally through a variety of approaches to teaching that are designed to give students greater voice and autonomy learner-centered teaching (Weimer, 2013) is foundational for relational pedagogy. By engaging in this approach, the instructor is implicitly telling students they respect their input, are confident of their choices, and most significantly are sending a message of mattering and trust. In other words, the students' contributions matter and the instructor trusts the students in sharing responsibility in the development of a successful teaching and learning experience. This teaching approach enhances learning through supportive relationships provided by the instructor and students, creates a sense of ownership and control over the learning experience, and helps establish a safe and trusting classroom environment for learning. Practically, it involves finding ways on a regular basis that provide students the opportunity to have input into how the course is managed and delivered (e.g., curriculum development, assignments, evaluation, instructional strategies).

6.3 Promoting Communities of Practice Inside and Outside the Classroom

Communities of practice refer to a group of people involved in informal relations through mutual engagement of a shared enterprise (Cox, 2005). In classroom settings, communities of practice involve students and teachers who share similar goals and practices related to a specific field/interest. These communities exist and evolve regardless of what the instructor and students do. The challenge for the instructor is to take advantage of this naturally evolving medium of social relations and be intentional at providing opportunities for fostering positive relationships among students and students and the instructor. Practically this means on a regular basis having students to work with each other collaboratively in and outside the classroom on activities related to the course. As students together grapple with ill-defined real-world problems associated with the course content and shared goals, students engage in more in-depth social relations, learning how to better work with others while at the same time more effectively learning the course material. The instructor's role shifts to more of a facilitator or coach, providing opportunities for "mattering," including student's experiences, opinions, and understanding in the course. For faculty, as a member of the community, it provides them an opportunity to engage in more personal social relations as well, by sharing personal experiences (relevant to the course topic), before and after class mingling with students inquiring about their everyday life and well-being and becoming more accessible to respond to individual student and group needs. Also, regularly, faculty should keep students informed and updated about the course over the semester through social media. This doesn't preclude the idea that the instructor could share as well, for example, insights and personal experiences concerning related research projects and endeavors.

6.4 Active Verbal and Nonverbal Communication

Active verbal and nonverbal communication are forms of communication that can foster a sense of immediacy with students (Frymier & Houser, 2000). The name "active" implies intentionality, where in verbal communication the teacher makes a point to verbally engage students in ways that foster positive teacher–student relationships. For example, the instructor would try to call as many students as possible by their names, ask students about their daily lives (when time allows), and/or request input from students about their opinion, thoughts, and suggestions concerning the topic of the course. These strategies also demonstrate that students "matter," such as who they are and what they have to contribute as being important to the success of the course. Another strategy involves remembering experiences that have impacted individual students as well as the class as a whole, such as welcoming a student back to class who has been absent due to an illness and/or recognizing a social/cultural event (e.g., demonstration on campus, sporting event) and allowing students time to share their reactions and feelings. Also, it is important for instructors to express themselves authentically about the course material through a range in voice modulation (excitement, disappointment, etc.). This is not only key to demonstrating genuineness but also gives permission for student to be more authentic as well as provides a basis for establishing positive relations. Active nonverbal communication compliments verbal communication and also enables immediacy and mattering when the instructor engages in "behaviors such as smiling at students, making eye contact" (p. 209). Nonverbal behavior is further clarified in the next strategy: embodied teaching.

6.5 Embodied Teaching

Traditional teaching creates a divide between the mind and the body, "regarding the body as little more than a subordinate to the mind" (Nguyen & Larson, 2015, p. 1). Embodied pedagogy foregrounds an instructional approach that attempts to join the body with the mind in the act of knowledge construction. As an approach/strategy of relational pedagogy, it means pragmatically having students engage their bodies in the process of learning. For example, this means the arrangement of learning "spaces designed to generate interaction collaboration, physical movement and social engagement as primary elements of student learning experience" (Jamieson, 2003, p. 121). By changing the learning spaces from a rigid and situated form that encourages passive learning to a more mobile space, it will help diminish the reified power dynamics of a traditional classroom (Nguyen & Larson, 2015). Students who learn collaboratively are often in closer proximity to each other, helping create a medium for more personal and productive social relations in the classroom. In addition, the faculty members use his or her body in ways to foster greater trust and accessibility with the students. Pragmatically it means leaving the frontal lecture position in the classroom and wandering the classroom or lecture hall in an effort to work in close physical proximity to the students (e.g., immediacy). As students work in small groups, the instructor willingly engages students (possibly kneeling while students are sitting or sitting next to a student who needs assistance or has a question).

6.6 Self-Disclosure

Self-disclosure by instructors in the classroom, although clearly a verbal strategy, deserves a separate discussion about its significance to developing positive student relationships. It is when instructors disclose personal aspects of their lives often to help illustrate course content, encourage student engagement, demonstrate credibility, and appear friendly to students (Miller, Katt, Brown, & Sivo, 2014). "Research has shown instructor self-disclosure to be positively related to students' interest in class material, affective learning, motivation to attend class, motivation to communicate with teachers and level of student participation in class" (p. 4). However, it is a matter of degree, where too much or hyper-opinionated self-disclosure has been found to have a negative impact on student behavior. Practically, self-disclosure is demonstrated by faculty sharing stories from their life with the intent to make the course content more relevant and meaningful. This can include both positive and negative information (not something that would question their credibility) often leading to a more positive learning environment and faculty being perceived as more approachable (Hosek & Presley, 2018). Three guiding principles include that self-disclosure should "relate to course content and class material; second, share positive attributes that humanize the instructor as being happy and competent; and third, an encourage relational affect among students" (p. 69).

7 Conclusion

Looking back over this chapter, the possibility exists that more questions have been raised than answered. Student–teacher relationships are still an ill-defined construct, as well as indicators of positive relationships and strategies for instructors to foster positive relationships in the classroom. Despite the limitations that exist, if instructors can begin to recognize and appreciate the import of student–teacher relationships, reflect on their own relationships with students, explore relationship building strategies, and seek feedback from their students, significant inroads can be made. Furthermore, as relationships are improved, the quality of the knowledge management within the course will be enhanced. Students will learn more effectively and with a greater degree of confidence in what is being taught and trust in themselves as a learner and the faculty as a teacher.

Let's return to the statistics instructor who was introduced at the beginning of this chapter. Here was an instructor who didn't know his students, mostly demonstrated by his characterization of them as a single homogenous group (all unmotivated and unengaged) without any appreciation or knowledge of individual differences that existed in his class. In many ways they didn't "matter" to him or did the course. Also, there was a lack of immediacy that existed between him and the students, such that he was at great distance from his students, physically, by remaining behind the podium and by his lack of self-disclosure. Students likely knew little about him personally and he knew little about them as well. Furthermore, there was a lack of passion revealed in his lectures, demonstrating a lack of commitment to the topic of the course, so in turn his students expressed little interest in the topic as well. In contrast to this instructor was his colleague, who also taught statistics but had students who were very engaged in the classroom. This was part and parcel because of the kind relationship she had with her students. She encouraged collaboration with and among students and students mattered in her class demonstrated by her immediacy, being physically close among students as she walked throughout the lecture hall. Students felt welcomed, trusted, and comfortable in her course despite the challenging topic, demonstrated by their tendency to mingle and not rush from class as it ended.

At this point the reader of this chapter might reflect and disagree, suggesting that all students have experienced a great teacher who they knew personally little about and was always at a distance both metaphorically and physically from students. This is true to a degree, but in many ways these powerful teachers, although rare, expressed their genuineness and interest in their students through a deep commitment to the topic of the course. By being highly committed and passionate to content, they were demonstrating that students mattered. And most often their passion for the topic was equaled by the passion for their students. However, these teachers who we long remember as being great educators, unfortunately, could have been even more so, if they had taken time to step out of the podium and share a bit of themselves and reach out to students on a more personal basis.

In the context of a classroom, teaching is synonymous with relationships; one cannot exist without the other. So as discussed earlier, the questions instructors need to continually ask themselves are: What kind of relationship do I have with my students? What kind of relationship do I want to have? What are ways I can intentionally improve my relationships with my students? Through ongoing reflection on teacher–student relationships and the foregrounding of relationships when considering how to teach, it will lead to more successful learning by both students and teachers.

References

Ayers, A. J. (2009). The right to be true. In R. Neta & D. Pritchard (Eds.), *Arguing about knowledge* (pp. 11–13). London: Routledge.

Brookfield, S. (1998). Critically reflective practice. *The Journal of Continuing Education in the Health Professions, 18*, 197–205.

Cox, A. M. (2005). What are communities of practice? A comparative review of four seminal works. *Journal of Information Science, 31*(6), 527–540. https://doi.org/10.1177/0165551505057016.

Cranton, P. (2006). Not making or shaping: Finding authenticity in faculty development. *To Improve the Academy, 24*(1), 70–85. https://doi.org/10.1002/j.2334-4822.2006.tb00451.x.

Cranton, P., & Carusetta, E. (2004). Perspectives on authenticity in teaching. *Adult Education Quarterly, 55*, 5), 5–5),22. https://doi.org/10.1177/0741713604268894.

Creasey, G., Jarvis, P., & Knapcik, E. (2009). A measure to assess student-instructor relationships. *International Journal for the Scholarship of Teaching and Learning, 3*(2). https://doi.org/10.20429/ijsotl.2009.030214.

Docan-Morgan, T. (2011). "Everything changed": Relational turning point events in college teacher-student relationships from teachers' perspectives. *Communication Education, 60*(1), 20–50. https://doi.org/10.1080/03634523.2010.497223.

Docan-Morgan, T., & Manusov, V. (2009). Relational turning point events and their outcomes in college teacher-student relationships from students' perspectives. *Communication Education, 58*(2), 155–188. https://doi.org/10.1080/03634520802515713.

Ei, S., & Bowen, A. (2016). College students' perceptions of student-instructor relationships. *Ethics and Behavior, 12*(2), 177–190.

Frymier, A. B., & Houser, M. L. (2000). The teacher-student relationship as an interpersonal relationship. *Communication Education, 49*(3), 207–219. https://doi.org/10.1080/03634520009379209.

Hagenauer, G., Gläser-Zikuda, M., & Volet, S. (2016). University teachers' perceptions of appropriate emotion display and high-quality teacher-student relationship: Similarities and differences across cultural-educational contexts. *Frontline Learning Research, 4*(3), 44–74. https://doi.org/10.14786/flr.v4i2.236.

Hagenauer, G., & Volet, S. E. (2014). Teacher–student relationship at university: An important yet under-researched field. *Oxford Review of Education, 4985*(November 2015), 370–388. https://doi.org/10.1080/03054985.2014.921613.

Haidet, P., & Stein, H. F. (2006). The role of the student-teacher relationship in the formation of physicians: The hidden curriculum as process. *Journal of General Internal Medicine, 21*(Suppl. 1), 16–20. https://doi.org/10.1111/j.1525-1497.2006.00304.x.

Hobson, J., & Morrison-Saunders, A. (2013). Reframing teaching relationships: From student-centred to subject-centred learning. *Teaching in Higher Education, 18*(7), 773–783. https://doi.org/10.1080/13562517.2013.836095

Hosek, A. M., & Presley, R. (2018). College student perceptions of the (in)appropriateness and functions of teacher disclosure. *College Teaching, 66*(2), 63–72. https://doi.org/10.1080/87567555.2017.1385587.

Jamieson, P. (2003). Designing more effective on-campus teaching and learning spaces: A role for academic developers. *International Journal of Academic Development, 8*, 119–133.

Jordan, J. V. (2017). Relational–cultural theory: The power of connection to transform our lives. *Journal of Humanistic Counseling, 56*(3), 228–243. https://doi.org/10.1002/johc.12055.

Jordan, J. V., Hartling, L. M., & Walker, M. (Eds.). (2004). *The complexity of connection: Writings from the Stone Center's Jean Baker Miller Training Institute*. New York: Guilford Press.

Karpouza, E., & Emvalotis, A. (2018). Exploring the teacher-student relationship in graduate education: A constructivist grounded theory. *Teaching in Higher Education*, 1–20. https://doi.org/10.1080/13562517.2018.1468319

Keeley, J., Smith, D., & Buskist, W. (2006). The teacher behaviors checklist: Factor analysis of its utility for evaluating teaching. *Teaching of Psychology, 33*(2), 84–91.

Kim, Y. K., & Sax, L. J. (2009). Student-faculty interaction in research universities: Differences by student gender, race, social class, and first-generation status. *Research in Higher Education, 50*(5), 437–459. https://doi.org/10.1007/s11162-009-9127-x.

Miller, J. B. (1986). *What do we mean by relationships?* Work in progress, no. 22. Working paper series. Wellesley, MA: Stone Center.

Miller, J. B. (1988). *Connections, disconnections, and violations*. Work in progress, no. 33. Working paper series. Wellesley, MA: Stone Center.

Miller, A. N., Katt, J. A., Brown, T., & Sivo, S. A. (2014). The relationship of instructor self-disclosure, nonverbal immediacy, and credibility to student incivility in the college classroom. *Communication Education, 63*(1), 1–16. https://doi.org/10.1080/03634523.2013.835054.

Murphy, M., & Brown, T. (2012). Learning as relational: Intersubjectivity and pedagogy in higher education. *International Journal of Lifelong Education, 31*(5), 643–654. https://doi.org/10. 1080/02601370.2012.700648

Nguyen, D. J., & Larson, J. B. (2015). Don't forget about the body: Exploring the curricular possibilities of embodied pedagogy. *Innovations in Higher Education, 40*(4), 331–344. https:// doi.org/10.1007/s10755-015-9319-6.

Pascarella, E. T. (1980). Student–faculty informal contact and college outcomes. *Review of Educational Research, 50*(4), 545–595.

Pascarella, E. T., & Terenzini, P. T. (2005). *How college affects students (volume 2): A third decade of research*. San Francisco, CA: Jossey-Bass.

Quinlan, K. M. (2016). *How higher education feels*. Boston, MA: Sense Publishers.

Richmond, V. P., McCroskey, J. C., & Mottet, T. (2006). Student incivility and resistance in the classroom. In T. P. Mottet, V. P. Richmond, & J. C. McCroskey (Eds.), *In the handbook of instructional communication* (pp. 235–252). New York: Routledge.

Rosenberg, M., & McCullough, B. C. (1981). Mattering: Inferred significance and mental health among adolescents. *Research in Community and Mental Health, 2*, 163–182.

Ryder, R., & Hepworth, J. (1990). AAMFT ethical code: "Dual relationships". *Journal of Marital and Family Therapy, 16*(2), 127–132.

Schwartz, H. L. 2013. "Dinner at Fitzwilly's: Intellectual mattering in developmental relationships." In Sixth annual mentoring conference proceedings: Impact and effectiveness of developmental relationship, edited by N. Dominguez and Y. Gandert. Albuquerque, NM: University of New Mexico. https://www.researchgate.net/publication/267694513_Dinner_at_Fitzwilly's_ Intellectual_Mattering_in_Developmental_Relationships

Seidel, S. B., & Tanner, K. D. (2013). "What if students revolt?"—Considering student resistance: Origins, options, and opportunities for investigation. *CBE Life Sciences Education, 12*, 586–595. https://doi.org/10.1187/cbe-13-09-0190.

Sidorkin, A. (2002). *Learning relations. Impure education, deschooled schools and dialogue with evil*. New York: Peter Lang.

Spilt, J. L., Koomen, H. M. Y., & Thijs, J. T. (2011). Teacher wellbeing: The importance of teacher-student relationships. *Educational Psychology Review, 23*(4), 457–477. https://doi.org/10.1007/ s10648-011-9170-y.

Strayhorn, T. (2016). Transition to higher education—In search of belonging. In K. M. Quinlan (Ed.), *How higher education feels* (pp. 23–52). Amsterdam: Sense Publishers.

Sutton, R. E., & Wheatley, K. F. (2003). Teachers' emotions and teaching: A review of the literature and directions for future research. *Educational Psychology Review, 15*(4), 327–358. https://doi. org/10.1023/A:1026131715856.

Taylor, J., & Turner, R. J. (2019). A longitudinal study of the role and significance of mattering to others for depressive symptoms. *Journal of Health and Social Behavior, 42*(3), 310–325.

Tiberius, R. G., Sinai, J., & Flak, E. A. (2002). The role of teacher-learner relationships in medical education. In *International handbook of research in medical education* (pp. 463–497). Great Britain: Kluwer Academic.

Titsworth, B. S. (2001). Immediate and delayed effects of interest cues and engagement cues on students' affective learning. *Communication Studies, 52*(3), 169–179. https://doi.org/10.1080/ 1051097010938855.

Titsworth, S., & Mazer, J. P. (2010). Clarity in teaching and learning: Conundrums, consequences and opportunities. In D. L. Fassett & J. T. Warren (Eds.), *The SAGE handbook of communication and instruction* (pp. 241–262). Thousand Oaks, CA: Sage.

Weimer, M. (2013). Learner-centered teaching and transformative learning. In E. W. Taylor & P. Cranton (Eds.), *Handbook of transformative learning: Theory, research and practice*. San Francisco, CA: Jossey-Bass.

Linking Active Learning and Capstone Projects in Higher Education

Tullio Vardanega and Monica Fedeli

Abstract This chapter reviews the results of a multi-year experience running a capstone project in a bachelor's degree program in computer science, at the University of Padua, Italy, designed and implemented using interactive learning methods. As part of that initiative, we explore how interactive practices such as cooperative learning and problem-based learning—components of the active learning framework—help foster more engaging and meaningful learning experiences for students, geared toward the development of personal employability and faster work transition. The evidence collected suggests that capstone projects form a natural and productive context for the successful deployment of interactive learning methods.

This chapter highlights the positive role played by capstone projects in higher education and the relation that they have with the theoretical background of active learning. As part of that, we discuss the challenges encountered in gracefully embedding a capstone project in a bachelor-level curriculum, we provide a quantitative evaluation of the results obtained over several years of operation, and finally we distil some lessons learned on key aspects of this project, with the intention of facilitating adoption in other organizations.

1 Capstone Projects in Higher Education

The presence of capstone projects in higher-education programs has been recorded for decades (Clear, Goldweber, Young, Leidig, & Scott, 2001; Hundhausen, 2015; Umphress, Hendrix, & Cross, 2002). With varying implementations, the capstone's core function is to afford students the opportunity to deploy the learning outcomes of their study career in a *collaborative* endeavor, meant to mark their curriculum significantly. According to Nelson and Bianco (2013), the instructional design of a capstone course should harness student responsibility and make students participate more actively in the acquisition of the basic abilities required to solve the kind of

---

T. Vardanega (✉) · M. Fedeli
University of Padova, Padova, Italy
e-mail: tullio.vardanega@unipd.it; monica.fedeli@unipd.it

© Springer Nature Switzerland AG 2019
M. Fedeli, L. L. Bierema (eds.), *Connecting Adult Learning and Knowledge Management*, Knowledge Management and Organizational Learning 8,
https://doi.org/10.1007/978-3-030-29872-2_5

nonstructured problems that they will encounter in their professional careers. For this reason, capstone courses form a context for the framework of active learning to find a natural field of application.

Prince (2004) sees active learning as "any instructional method that engages students in the learning process" (p. 223). Likewise, Nelson and Bianco (2013) situate it "where the student is involved in generating content and ideas, sharing their learning with others, and drawing inferences and conclusions beyond that which were presented during the course" (p. 269).

The educational literature in numerous domains including STEM (science, technology, engineering, and mathematics) links capstone projects with interactive learning methods (Dunlap, 2005; Reinicke & Janicki, 2010; Wosinski et al., 2018), making the link with the active learning framework apparent.

Accordingly, in this work, which updates and extends the material published in Vardanega and Fedeli (2018), we discuss the design and implementation of a two-staged capstone project embedded in a bachelor curriculum in computer science (CS) at the University of Padua, Italy, casting it comprehensively into the theoretical framework of active learning.

The said curriculum, inaugurated in October 2001, was designed to comply with the legislative reform of education promulgated in Italy in February 2000, with the intention of narrowing the gap, for acquired skills and duration, between the student's traversal of the education path and the start of a fulfilling professional life. That divide used to be very large: on the cognitive end, for insufficient dialogue between the university and the workplace, and on the temporal side, for excessive duration of the study path, compounded by a low rate of retention. The insertion of a capstone course in the BSc study path was at the center of the curricular design adopted by the faculty in 2001. This opportunity arose in view of the decision by the hosting institution, the Department of Mathematics, to transform the earlier diploma degree in computer science into a BSc curriculum proper, starting from the academic year 2001, therefore falling within application of the cited legislative reform. Before that moment, computer science education featured as a lateral addition to mathematical studies. Subsequently instead, it acquired a visibility of its own, motivating the slow but steady recruitment of a number of instructors sufficient to sustain the curriculum.

Since inauguration, 15 cohorts of 1100 graduates in total have majored in that curriculum. Over 800 of them have entered employment immediately after graduation. This data record is precious in two ways. It supports analytic reasoning on the success of the curriculum concept and of its distinguishing traits. Additionally, it allows learning lessons worth sharing with the teaching community, from the use of interactive learning methods in the realization of the capstone.

2   Connecting Active Learning and Capstone Projects

Goldstein and Fernald (2009) suggested that capstone courses should have five components: (1) student-centered learning, (2) empathic listening, (3) affective and experiential learning, (4) collaborative learning and self-disclosure, and

(5) assignments that focus on personal and professional growth. Components (1), (3), (4), and (5) correlate strongly with the objectives attached to our capstone insert and therefore provide solid inspiration for its design. Moreover, these instructional components carry very explicit relations to two of the three forms of interactive learning that Prince (2004) discussed in a comprehensive taxonomy and review of the relevant research. We recap them briefly, before highlighting the slant on active learning that our capstone course design took from the outset.

Active Learning (AL) Active learning engages students in performing learning activities that cause them to actively think about what they are doing (Bonwell & Eison, 1991). While in principle this definition could include traditional homework-type assignments, AL is understood to refer to activities that also take place in the classroom and therefore require a different style of teaching. AL traces back to one of the "Seven Principles for Good Practice" (Chickering & Gamson, 1987):

1. Encourage contact between students and faculty
2. Develop reciprocity and cooperation among students
3. Encourage active learning
4. Give prompt feedback
5. Emphasize time on task
6. Communicate high expectations
7. Respect diverse talents and ways of learning

Different AL methods exist, which suggests that AL should be regarded more as an approach than as a method, and each method should be assessed separately. To determine whether AL "works," a broad range of outcomes should be considered, including measures of factual knowledge, relevant skills and attitudes, and pragmatic factors such as student retention in academic programs. The work of Prince (2004) recognized three forms of AL: collaborative learning, cooperative learning, and problem-based learning.

The principal trait of *collaborative learning*, which encompasses all group-based instructional methods, where students work together in small groups toward a common goal, is that it places groups above individuals**.** In the remainder of this chapter, we do not discuss this particular form of AL as its philosophy has goals that exceed those of interest to this work.

Cooperative Learning (CL) Cooperative learning is a structured form of *group work*, where students pursue common goals while being assessed individually. The most common model of CL in the engineering literature lists five specific tenets (Johnson, Johnson, & Smith, 1998):

(a) Individual accountability
(b) Mutual interdependence
(c) Face-to-face promotive interaction
(d) Appropriate practice of interpersonal skills
(e) Regular self-assessment of team functioning

Whether CL effectively develops interpersonal skills is a difficult question. Part of this difficulty is tied to how one defines and measures team skills. Still, there is reason to think that CL is effective in this area. The cited authors recommended explicitly training students in the skills needed to be effective team members, when using CL groups. It is reasonable to assume that the opportunity to practice interpersonal skills coupled with explicit instructions in these skills is more effective than traditional instruction that rests on individual learning and has scarce explicit exposure to teamwork.

Problem-Based Learning (PBL) Problem-based learning is an instructional method that introduces relevant problems at the beginning of the instruction cycle and uses them to provide the context and motivation for the learning that follows. PBL is always active and usually, but not necessarily, cooperative. PBL typically involves significant amounts of self-directed learning on the part of the students. According to Woods, Felder, Rugarcia, and Stice (2000), there exist several variants of PBL instructional methods, which include:

- Lecturing
- Instructor-facilitated discussion
- Guided decision-making
- Cooperative learning

In PBL settings, student groups receive assignments to perform any of the learning tasks listed above, inside or outside of class. In the latter case, three approaches may help the groups to stay on track and to monitor progress: (a) give the groups written feedback after each task; (b) assign a tutor or teaching assistant to each group, knowing that Prince (2004) reports a significant negative effect size with non-expert tutors; and (c) create fully autonomous, self-assessed "tutorless" groups, for which Prince (2004) reports a small negative effect with both self-paced and self-directed learning. PBL is active and engages students in collaboration. It is also inductive and generally self-directed (although cautiously so, given the cited risk) and often includes explicit training in necessary skills. Which such element is common or decisive in it is an interesting question.

While PBL and CL are distinct approaches, there is a natural synergy between them. Real problems of the sort used in PBL require teams to solve effectively. At the same time, the challenge presented by realistic problems can provide some of the mutual interdependence that is one of the five tenets of CL, and it is designated to promote interpersonal skills. We leveraged that synergy considerably in our capstone design.

While practice is crucial for mastering skills such as problem-solving, greater gains are realized through explicit instruction of such skills: we valued this observation, and made room for explicit instruction, as part of the capstone itself.

No evidence proves that PBL enhances academic achievement as measured by exams, and we have none to offer. However, experience—including ours—shows that PBL does indeed "work" for achieving other important learning outcomes, including problem-solving and lifelong learning skills.

The instructional design of the capstone course presented in this chapter centers on four of the five components suggested by Goldstein and Fernald (2009). It solicits student's engagement (which corresponds to component 1, student-centered learning) in return for measurable acquisition of personal and professional skills (component 5, focus on personal and professional growth). Moreover, a considerable proportion of its learning activities are experiential (component 3) and collaborative,

Linking Active Learning and Capstone Projects in Higher Education

Table 1 Distinguishing traits of our capstone course design in relation to the inspiring principles from the state of the art (the cells on the same rows across columns refer to traits that are related across methods)

Capstone components	Good practice principles	Collaborative learning traits	Problem-based learning	
			Instructional methods	Monitoring of out-of-class work
Student-centered learning	Active learning		Instructor-facilitated discussion	
Experiential learning		Practice of interpersonal skills	Guided decision-making	
Collaboration and reciprocity	Reciprocity and cooperation	Mutual interdependence	Collaboration	
Personal and professional growth	Prompt feedback	Individual accountability	Lecturing	Prompt written feedback after each task
	Emphasis on task timeliness			
	Raising expectations	Regular self-assessment		

with a dynamic that emphasizes reciprocity (component 4, collaborative learning and self-disclosure).

The above traits directly encompass principles (2) and (3) of the Seven Principles for Good Practice in Chickering and Gamson (1987), enumerated earlier in this chapter, that is, encouraging direct contact between students and faculty and active learning. In addition to that set of objectives, our instructional design especially seeks to apply three further Principles of Good Practice, that is, (4) giving prompt feedback, (5) placing emphasis on task timeliness, and (6) raising expectations.

Of the common characteristics of collaborative learning, not implicitly met by the traits recalled above, our capstone course places explicit emphasis on (a) individual accountability, (c) face-to-face promotive interaction, and (e), regular self-assessment of team functioning, providing students with direct instruction in the basics of the relevant skills.

Further, we use, with various degrees of intensity, all variants of the problem-based learning (PBL) instructional methods described in Woods et al. (2000) and enumerated earlier in this chapter. For the monitoring of outside-of-class activities, which form the bulk of our capstone, we use approach (a) giving each group written feedback after each task, which is the most taxing for the instructor but also the one that incurs the least risk. Our choice of problems for the PBL element of our capstone emphasizes realism (the problem must be presented by a business professional), ambition (solving the problem would foster product or service innovation), and responsibility (the student teams choose the problem out of their own volition from a set provided by the instructor).

Table 1 summarizes the distinguishing traits that our capstone course design seeks, pairing them across all dimensions of the taxonomy discussed in this section.

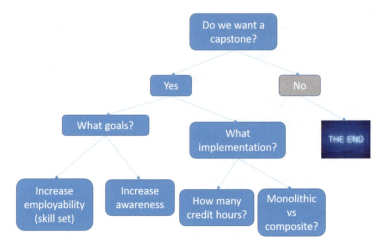

Fig. 1 Summary of the top-level decision points regarding capstones

3 Taxonomy of Implementation Challenges

The realization of effective capstone projects for BSc curricula raises several challenges, which correspond to the top-level decision points illustrated in Fig. 1. Some of those challenges relate to the height of the capstone goals and others to the fabric of the capstone itself and its integration in the curriculum. All of them ultimately stem from the discontinuity in learning methods and required level of engagement that the capstone insert may confront the students with in relation to the rest of the curriculum. In this work, we discuss emblematic instances of such challenges for each of those two fronts and discuss how we addressed them—with the help of interactive learning methods—and with what outcomes.

Regarding goals, capstones should measurably raise employability (Hall, 2002), that is, the skill set of BSc graduates whom the computer science labor market needs massively, but who are at risk of a low-value recognition, critically inferior to their MSc senior correspondents. Furthermore, by narrowing the gap between the study path and the workplace, capstones should also motivate students to reflect more thoroughly on whether to continue their study career pursuing a MSc degree, with more profound awareness of the alternatives, and sharper motivation in the choice, with more consequent goals and ambitions.

Regarding the design challenge, the work-related nature of the interactive learning traits given to the capstone should blend without hard tension and friction even in situations where the traditional content-centered teaching (Kember, 2009) permeates BSc curricula, especially so when they are seen as merely preparatory to MSc culmination.

One delicate element of that equation is to decide the quantity of credit hours that can be allotted to the capstone. They rarely can be many, especially in traditional content-centered teaching settings. Typically, capstones can seize only a modest fraction of the total. Another question is how to best use the allotted space, whether for a monolithic activity, such as an internship or a project embedded in a third-year course, or for a composite experience. The next two sections review our design decisions in all of those regards.

4 Local Constraints and Rationale

Our design had to balance two opposite forces. Traditional content-centered teaching wanted to compress as much learning material as possible of the previous 4–5-year curriculum duration in place before the February 2000 national reform, in the 3 years of the BSc program, with the intention that the knowledge level of future graduates would not be critically inferior to that attainable with the earlier curriculum. In contrast with that, the work-related learning innovation drive (Dirkx, 2011; Litchfield, Frawley, & Nettleton, 2010), solicited in the cited reform, wanted the 3-year duration to make room for situated learning opportunities (Lave & Wenger, 1991), directed toward some form of professional apprenticeship, to be deployed with interactive learning methods.

The faculty opted for reserving 25 out of the 180 credit hours of the overall curriculum[1] for a composite (hence *not* monolithic) mandatory capstone project, scheduled to occur in the final year, prior to the final exam. Although taking a modest fraction of the total student effort over the 3 years, the mandatory nature of the capstone inserts marked the curriculum with a trait that was unique across all the equivalent contemporary curricula majoring in computer science or information engineering countrywide and still is to date.

Before engineering the capstone internals, faculty consensus on the curriculum design was that it should culminate with a mandatory individual full-time internship at an organization external to the department and preferably to the university. That provision was the prime "gap-narrowing" trait of the curriculum, and it earned much attention from the pool of enterprises that the law required consulting ahead of the act of institution.

With the internship positioned at the tail end of the curriculum, we styled the final exam as the candidate's critical review, in writing and by a public presentation, of the internship experience. That arrangement aimed to facilitate the students' entry into the labor market in two ways. Boosting their motivation with fresh experience of what professional work is like made close to ending the BSc program, hence directly evocative of the reality ahead. Providing an accurate picture of the available job openings, for types, technology trends, and sought profiles, always correlate well with the internship projects on offer.

---

[1] One credit hour corresponds to a total of 25 hours of student work so that 60 credit hours correspond to the full-time equivalent of 1 year of student work.

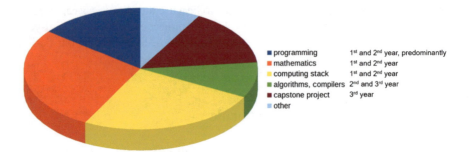

Fig. 2 Breakdown of the curriculum, for subject matters, relative proportion of class hours, and schedule across the 3-year study path

Mandating an internship in the curriculum should not incur negative impact on throughput, hence not slowing progress down with excess workload and duration. The 25 credit hours set aside for the capstone project overall correspond to 625 hours of work for the student, 16.7% less than the traditional 6-month full-time equivalent of voluntary (typically extracurricular) internships of other institutions. This observation vouched against having a traditional content-centered learning path abruptly transition into a compressed internship, for a "cold-fusion" effort at risk of poor outcome. Our design challenge was thus to retain a mandatory (short) internship at the tail end of the curriculum while making it as productive for students as effective for the hosting organizations, in spite of a compressed duration.

A further factor effected our design, which we should remark before illustrating our implementation decisions. Like most curricula in Italy, our regulatory statutes do not place blocking barriers on the passage of years but only set preconditions on access to some specific courses. One consequence of that arrangement is that students may incur an irregular progression of studies. The students who do may have access to the capstone project before completing all other exams and also with variable-length intermissions in its execution, contingent on the speed with which they are able to progress the backlog that they have cumulated. This structural vulnerability correlates with throughput statistics (University of Padua, 2017), which show that less than 15% of the students complete the BSc program in 3 years, while twice as many do need up to 1 more year for it.

Figure 2 provides a pictorial representation of the curriculum breakdown for subject matters, their relative weight in terms of credit hours, and schedule across the 3 years of the study path.

5 Implementation Decisions

Our ambition was to expose the final-year students to a continuum of learning experience, constituted by two subsequent but distinct and separately graded segments of activity, one preparatory to the other.

Fig. 3 Structure of the capstone project for parts, volume of effort, and calendar-time duration

The first part, "stage 1," of our two-staged capstone project centers on group work performed as a *learning-for-work* collaborative laboratory (Little & Brennan, 1996) aimed at the acquisition of soft skills (Freudenberg, Brimble, & Cameron, 2011), and exposure to technology and market innovation challenges, uniting elements of PBL and CL.

The second part, "stage 2," is a PBL-based *learning-through-work* (Subramaniam & Freudenberg, 2007) internship proper, hosted at a partner organization, aimed at aiding students to associate theoretical contents with professional problems and practices.

The first part is longer in duration (ca. 6 elapsed months), but part-time in actuation, overlapping with other class activities for the first 3 calendar months, upper-bounded at 180 hours of collaborative project work per student, accompanied by 75 class hours of lecturing, instructor-facilitated discussion, and guided decision-making, and another 75 hours of preparatory self-learning.

The second part is shorter in duration (ca. 2 elapsed months), but full-time in execution, for a total of 320 hours, 8 full-time equivalent weeks per student, immersed in a real-world PBL-based project, supervised by business professionals in an external organization.

The duration of the two parts combined nears 9 elapsed months in total, destined to the last three-quarters of the third and final year. The expanse of our capstone matches the state-of-the-art tendency to span it over two semesters (Flowers, 2008), to afford sufficient time to the exposure, the elaboration, and the absorption of the key ingredients of the intended trajectory (Fig. 3).

5.1 Design of Stage 1

The first part of the capstone found natural collocation in a software engineering course. The tight interplay between those two elements is vastly acknowledged in the literature (Flowers, 2008; Vanhanen, Lehtinen, & Lassenius, 2012). The distinctive trait of that bond in our context is that the learning outcomes of stage 1 are immediately deployed *within* the BSc study path and exposed to evaluation by a professional outside of faculty, in the stage 2 internship, with direct impact on the final exam. The students appear to value the reputation they earn among professionals through their capstone, which strengthens their dedication.

Our implementation of stage 1, which combines PBL and CL, has three main goals, which relate to the taxonomy in (Clear et al., 2001): (a) to develop the students' capability, confidence, and maturity, favoring active integration of previous knowledge; (b) to immerse them in their first team-based "programming in the large" experience (DeRemer & Kron, 1976), with guided reference to professional practices, with a process-centered style, similar to (Vanhanen et al., 2012), and explicit links to individual accountability and schedule obligations; and (c) to foster their endowments of soft skills.

To highlight the link with stage 2, the project sponsors are selected from members of the internship partnering program who are willing to play that role and have themes and mentoring resources to provide for it. Interestingly, after the initial investment of effort in seeding awareness of this model among enterprises, this machinery has become self-sustaining: most sponsors come forward on their own resolve, sometimes on push from the alumni among their staff.

To stimulate self-learning, the drive in stage 1 is to promote the exploration of technology and product innovation and process-related practices, outside of the students' prior knowledge. The project sponsors collaborate to this scheme enthusiastically, with PBL instruction that helps the students steer their self-learning efforts.

Multiple projects are proposed to the students, one project per sponsor. By explicit request of the instructor, all such projects are designed to seek significant product or service innovation, which goes significantly beyond the students' knowledge, and therefore require considerable self-learning on their part. A few weeks into the class part of stage 1, the representatives of the selected sponsors present their projects to the students in a public, open session. A typical example project may ask students to use very fresh software technology to implement innovative services or products. For example, months before Google's launch of their Hangouts communication platform in 2013, one of our projects called for a prototype implementation of the client side of it.

To create conditions as favorable as those discussed in Gorka, Miller, and Howe (2007), multiple teams, up to a limit agreed with the sponsor, are allowed to undertake the same project. This provision motivates the sponsors to devise themes that enable complementary explorations, and therefore compensates the extra load that they take on in interacting with more student teams.

By design, the project offering always exceeds the quantity of student teams, so that the students have ample room for choice (Whalley, Goldweber, & Ogier, 2017). In that manner, the students signing up to a team and to a project incur less risk of losing interest and motivation along the way. The sponsors are not allowed to reject teams whose bid has been accepted at project start.

The teams are composed of peers and count 6–8 members: a slightly smaller contingent and with a different composition than in Vanhanen et al. (2012). That empirical threshold is designed to exceed the average student's prior experience with teamwork.

Up to the 2017 cohort, the students were allowed to form their teams freely, after common interest for project themes and schedule constraints. The group formation process was constantly reflected on a public digital document monitored by the instructor to allow intervening in case of critical situations. This strategy produced fairly balanced teams, much like the experience reported in Whalley et al., (2017), while requiring less supervisory control. Prior personal relations among students (frequently unrelated to skills), however, inevitably played a role in that process, occasionally keeping off some individuals from specific "inner circles." From the 2018 cohort, we switched to a lottery-based scheme: the outcomes of that choice suggested confirming this policy for the subsequent cohorts, taxing the students more in the practice of interpersonal skills, and becoming more acutely aware of the complex interplay between individual accountability and mutual interdependence in the realization of complex collaborative tasks.

Maximizing students' exposure to the principal dimensions of project work is one of the learning outcomes of stage 1. To this end, each team must explicitly plan for all members to traverse all project roles (e.g., coordinator, administrator, designer, programmer, tester), at least once for a sizable span of time, and to report on that front regularly.

This provision creates natural conditions to foster mutual interdependence, in the sharing of experience and lessons learned from project roles and in subdividing tasks to leverage parallelism in their execution. This provision however also incurs two known negatives, whose incidence requires constant monitoring. It increases the level of student stress by moving them out of their comfort zone, and it causes process-related overhead in the execution of the project. On balance, the benefits accrued with this scheme much outweigh the downside.

Grading in stage 1 has two components that yield a single final mark (Farrell, Ravalli, Farrell, Kindler, & Hall, 2012): one reflects group output and the other the individual understanding of and contribution to it. The grading of the group component addresses the three P's, product, process, and progression in learning, after Clear (2009), and it is assigned incrementally, at bid time, at delivery, and at two intermediate milestones agreed with each team at the moment of signing them in, all factored in a single mark. The grading at every milestone is accompanied by written detailed feedback for each group. When the final group grading reflects on the individual, the instructor applies a small correction factor to reflect the magnitude of that student's contribution to the project outcome, measured in terms of quantity of work falling in an allowable range of excess. That range is strictly upper-bounded to avoid the risk of overwork, which might undermine the student performance in other curricular activities. The individual quantity of project work is recorded, for the whole team, in a journal shared with the instructor. The intellectual value of individual contribution to group work is meant to emerge in the solo grading, which measures students against technical questions pertinent to the body of knowledge experienced in the project work. This system of grading is a complex task indeed, which requires constant maintenance, for which we use the criteria described in Hayes, Lethbridge, and Port (2003).

5.2 Design of Stage 2

With a mandatory internship, the burden of finding opportunities should not be on the students, who however should be free to go seek them on their own as long as certain basic conditions are met. To support this process, the department runs an internship partnering program: since the inception of the BSc curriculum, that program has affiliated nearly 200 external organizations in total. Besides legal clauses, the technical prerequisite to be fulfilled for joining the program is that the candidate hosts have personnel qualified to supervise the interns, able to provide students with the necessary PBL formation (on tools, methods, and practices), and whose job can be assigned supervision tasks explicitly, so that the supervisor's attention is secured with sufficient intensity.

The department organizes an annual internship fair, open to neighboring curricula from the region, in which selected members of the partnering program are invited to present their proposals and meet face-to-face with the students who have to undertake the internship. To maximize throughput, this event is scheduled to occur around 4 calendar months before the earliest opportunity of final exam. This provision allows students to select, agree, and perform their internship of choice right after the fair day and continue straight through to graduation. Interestingly, the yearly offering for that event provides an accurate indicator of the software technology and application trends in the marketplace, which course instructors may use to refresh their syllabus.

All the internship projects present PBL tasks designed for a single intern, who is expected to interact with a team of professionals at the host organization. That team may preexist, for internship projects that map onto real enterprise undertakings or may be formed ad hoc, to accompany the students in their work. The former arrangement is prevalent. We firmly direct host organizations to avoid teams formed exclusively of interns. With the progressive recruitment of alumni from our curriculum in enterprises from the partnering program, increasingly often the host teams include alumni. We welcome their presence, as the alumni's direct experience of the hardship of internships operates as a natural facilitator.

The students pick the host of their internship after personal interest, technical curiosity, and career strategy. Internships start asynchronously, when the student has fulfilled the prerequisites. The internship ends with the supervisor's assessment of the intern along two axes. One addresses the quality of the student's contribution to the material outcome of the internship project. The other addresses the degree of autonomy, maturity, and proactivity shown at work, and the tension toward interpersonal skills, to match the recruitment factors discussed in Zheng, Zhang, and Li (2015).

6 Evaluation

To conclude this chapter, we first evaluate the curriculum performance against student satisfaction, surveyed with anonymous questionnaires filled for all courses, as well as with findings from nationwide polls on the opinion of graduates, taken 1, 2, and 3 years after graduation.[2]

The average student satisfaction with the curriculum overall, recorded on an annual basis, has been stable over time: the latest available result, referred to the 2016/2017 academic year (University of Padua, 2017), has it at 7.46/10, only marginally inferior to the 7.72/10 average value computed across the 200+ BSc curricula hosted at the University of Padua. The capstone project itself regularly scores high for the students' appreciation of its contents, organization, and value for learning. Stage 1's grade median is stable above 7/10, but it also collects occasional discomfort—varying across cohorts—with the intensity of the workload required. Reportedly, part of this frustration stems from the acute perception of discontinuity in the style of learning that the third-year students are confronted with.

The postgraduation surveys constantly reveal higher satisfaction in our study path than for other provenances, higher correspondence between the current job and the curriculum profile, and higher employment rate. For example, the 2016 survey data report: +3.3% higher appreciation rate than for equivalent curricula in the region, +27.1% higher appreciation rate than BSc graduates in electronic engineering (the closest topic at the same University of Padua), +18.1% higher employment rate than equivalent curricula from other provenances, and +15.1% higher employment rate than for BSc graduates in electronic engineering from the same university.

Next, we assess whether the capstone experience affords the graduates who seek recruitment a jump-start entry, for productivity and integration, at the workplace. We addressed this question in three ways. First, we submitted an online questionnaire[3] to the 82 organizations that attended the 2017 internship fair, 69.5% of which were recurrent. That yielded 61 partial returns, 35 from small-sized enterprises, 26 from medium to large ones. The 40 returns that were complete came from employers that collectively had hosted 136 of our internships in the previous 2 years, out of the total 210 in that period, and recruited 208 of our BSc graduates over the previous 5 years, out of the total 326 in that period. Their feedback was unanimously positive, so we do not discuss it further. Second, we held a focus-group meeting with 10 employers with a long record of participation in our partnership program and inquired them on the following three fronts:

(Q1) What factors increase the productivity of new recruits
(Q2) The fresh BSc graduates' familiarity with problem-solving and self-learning
(Q3) The new recruits' skills for planning, oral and written communication, and interpersonal skills

---

[2]http://www.almalaurea.it/universita/occupazione/occupazione15

[3]https://www.surveymonkey.com/r/STAGE-IT_2017

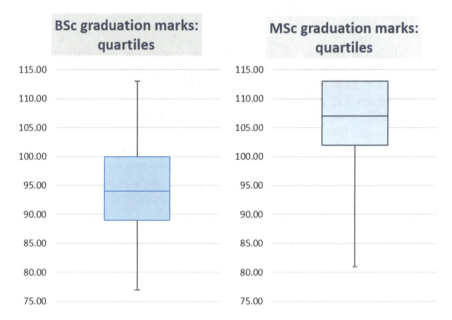

Fig. 4 Quartiles of graduation marks for our full population of BSc and MSc graduates: 1100 and 263 individuals, respectively (higher is better)

Regarding (Q1: *what factors increase the productivity of new recruits*), participants concurred that all types of graduates, including BSc, should be familiar with collaborative work, which all curricula ought to promote before leaving it to mature from exposure to the workplace practices. In that regard, the participants declared preferring candidates who had taken active roles in curricular experiences of collaboration.

When presented the finding from the online questionnaire that the first-time recruits from our curriculum required less time than peers from other provenances (an average of 7.38 vs. 9.66 elapsed months) to reach satisfactory operational maturity, the focus-group participants had split opinions: the representatives of small organizations rated that trait higher than for larger ones; presumably, the latter can attenuate lesser individual yield with larger volume. All participants acknowledged that the capstone project does indeed exercise productivity factors visibly and makes our graduates stand out from peers off other equivalent provenances.

Regarding (Q2: *the fresh BSc graduates' familiarity with problem-solving and self-learning*), participants observed that MSc graduates are intrinsically more equipped for self-learning and problem-solving, which makes them attractive targets of recruitment. Figure 4 provides a vivid indicator of the superiority of MSc graduates over BSc ones, by paralleling the quartiles of graduation marks for their respective total population so far. Preferring MSc graduates however has the drawback that their study career is 3.2 years longer on average than the BSc path duration for computer science and engineering curricula at this university (similar figures regionally).

The focus-group participants also noted that the self-learning and problem-solving skills need the complementary ability to communicate findings, both orally and in writing, lamenting that such ability is insufficiently exercised in most curricula. In order for that ability to reach a satisfactory level by the time of graduation, the corresponding training should extend *beyond* the capstone project.

Regarding (Q3: *the new recruits' skills for planning, oral and written communication, and interpersonal skills*), participants agreed that the planning ability, intrinsically limited in new recruits, naturally improves with experience. As such, it should *not* be placed among the primary objectives of the capstone project (and, transitively, of the overall curriculum). Conversely, participants regarded *interpersonal skills* as the most critical factor, which, while very positively exercised by the capstone course, should be more actively stimulated by the curriculum as a whole. In that ambit, MSc graduates, more equipped to earn trust, tend to configure as "leaders" and BSc ones as "followers." It is obviously easier (for energy and yield) to team up with the former, but they are needed in far smaller quantity than the latter. Interestingly, the participants reported finding noticeable positive tension toward earning trust in BSc graduates from our curriculum.

Last, we considered the perspective of the more "disadvantaged" BSc students. We sampled them from the full population of BSc graduates since inception, picking those with graduation marks *below* the overall median shown on the left of Fig. 4, and then determined how they were rated by the business professional who supervised them in their stage 2 internship. To this end, we randomly sampled 100 internships from the 2013 to 2017 cohorts to which we had prompt digital data access, discarding those that had incomplete record data. That left us with 91 internships that took place at 52 unique employers. The sample population collectively had median, first quartile, and third quartile, all *lower* than the full BSc population. 41.8% of the sample (group A) had graduation marks *above* the median of the full population, while 58.2% (group B) had them *below* the median. Interestingly, a large subset of group B (22 of 53, 41.5%), supposedly disadvantaged, earned very high marks on the capstone's internship, nearly as many in quantity as group A (25 of 38, 65.8%, which include the highest-scoring case). As the employers' evaluation is based on professionally relevant skills, this evidence suggests that the capstone boosts the employability of disadvantaged graduates, without affecting negatively that of higher-performing ones. Only a small fraction of group B (7 of 53, 13.2%) had low marks on the internship, which shows that those inclined to fail do find ways to fail, and the capstone is no ultimate salvation. Notably, being from group A (hence with graduation marks above the overall median) does not exempt from earning low internship marks either (1 of 38, 2.6%, with the lowest mark of all). Figure 5 summarizes the quartiles corresponding to those findings.

These findings support the argument that the capstone insert has a quantifiably positive effect on the quality of the curriculum output, which sets it apart from comparable offerings. We should also note that our current statistics show that 90% of the students who enter the capstone project regularly, as the last leg of the third

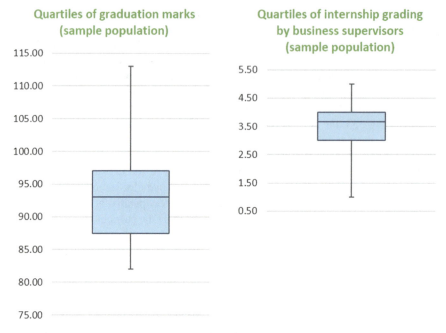

Fig. 5 Quartiles of graduation marks vs. employers' evaluation at the end of capstone for a random sample of 91 individuals on a total population of 1100 BSc graduates

year, graduate within the next 9 calendar months. Since 9 months is the designed duration of the capstone, we can conclude that its implementation causes students *no further delay* in their traversal of it.

7 Conclusions

This chapter has illustrated the distinguishing characteristics of a capstone implementation and rationale of the decisions we made to design it: this information should allow others to find inspiration in designing and implementing their own capstone programs. In the discussion, we have highlighted the evident relations between active learning and the instructional design of the capstone. The group work that stage 1 of our capstone requires, lends itself well to the application of collaborative learning. Stage 1 also has distinct problem-based learning traits that prepare the students to the stage 2 internship. The ensuing gradualness caters for a smoother and more effective transition into the workplace, which mitigates the risk of the compressed duration that we could afford for the internship proper. That measure of gradualness however does not seem to suffice, as the step into the capstone still appears to be steep for most students, who find discomfort in the radical difference of learning style applied in it: the students like interactive learning, but some also consider it "too taxing." The obvious solution to that problem is to devolve some of the capstone's learning outcomes to earlier classes. Finding suitable classes and fitting contents for them, as well as willing instructors, is the harder part. The other factor of risk is the extra load on the instructor that stems from designing, executing, and maintaining the capstone course. Running the whole endeavor consistently with active learning principles, thus facilitating discussion, guiding the students' decision-making, stimulating individual accountability, giving prompt and regular feedback, while earning and motivating trust, is a very big challenge. Most of that load falls on the instructor: offloading part of it requires absolute alignment of style, vision, and intent with the teaching assistants, which takes a long time to build, and is difficult to preserve. The response from the students and the lasting appreciation by the alumni and the employers are the currency that pays back the instructor overwhelmingly.

References

Bonwell, C., & Eison, J. (1991). Active learning: Creating excitement in the classroom. *American Association for Higher Education Bulletin* (ERIC Number ED336049), 121. Retrieved 2019-01-04, from https://eric.ed.gov/?id=ED336049.

Chickering, A., & Gamson, Z. (1987). Seven principles for good practice in undergraduate education. *American Association for Higher Education Bulletin* (ERIC Number ED282491), 3–7. Retrieved 2019-01-04, from https://eric.ed.gov/?id=ED282491.

Clear, T. (2009). Thinking issues: The three p's of capstone project performance. *ACM SIGCSE Bulletin, 41*(2), 69–70. https://doi.org/10.1145/1595453.1595468.

Clear, T., Goldweber, M., Young, F., Leidig, P., & Scott, K. (2001). *Resources for instructors of capstone courses in computing.* In Working group reports from ITiCSE on Innovation and Technology in Computer Science Education (pp. 93–113). ACM. https://doi.org/10.1145/572133.572135.

DeRemer, F., & Kron, H. (1976). Programming-in-the-large versus programming-in-the- small. *IEEE Transactions on Software Engineering, 2*(2), 80–86. https://doi.org/10.1109/TSE.1976.233534.

Dirkx, J. (2011). Work-related learning in the United States: Past practices, paradigm shifts, and policies of partnerships. In *The SAGE handbook of workplace learning* (pp. 293–306). London: Sage. https://doi.org/10.4135/9781446200940.n21.

Dunlap, J. (2005, March). Problem-based learning and self-efficacy: How a capstone course prepares students for a profession. *Educational Technology Research and Development, 53*(1), 65–83. https://doi.org/10.1007/BF02504858.

Farrell, V., Ravalli, G., Farrell, G., Kindler, P., & Hall, D. (2012). Capstone project: Fair, just and accountable assessment. In *Proceeding of the 17th ACM Annual Conference on Innovation and Technology in Computer Science Education* (pp. 168–173). ACM. https://doi.org/10.1145/2325296.2325339.

Flowers, J. (2008). Improving the capstone project experience: A case study in software engineering. In *Proceedings of the 46th Southeast Regional Conference* (pp. 237–242). New York: ACM. https://doi.org/10.1145/1593105.1593167.

Freudenberg, B., Brimble, M., & Cameron, C. (2011). WIL and generic skill development: The development of business students' generic skills through work- integrated learning. *Asia-Pacific Journal of Cooperative Education, 12*(2), 79–93.

Goldstein, G., & Fernald, P. (2009). Humanistic education in a capstone course. *College Teaching, 57*(1), 27–36. https://doi.org/10.3200/CTCH.57.1.27-36.

Gorka, S., Miller, J., & Howe, B. (2007). Developing realistic capstone projects in conjunction with industry. In *Proceeding of the 8th ACM SIGITE Conference on Information Technology Education* (pp. 27–32). New York: ACM. https://doi.org/10.1145/1324302.1324309.

Hall, D. T. (2002). *Careers in an out of organizations*. London: Sage. https://doi.org/10.4135/9781452231174.

Hayes, J., Lethbridge, T., & Port, D. (2003). *Evaluating individual contribution toward group software engineering projects*. In 25th International Conference on Software Engineering, 2003 (pp. 622–627). https://doi.org/10.1109/ICSE.2003.1201246.

Hundhausen, C. (2015). Special issue on team projects in computing education. *ACM Transactions on Computing Education, 15*(4). https://dlnext.acm.org/toc/toce/2015/15/4

Johnson, D., Johnson, R., & Smith, K. (1998). *Active learning: Cooperation in the college classroom*. Edina, MN: Interaction Book Company.

Kember, D. (2009). Promoting student-centred forms of learning across an entire university. *Higher Education, 58*(1), 1–13. https://doi.org/10.1007/s10734-008-9177-6.

Lave, J., & Wenger, E. (1991). *Situated learning: Legitimate peripheral participation*. Cambridge: Cambridge University Press.

Litchfield, A., Frawley, J., & Nettleton, S. (2010). Contextualising and integrating into the curriculum the learning and teaching of work-ready professional graduate attributes. *Higher Education Research and Development, 29*(5), 519–534. https://doi.org/10.1080/07294360.2010.502220.

Little, B., & Brennan, J. (1996, October). *A review of work-based learning in higher education*. Retrieved from http://oro.open.ac.uk/11309/.

Nelson, D., & Bianco, C. (2013). Increasing student responsibility and active learning in an undergraduate capstone finance course. *American Journal of Business Education (AJBE), 6*(2), 267–278. https://doi.org/10.19030/ajbe.v6i2.7692.

Prince, M. (2004). Does active learning work? A review of the research. *Journal of Engineering Education, 93*(3), 223–231. https://doi.org/10.1002/j.2168-9830.2004.tb00809.x.

Reinicke, B., & Janicki, T. (2010). Increasing active learning and end-client interaction in the systems analysis and design and capstone courses. *Information Systems Education Journal, 8*(40), 3–10. Retrieved from http://isedj.org/8/40/.

Subramaniam, N., & Freudenberg, B. (2007). Preparing accounting students for success in the professional environment: Enhancing self-efficacy through a work integrated learning programme. *Asia-Pacific Journal of Cooperative Education, 8*(1), 77–92.

Umphress, D., Hendrix, T., & Cross, J. (2002). Software process in the classroom: The capstone project experience. *IEEE Software, 19*(5), 78–81. https://doi.org/10.1109/MS.2002.1032858.

University of Padua. (2017, September). *Periodic assessment of curricula: 2013–2015*. (Internal).

Vanhanen, J., Lehtinen, T., & Lassenius, C. (2012, June). *Teaching real-world software engineering through a capstone project course with industrial customers*. In 2012 First International Workshop on Software Engineering Education Based on Real-World Experiences (edurex) (p. 29–32). Zurich. https://doi.org/10.1109/EduRex.2012.6225702.

Vardanega, T., & Fedeli, M. (2018). A two-staged capstone project to foster university-business dialogue. In *Proceedings of the 23rd Annual ACM Conference on Innovation and Technology in Computer Science Education, ITiCSE 2018* (pp. 272–277). https://doi.org/10.1145/3197091.3197130.

Whalley, J., Goldweber, M., & Ogier, H. (2017). Student values and interests in capstone project selection. In *Proceeding of the 19th Australasian Computing Education Conference* (pp. 90–94). New York: ACM. https://doi.org/10.1145/3013499.3013508.

Woods, D., Felder, R., Rugarcia, A., & Stice, J. (2000). The future of engineering education III. Developing critical skills. *Chemical Engineering Education, 34*, 108–117.

Wosinski, J., Belcher, A. E., Dürrenberger, Y., Allin, A. C., Stormacq, C., & Gerson, L. D. (2018). Facilitating problem-based learning among undergraduate nursing students: A qualitative systematic review. *Nurse Education Today, 60*, 67–74. https://doi.org/10.1016/j.nedt.2017.08.015.

Zheng, G., Zhang, C., & Li, L. (2015). Practicing and evaluating soft skills in it capstone projects. In *Proceeding of the 16th Annual Conference on Information Technology Education* (pp. 109–113). New York: ACM. https://doi.org/10.1145/2808006.2808041

Teaching for Globalization: Implications for Knowledge Management in Organizations

Maria Cseh, Oliver S. Crocco, and Chilanay Safarli

Abstract Global workforce mobility and the technologies that support collaborative work across the globe lead to the need of knowledge management systems that take into account how adults with various national and ethnic backgrounds learn and share knowledge, and that incorporate both the professional and technical knowledge in organizations, and the diversity of thought and worldviews of their employees. It is incumbent on learning facilitators, instructional designers, and developers of knowledge management systems to enable and empower employees to think at a global level and use and share their knowledge and skills in their organizations to address the global challenges they face. Thus, teaching for globalization is considered both an antecedent and an outcome of knowledge management systems in organizations. This chapter discusses the (a) global context of education and work (the "whys" for teaching for globalization), (b) importance of knowledge management in today's organizations (the "whys" for knowledge management designed for the global environment), (c) global systems thinking and global mindset (the "whats" of teaching for globalization), and (d) cultivating global systems thinking and global mindset (the "hows" of teaching for globalization). The chapter concludes with implications for the design of knowledge management systems to support continuous learning in organizations, and nurture engaged, creative, and responsible global professionals.

As cultures and economies are increasingly interconnected, the presence of globalization is visible in nearly every aspect of life and work (Giddens, 2002; Hirst, Thompson, & Bromley, 2009). Global workforce mobility has led to workplaces around the globe becoming more diverse with people bringing their various worldviews and identities to work (Cseh & Coningham, 2012). Findings of the Global

---

M. Cseh (✉) · C. Safarli
The George Washington University, Washington, DC, USA
e-mail: cseh@gwu.edu

O. S. Crocco
Louisiana State University, Baton Rouge, LA, USA

© Springer Nature Switzerland AG 2019
M. Fedeli, L. L. Bierema (eds.), *Connecting Adult Learning and Knowledge Management*, Knowledge Management and Organizational Learning 8,
https://doi.org/10.1007/978-3-030-29872-2_6

Skills Gap report (Think Global & British Council, 2011) show that in countries like those in the UK, high-school graduates are not competent enough to work in globalized and cross-cultural environments. Preparing students and professionals to work in every discipline from anthropology to zoology requires a nuanced understanding of the impact of globalization both in the disciplinary content and the methods used to facilitate learning. It is incumbent on learning facilitators, instructional designers, and developers of knowledge management systems whether in higher education, organizations, or communities to enable and empower participants to think at a global level and use and share their knowledge and skills in their organizations to address the global challenges they face.

Within the ongoing and changing realities of globalization, organizations and individuals are asking questions such as: *What should we know to be successful contributors to our global community? How should we be as human beings in our global environment? What kinds of skills, abilities, and attitude should we develop and how? How do we become global system thinkers? How can we enrich our global mindset? How can we engage learners in global knowledge creation? What strategies for learning and teaching will lead to engaged learners who will share their knowledge, skills, and ways of thinking in the global workplace and community?* These questions guide the content of this chapter, which is organized in the following sections: (a) the global context of education and work (the "whys" for teaching for globalization), (b) the importance of knowledge management in today's organizations (the "whys" for knowledge management designed for the global environment), (c) global systems thinking and global mindset (the "whats" of teaching for globalization), and (d) cultivating global systems thinking and global mindset (the "hows" of teaching for globalization). The chapter concludes with implications for the design of knowledge management systems to support continuous learning in organizations and nurture engaged, creative, and responsible global professionals.

1 The Global Context of Education and Work

Globalization is the increasing interrelatedness and interconnection of the modern world through the flow of services, people, knowledge, goods, and information across international boundaries (Department of International Development, 2000). When we think of globalization, our minds tend to conjure images of Japanese trucks driven across Europe or American soft drinks consumed in rural African villages. This emphasis on the flow of goods in globalization downplays the impact and importance of the flow of people with their diverse cultures across the world, both face-to-face and digitally.

The increasing trend in global mobility is a key development in globalization that requires thoughtfulness to prepare people for global work. According to the World Migration Report 2018 by the United Nation's International Organization for Migration (2017), there are roughly 244 million international migrants (i.e., those people living outside the country of their birth), who represent over 3% of the world's population. According to the International Labour Organization (2015), migrant workers comprise nearly 64% of the world's international migrant population, only half of whom (48.5%) work in North America and Northern, Southern, and Western Europe. Nearly 12% of these migrant workers are located in Arab states, 9.2% live and work in Eastern Europe, and the rest are located elsewhere. Understanding the human element of globalization around the world, however, should not be limited to considerations of global mobility. Many people work on international projects within groups comprised of members from various backgrounds and cultures, which necessitates a different mindset and set of skills for communicating and understanding others' perspectives to work effectively in these multicultural environments.

There is also an increase in the mobility of international students. International student mobility reached 2.5 million students in 2006, which represented an increase of 41% from 1999 (Bhandari & Blumenthal, 2010). The Education at a Glance 2017 report by OECD (2017) also highlights the rapid growth in global student mobility, particularly during 1990–2010, and as of 2017, it was estimated at approximately 5 million. OECD (2017) projects that the total number of internationally mobile students will reach 8 million by 2025. According to Bhandari (2017), with the increasing growth of the global workplace, some countries use higher education institutions to recruit qualified and culturally competent students. In line with this focus, many developed countries such as Canada, Germany, Japan, and China have updated their policies to attract international students and provide them with job opportunities upon graduation.

According to Deloitte (2016), globalization is one of the key factors driving change in today's workforce. This change requires organizations to continually adapt their business processes and policies to accommodate the increasing number of employees coming from different cultures and backgrounds. Employers across industries are also seeking out employees who are equipped to work effectively in the global reality facing organizations. In a 2015 report by the Asia Society, 80% of US executives representing a variety of industries believe that having staff members with international experience will positively contribute to their business (Monthey, Singmaster, Manise, & Kreamer, 2015). This is not only true for large-size companies but also mid-size and small companies, which see international skills as critical at both entry and management levels (Monthey et al., 2015). A desire for globally engaged employees is not only applicable to US executives. In a study on work and culture in over 100 countries, employers from around the world were found to look for employees who are not only technically savvy but also culturally intelligent to work in a global work environment (British Council, 2013). The study also revealed that the ability to understand and respect other cultural viewpoints and speak a foreign language are skills that are prioritized by employers while hiring and retaining their employees.

As employers seek out globally minded employees, higher education institutions are also seeking to produce globally minded graduates. A study conducted by the Association of American Colleges and Universities (2018) found that 65% of business executives and 73% of hiring managers rank the ability to "[a]nalyze/solve problems with people from different backgrounds/cultures" as "very important skills for recent college graduates," which represents an 18-point increase from 2014 (p. 13). The report added that business executives and hiring managers would be 29% and 37%, respectively, more likely to hire someone with experience in working on community-based projects that involved people from different backgrounds/cultures.

Considering the reality that current and future students will work in a global market and workplace, higher education institutions must prepare students with the knowledge, skills, and abilities needed to compete in the global workforce (Richardson, 2012). As Richardson (2012) noted, "As jobs continue to be transferred overseas, institutions of higher learning are placed at the forefront of training bilingual and culturally astute workers for the global market" (p. 43). And preparing globally minded graduates is no longer confined simply to the field of business—globalization is impacting work and life of nearly every field of study (White & Toms, 2009). In their research on globalization's impact on higher education, Meyer, Bushney, and Ukpere (2011) emphasize that higher education institutions must adapt to the fact that employers of all kinds are seeking graduates with a global mindset as a source of competitive advantage in the global workplace. They point out, however, that most higher education institutions are nowhere near adequately preparing students for the new global reality (Meyer et al., 2011). As a result, now more than ever designers and facilitators of learning in higher education are called to consider curricular and cocurricular reforms to prepare graduates to make effective contributions in the global systems in which they work and live.

2 Knowledge Management in the Global Environment

Due to the transition to the knowledge economy, increasing advancement of the technology, and globalization, knowledge management has become an inevitable factor in the life of organizations to ensure their competitive advantage in the global market (Pauluzzo & Cagnina, 2017). The major premise of knowledge management is to build organizations' capacity "to search, acquire, create, organize, share and transform knowledge towards the identification and exploitation of competitive advantage" (Sharma, Chadee, & Roxas, 2016, p. 1270). Bollinger and Smith (2001) present the importance of two forms of knowledge in organization—explicit knowledge (codified and kept in a database and easily accessible by people in the organization) and tacit knowledge (the knowledge that resides within an employee and is hard to access). The importance of tacit knowledge and the employees who possess it is recognized in the literature. For example, according to Joe, Yoong, and Patel (2013), when employees leave an organization, the loss due to the knowledge they take from the organization is detrimental to the organization. Robert Reich, former US Labor Secretary, noted,

> Nowadays, any competitor can get access to the same information technology, the same suppliers, the same distribution channels, and often the same proprietary technology. The only unique asset that a business has for gaining a sustained competitive advantage over its rivals is its workforce—the skills and dedication of its employees. There is no other sustainable competitive advantage in the modern, high tech global economy. (Bingham & Galagan, 2006, p. 32)

These statements highlight the importance of knowledge management systems that incorporate not just the professional, technical knowledge in organizations, but the diversity of thought and worldviews of employees, especially for organizations that operate in a global environment (Paci, Lalle, & Chiacchio, 2010). Bubel (2015) noted that global companies should become proficient in knowledge management. Despite the increasing importance of knowledge management, according to Ernst & Young (as cited in King, 2007), 44% of employees are inefficient at transferring knowledge. One of the reasons for the inefficiency for the transfer of knowledge is a lack of communication between departments in organizations and unawareness about the existing resources, as described by Goodman and Schieman (2010). The authors discuss that situation as follows: "Corporations, especially large global corporations, are needlessly spending money on training and development to 'gain' knowledge that they already have" (p. 112). Besides the size of the organization, another challenge for organizations in their efforts of managing knowledge is the complexity that comes with globalization, including language barriers, sociopolitical factors, and distance (Moitra & Kumar, 2007). All of these factors demand the development and maintenance of a knowledge management system that leverages the knowledge, experience, and worldviews of the organizations' employees.

3   Global Systems Thinking and Global Mindset

In this section, we sought answers to the following questions: What should we know to be successful contributors to our global community? How should we be as human beings in our global environment? What kinds of skills, abilities, and attitude should we develop?

To answer these questions, we must begin with the foundations of our learning and how it changes over time with increased complexity. From the moment we are born, we begin making sense of the world in terms of simple, causal relationships. We learn to isolate and oversimplify ours and others' experiences, and we ascribe one-dimensional causes to those experiences. Touching a hot stovetop brings pain, eating our favorite dessert makes us happy, and laughing with friends produces joy. This type of mechanistic thinking comes easy to us and serves us well in our early development. A problem emerges in adulthood when we apply this thinking to sets of variables that are functioning within more complex systems. Systems thinking provides a way for us to make sense of this complexity (Checkland, 1981; Gharajedaghi, 2011). Systems thinking is built on the idea that people, organizations, and societies are not understood best as independent variables but interdependent variables (Gharajedaghi, 2011). Systems represent dynamic contexts—such as collections of people, cells, ecosystems, weather, etc.—in which variables interact and eventually generate patterns of behavior (Meadows, 2008). As a result of this complexity, ascribing simplistic causal explanations to phenomena occurring within systems becomes inaccurate at best and dangerous at worst. Consider the following example: A manager has been tasked with understanding the lack of motivation to learn in her workplace. Perhaps she asks herself, "What is causing this lack of motivation? How can I make this person more motivated?" Taking what we know of systems, it behooves this manager to isolate the

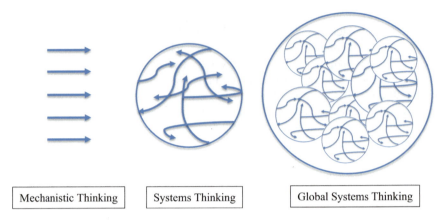

Fig. 1 Global systems thinking

phenomenon of motivation at the individual level and seek out individual-level interventions without taking into consideration how other sets of variables in the context are interconnected. A systems thinker will consider how individual characteristics and dispositions interplay with organizational culture and other environmental factors to generate patterns around motivation to learn (Wlodkowski & Ginsberg, 2017).

When we consider globalization, a non-systems thinking perspective would assume that globalization represents a one-way interaction (i.e., that the free flow of goods and services from large corporations are dispersed throughout the world and impact local populations). A systems thinking perspective of globalization, however, takes into consideration the interplay between global and local while recognizing the interconnectedness of systems and sub-systems around the world. As a result, even small actions can have a significant impact within larger systems. This idea, also known as the *Butterfly Effect*, helps us to recognize the infinite connections within the world that continuously emerge and interact together. In organizational settings, each person represents "a larger collective that does not go away when that person is at work" (Cseh & Coningham, 2012, p. 298). Individuals bring their whole selves to the workplace or classroom, and even small aspects of their being can influence the whole. This understanding moves us from seeing relationships and organizations as mechanistic processes to seeing them as part of local systems and ultimately part of global systems. With mechanistic thinking, we might make sense of the world in terms of linear, disconnected, and unidimensional variables. In global systems thinking, local systems are interconnected with one another around the world creating a global system of interrelated variables (See Fig. 1).

To further demonstrate the difference between systems thinking and global systems thinking, take an often-cited example in systems thinking: obesity. While a mechanistic thinker would ascribe obesity simply to the poor lifestyle choices of individuals, a systems thinker recognizes there are many factors interacting within this local system. These might include a series of factors such as access to high-quality health care, family culture, community resources, genetics, physiology, and psychological disposition. Further still, a global systems thinker understands how this somewhat local system is interconnected with systems around the world. Take the example of the rise of obesity in Thailand. All previous factors mentioned apply, but there are additional global factors at play such as the introduction of complex carbohydrates and dairy from the West into the Thai diet, which until recently relied mostly on rice, vegetables, pork, and chicken. A global systems thinker understands how perceptions of the West as affluent lead to the association of these new foods with wealth; how globalization has led to over 8000 7-Eleven stores throughout Thailand, for example, making these products available on nearly every street corner; and how increases in technology and advertising have allowed these corporations to market their products throughout the country.

To understand global systems thinking we must consider the connection between systems thinking and global mindset. There are many concepts that describe what it means to live and work effectively across cultures such as intercultural competence (Deardorff, 2009), global mindset (Beechler & Javidan, 2007), cosmopolitanism (Appiah, 2010), and global competence (Caligiuri & Santo, 2001). These concepts tend to focus on the knowledge, skills, abilities, and dispositions of individuals as they interact with people from other cultural contexts. For example, Beechler and Javidan (2007) described the global mindset needed for understanding and facilitating change within global contexts as "an individual's stock of knowledge, cognitive, and psychological attributes that enable him/her to influence individuals, groups, and organizations from diverse sociocultural systems" (p. 152). This mindset includes certain qualities such as "a curiosity for and a drive to place the current tasks against the backdrop of historical past as well as probable future" (Srinivas, 1995, p. 30). The concept of cultural intelligence (Earley & Ang, 2003) includes an additional component of metacognition, which goes beyond effectiveness in a single cross-cultural or multicultural context and helps individuals "facilitate problem-solving and pattern recognition across cultures" (Earley, Murnieks, & Mosakowski, 2007, p. 99). However, one shortfall of global mindset as a construct is that it pertains to leadership and change within certain cross-cultural contexts and does not necessarily include the kind of global systems thinking we believe is required for today's workforce.

When we consider the questions at the beginning of this chapter about how we should be and what we should know in global systems, we can start to identify the components essential in becoming global system thinkers. These components include combinations of global knowledge, self-knowledge of one's worldview and the worldviews of others, skills for interacting with others, and ongoing critical reflection about one's meaning-making processes.

The first key component, which is particularly under the purview of education and learning, is knowledge. A global systems thinker is someone who continually seeks more knowledge about the cultures, people, and processes in the world around them. The key driver of knowledge is curiosity, which is often lost during socialization into formal schooling. Becoming a global systems thinker requires an almost childlike curiosity to learn more about why people are the way they are, why certain processes work the way they do, and why communities and societies around the world exist as they do. Each of us must function like emerging cultural anthropologists not only in foreign environments but in our own local environments as well.

This results in the accumulation of important knowledge about the existence of other ways of thinking and behaving in the world.

As learners acquire more knowledge about the world around them, facilitators must also push them to cultivate a deeper understanding of themselves and their own worldviews as well. A worldview represents the set of presuppositions about the nature of reality with which we operate as we interact with and make meaning of the world around us. To be a global systems thinker means that we seek not only to understand our worldview and the set of experiences that shape our worldview but also the worldviews that drive others. We can explore concepts such as cultural value dimensions (Hofstede, 2001; Hofstede, Hofstede & Minkov, 2010; Trompenaars & Hampden-Turner, 2012) and see how they manifest themselves in our practice. We acknowledge the fact that we make sense of the world through a limited set of assumptions based on our limited life experiences and that others do the same. This reflective disposition can be cultivated in a variety of reflective exercises but it can also be done through service-learning integration in which critical reflection is often a key component (Jacoby, 2014).

As learners gain knowledge about the people, processes, and cultures of the world, they must also nurture a set of skills and abilities associated with living and working effectively in cross-cultural and multicultural environments. There is no single set of behaviors that is applicable to all cultural contexts, so part of the development of cross-cultural skills comes with an understanding of the highly contextual nature of behavior and the meaning that others ascribe to it. If learners know that behavioral norms are the result of contextual factors, they are able to seek out the learning necessary to understand appropriate behavior for the context at hand. Therefore, a certain ability to be flexible is also necessary. Flexibility and openness have long been core components of cross-cultural adaptability (Kelley & Meyers, 1995).

To facilitate the continual deepening of one's global knowledge and skills, facilitators of learning in both higher education and workplace contexts must seek not only to develop their learners' global mindset, but also create conditions in which adults can develop and enrich the way they make meaning of the world. While adults are capable of learning new content in terms of knowledge, skills, and abilities, adults are also capable of developing more complex meaning-making structures (Kegan, 2009). The ways in which our knowledge, skills, and abilities are constructed can be charted along a developmental path. This idea forms the foundation of Constructive Developmental Theory which states that humans construct meaning of their experiences and that these meaning-making structures can change to become more complex (Kegan, 1980). Kegan (1980) noted that the nature of this complexity of meaning making is in the extent to which adults are able to make object that which is subject to them such as their needs, interests, and even identity. When learners are first developing their global mindset, their own culture is subject to them, meaning that it is perceived to be who they are, not something that they have as a result of their experiences. Then, as they learn about other cultures and reflect on their worldviews, they begin to take their own culture as object. They can hold it apart from themselves. Their cultural identity is no longer something that they are but something that they have. Thus, becoming a global systems thinker is ultimately a process that is continually enriched with deeper knowledge and more complex meaning making throughout one's life (See Fig. 2).

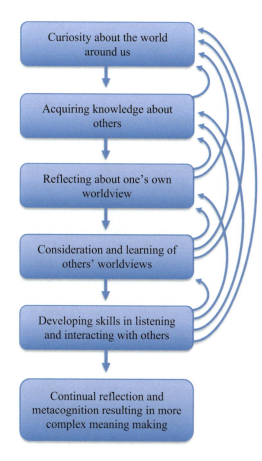

Fig. 2 Global mindset development process

4 Cultivating Global Systems Thinking and Global Mindset

In this section, we sought answers to the following questions: How do we become global system thinkers? How can we enrich our global mindset? How can we engage learners in global knowledge creation? What strategies for learning and teaching will lead to engaged learners in the global workplace and community?

The first step in teaching for globalization in our classrooms and organizations is to begin by enriching our own global mindsets as facilitators. This means that we should critically reflect on our own assumptions about the world and how those assumptions emerged from our unique set of limited experiences. We can role model this reflection through critically reflective exercises. We can also foster discussions around systems that are discipline-specific to help learners see the many variables interacting within the given context. We can provide unstructured times where learners are encouraged to allow their curiosity on a topic to lead them in a multitude of directions.

We can seek out readings and materials that represent ideas from around the world and reflect together with our learners about the Western influences in higher education and how those roots inform our assumptions about the purpose of education today. Designers and facilitators of learning experience in global organizations as well can be reflective about their choice of materials and ensure a capacious view of knowledge and wisdom that encompasses a spectrum of cultures. When we facilitate learning, we should come at it with a sense of humility about the nature of our knowledge.

Methods of facilitation can also be broadened to include global perspectives. As technology develops, resources are allowing access to research informed by global perspectives. Instructors are no longer strapped to teacher-centered methods of instruction and can now facilitate learning through technology in a way where learners can have authentic cross-cultural experiences. This can be done through videos and research available online as well as through in-person global experiences. As a result of global mobility, many of our cities and communities include vibrant diasporas that can provide rich cross-cultural learning experiences either through community-based project to allow for mutual learning or through invitation extended to members of these local communities to share their experiences.

There is ample literature dealing with the critical role of a global mindset in effective operation of the organization (Sharma et al., 2016). According to the Future Work Skills 2020 report (2011) developed by the Institute for the Future, in today's fast-paced globalized world, people are much more likely to move between jobs in various locations. In order to be successful at those jobs and navigate those diverse workplaces, individuals need to develop their global mindset to adapt to changing circumstances and to collaborate and work effectively with people from various backgrounds and cultures.

Global mindset also comes into play while thinking of suitable conditions for knowledge management. As organizations go global, they face challenges to develop systems that allow for knowledge sharing among employees with diverse cultural backgrounds. Therefore, developers of knowledge management initiatives should be aware of those cultural differences. Besides, Moitra and Kumar (2007) argue that it is an equally strong need to recognize how adults learn and the influence of diverse cultures in this process and to act accordingly. Otherwise, as indicated by Nissen (2007), those cultural variations can significantly hinder the knowledge flow and thus the competitive advantage of the organization. Hence, people who facilitate knowledge management in organizations should "diagnose and dissolve intercultural clumps and clots that impede the healthy circulation of the knowledge" (p. 211). Overall, one of the most vital antecedents for creating flexible knowledge management systems is recognizing differences and similarities between knowledge sharing practices of diverse people informed by their values (Ardichvili, Maurer, Li, Wentling, & Stuedemann, 2006).

Many scholars agree that shared understanding of the benefit of knowledge sharing, leadership encouragement, and conducive organizational culture supportive of knowledge sharing are prerequisites for the successful design of knowledge management systems (Bollinger & Smith, 2001). If these conditions are absent, no

Teaching for Globalization: Implications for Knowledge Management in... 115

matter how sophisticated the technologies, tools, platforms, or channels are, knowledge management initiatives will not be as effective as desired. In addition to that, Bollinger and Smith (2001) noted that, "Whereas traditional knowledge management systems focus on know-what and know-how, loyalty and caring reflect the care-why, which is the essence of a successful knowledge management system" (p. 7).

Transdisciplinarity is another critical factor contributing to the success of knowledge management systems. According to Future Work Skills 2020 report (2011), being an expert in one discipline is not enough to resolve the complex problems of today's rapidly changing organizations. Consequently, one way to do this is by developing a transdisciplinary approach. According to Howard Rheingold (as cited in Future Work Skills 2020 report (2011)), "Transdisciplinarity goes beyond bringing together researchers from different disciplines to work in multidisciplinary teams. It means educating researchers who can speak languages of multiple disciplines—biologists who have understanding of mathematics, mathematicians who understand biology" (p. 11). To gain a transdisciplinary approach, people should continuously learn, and to do this, individuals should have the curiosity and enthusiasm to learn beyond formal education (Future Work Skills 2020, 2011).

5 Implications for Knowledge Management

In their discussion of knowledge management in global organizations, Moitra and Kumar (2007) noted that it is not enough to have useful technologies and practices. It is also essential to be conscious about how adults with various national and ethnic backgrounds learn and share knowledge. Organizations should think about how to create knowledge management systems that are flexible and adaptable based on adult learning principles. According to the authors, one of the ways to create those effective knowledge management systems can be achieved through a "managed socialization." Managed socialization is about developing platforms that will encourage communication and knowledge sharing among all employees. Vij and Farooq (2015) also emphasize the role of communities of practice within the organization to achieve knowledge sharing among employees and to stimulate continuous learning. Communities of practice are defined as informal groups of people who share their knowledge and opinions through various ways such as storytelling, lunch and learn sessions, seminars, and workshops (Tyagi, Cai, Yang, & Chambers, 2015). According to Nathan (2008), interactive online platforms and blogs can also enable knowledge generation and exchange in organizations with employees working in various countries separated by time and distance. However, having the necessary skills to use those technologies and be involved in virtual learning is equally important.

Teaching for globalization should be both an antecedent and an outcome of knowledge management systems in organizations working in global environments. Ways to design knowledge management systems should be a part of the toolbox of

HRD practitioners, organizational leaders, consultants, educators, and all other responsible parties who want to contribute to the well-being of their organizations. Bringing a global systems thinking approach to knowledge management will allow individuals and organizations to learn, thrive, and stay competitive in the rapidly changing global environment.

References

Appiah, K. A. (2010). *Cosmopolitanism: Ethics in a world of strangers*. New York: WW Norton.

Ardichvili, A., Maurer, M., Li, W., Wentling, T., & Stuedemann, R. (2006). Cultural influences on knowledge sharing through online communities of practice. *Journal of Knowledge Management, 10*(1), 94–107. https://doi.org/10.1108/13673270610650139.

Association of American Colleges and Universities. (2018). *Fulfilling the American dream: Liberal education and the future of work*. Retrieved from https://www.aacu.org/sites/default/files/files/LEAP/2018EmployerResearchReport.pdf

Beechler, S., & Javidan, M. (2007). Leading with a global mindset. In M. Javidan, R. M. Steers, & M. A. Hitt (Eds.), *The global mindset* (pp. 131–169). Bingley, UK: Emerald.

Bhandari, R. (2017). *A world on the move: Trends in global student mobility*. Retrieved from https://vtechworks.lib.vt.edu/bitstream/handle/10919/83142/GlobalStudentMobility.pdf?s

Bhandari, R., & Blumenthal, P. (2010). *International students and global mobility in higher education: National trends and new directions*. New York: Palgrave Macmillan.

Bingham, T., & Galagan, P. (2006). Preparing the workforce. *Training and Development, 60*(9), 31–35. https://doi.org/10.1111/j.1748-8583.2006.00011.x.

Bollinger, A. S., & Smith, R. D. (2001). Managing organizational knowledge as a strategic asset. *Journal of Knowledge Management, 5*(1), 8–18. https://doi.org/10.1108/13673270110384365.

British Council. (2013). *Culture at work: The value of intercultural skills in the workplace*. Retrieved from https://www.britishcouncil.org/sites/default/files/culture-at-work-report-v2.pdf

Bubel, D. (2015). Globalization and knowledge management in projects. *Foundations of Management, 7*(1), 19–28. https://doi.org/10.1515/fman-2015-0022.

Caligiuri, P., & Santo, V. (2001). Global competence: What is it, and can it be developed through global assignments? *Human Resource Planning, 24*(3), 27–35.

Checkland, P. B. (1981). *System thinking, system practice*. Chichester, UK: Wiley.

Cseh, M., & Coningham, B. (2012). Working in multicultural and multilingual environments: HRD professionals as learning and change agents in the global workplace. In J. P. Wilson (Ed.), *International human resource development: Learning, education and training for individuals and organizations* (3rd ed., pp. 297–309). London: Kogan Page.

Deardorff, D. K. (Ed.). (2009). *The SAGE handbook of intercultural competence*. Thousand Oaks, CA: Sage.

Deloitte. (2016). *The future of the workforce: Critical drivers and challenges*. Retrieved from https://www2.deloitte.com/content/dam/Deloitte/au/Documents/human-capital/deloitte-au-hc-future-of-workforce-critical-drivers-challenges-220916.pdf

Department of International Development. (2000). *Eliminating world poverty: Making globalization work for the poor. White paper on international development*. London: DfID. Retrieved from https://webarchive.nationalarchives.gov.uk/+/http:/www.dfid.gov.uk/policieandpriorities/files/whitepaper2000.pdf

Earley, P. C., & Ang, S. (2003). *Cultural intelligence: individual interactions across cultures*. Stanford, CA: Stanford University Press.

Earley, P. C., Murnieks, C., & Mosakowski, E. (2007). Cultural intelligence and the global mindset. In M. Javidan, R. M. Steers, & M. A. Hitt (Eds.), *The global mindset* (pp. 75–103). Bingley, UK: Emerald.

Gharajedaghi, J. (2011). *Systems thinking: Managing chaos and complexity* (3rd ed.). Burlington, MA: Elsevier.

Giddens, A. (2002). *Runaway world: How globalization is reshaping our lives* (2nd ed.). New York: Routledge.

Goodman, N., & Schieman, J. (2010). Using knowledge management to leverage training and development initiatives. *Industrial and Commercial Training, 42*(2), 112–115. https://doi.org/10.1108/00197851011026108.

Hirst, P., Thompson, G., & Bromley, S. (2009). *Globalization in question* (3rd ed.). Cambridge, UK: Polity Press.

Hofstede, G. (2001). *Culture's consequences: Comparing values, behaviors, institutions and organizations across nations* (2nd ed.). Thousand Oaks, CA: Sage.

Hofstede, G., Hofstede, G. J., & Minkov, M. (2010). *Cultures and organizations: Software of the mind*. New York: McGraw Hill.

Institute for the Future. (2011). *Future work skills 2020*. Retrieved from https://uqpn.uq.edu.au/files/203/LIBBY%20MARSHALL%20future_work_skills_2020_full_research_report_final_1.pdf

International Labour Organization. (2015). *ILO global estimates of migrant workers and migrant domestic workers: Results and methodology*. Retrieved from https://www.ilo.org/wcmsp5/groups/public/@dgreports/@dcomm/documents/publication/wcms_436343.pdf

International Organization for Migration. (2017). *World migration report 2018*. Geneva: International Organization for Migration.

Jacoby, B. (2014). *Service-learning essentials*. San Francisco, CA: Jossey-Bass.

Joe, C., Yoong, P., & Patel, K. (2013). Knowledge loss when older experts leave knowledge-intensive organisations. *Journal of Knowledge Management, 17*(6), 913–927. https://doi.org/10.1108/JKM-04-2013-0137.

Kegan, R. (1980). Making meaning: The constructive-developmental approach to persons and practice. *The Personnel and Guidance Journal, 58*(5), 373–380.

Kegan, R. (2009). What "form" transforms? A constructive developmental approach to transformative learning. In K. Illeris (Ed.), *Contemporary theories of learning* (pp. 43–60). New York: Routledge.

Kelley, C., & Meyers, J. (1995). *CCAI: Cross-cultural adaptability inventory*. Minneapolis, MN: National Computer Systems.

King, W. R. (2007). A research agenda for the relationships between culture and knowledge management. *Knowledge and Process Management, 14*(3), 226–236. https://doi.org/10.1002/kpm.281.

Meadows, D. H. (2008). *Thinking in systems: A primer*. White River Junction, VT: Chelsea Green.

Meyer, M., Bushney, M., & Ukpere, W. I. (2011). The impact of globalization on higher education: Achieving a balance between local and global needs and realities. *African Journal of Business Management, 5*(15), 6569–6578.

Moitra, D., & Kumar, K. (2007). Managed socialization: How smart companies leverage global knowledge. *Knowledge and Process Management, 14*(3), 148–157. https://doi.org/10.1002/kpm.278.

Monthey, W., Singmaster, H., Manise, J., & Kreamer, K. B. (2015). *Preparing a globally competent workforce though high-quality career and technical education*. Retrieved from http://asiasociety.org/sites/default/files/preparing-a-globally-competent-workforce-june-2016.pdf

Nathan, E. P. (2008). Global organizations and e-learning: Leveraging adult learning in different cultures. *Performance Improvement, 47*(6), 18–24. https://doi.org/10.1002/pfi.20004.

Nissen, M. E. (2007). Knowledge management and global cultures: Elucidation through an institutional knowledge-flow perspective. *Knowledge and Process Management, 14*(3), 211–225. https://doi.org/10.1002/kpm.285.

OECD. (2017). *Education at a Glance 2017: OECD Indicators*. Retrieved from https://www.oecd-ilibrary.org/docserver/eag-2017-en.pdf?expires=1555647219&id=id&accname=guest&checksum=1703622D7C20E13E998970DB2C53438C

Paci, A. M., Lalle, C., & Chiacchio, M. S. (2010). Knowledge management for open innovation: Collaborative mapping of needs and competencies. *Journal of Knowledge Management Practice, 11*(1), 30–39.

Pauluzzo, R., & Cagnina, M. R. (2017). Bridging the divide: Intercultural competences to reconcile the knowledge transfer dilemma in multinational contexts. *Knowledge Management Research & Practice, 15*(4), 542–550. https://doi.org/10.1057/s41275-017-0073-7.

Richardson, D. (2012). Teaching with a global perspective. *Inquiry: The Journal of the Virginia Community Colleges, 17*(1), 43–50. Retrieved from https://files.eric.ed.gov/fulltext/EJ974773.pdf.

Sharma, R. R., Chadee, D., & Roxas, B. (2016). Effects of knowledge management on client-vendor relationship quality: The mediating role of global mindset. *Journal of Knowledge Management, 20*(6), 1268–1281. https://doi.org/10.1108/JKM-03-2016-0099.

Srinivas, K. M. (1995). Globalization of business and the third world: Challenges of expanding the mindsets. *Journal of Management Development, 14*(3), 26–49. https://doi.org/10.1108/02621719510078957.

Think Global & British Council. (2011). The global skills gap: Preparing young people for the new global economy. Retrieved from https://think-global.org.uk/wp-content/uploads/dea/documents/BusinessPoll_online_TG.pdf

Trompenaars, F., & Hampden-Turner, C. (2012). *Riding the waves of culture: Understanding diversity in global business* (2nd ed.). New York: McGraw-Hill.

Tyagi, S., Cai, X., Yang, K., & Chambers, T. (2015). Lean tools and methods to support efficient knowledge creation. *International Journal of Information Management, 35*(2), 204–214. https://doi.org/10.1016/j.ijinfomgt.2014.12.007.

Vij, S., & Farooq, R. (2015). The relationship between learning orientation and business performance: Do smaller firms gain more from learning orientation? *IUP Journal of Knowledge Management, 13*(4), 7–28. https://doi.org/10.19030/jss.v5i1.6940.

White, G. W., & Toms, L. (2009). Preparing college of business students for a global world. *International Journal for Professional Educators, 75*(4), 11. Retrieved from http://www.deltakappagamma.org/NH/BulletinSummer09June16.pdf.

Wlodkowski, R. J., & Ginsberg, M. B. (2017). *Enhancing adult motivation to learn: A comprehensive guide for teaching all adults* (4th ed.). San Francisco, CA: Wiley.

Knowledge Management for Organizational Success: Valuing Diversity and Inclusion Across Stakeholders, Structures, and Sectors

Tomika W. Greer and Toby M. Egan

Abstract Knowledge is a core source of energy for any organization and has been repeatedly highlighted as a critical element for organizational survival in our increasingly dynamic world. With the increased importance of knowledge comes the importance that it be managed effectively for organizational success and innovation. Desired organizational performance outcomes can be enhanced by including diverse knowledge and perspectives in knowledge sharing practices throughout the organization. In this chapter, we highlight the use of communities of practice as a tool to leverage human diversity and structural diversity to optimize knowledge management and improve organizational outcomes in a variety of organizational contexts.

1 Introduction

Over the past 40 years, a radical alteration from a manufacturing-based economy to a knowledge economy has occurred. This economic shift has mirrored the sharp increase in technological advancement across all industries and sectors worldwide. In a knowledge economy, economic prosperity is dominated by the exchange of services, making human capital and knowledge valuable economic, social, and political differentiators. Mastering the management of knowledge is key to the effectiveness of all modern organizations across all sectors (for-profit, governmental, and nonprofit/nongovernmental). Though there is abundant debate among researchers regarding what constitutes knowledge (Sen, 2019), a general understanding of knowledge is essentially the body of useful information and skills that one has obtained through education and previous experiences. The management of knowledge has been recognized as an important factor in this accelerated rate of economic change (Adelstein, 2007).

T. W. Greer (✉)
University of Houston, Houston, TX, USA
e-mail: twgreer@uh.edu

T. M. Egan
University of Maryland, College Park, MD, USA

© Springer Nature Switzerland AG 2019
M. Fedeli, L. L. Bierema (eds.), *Connecting Adult Learning and Knowledge Management*, Knowledge Management and Organizational Learning 8,
https://doi.org/10.1007/978-3-030-29872-2_7

Knowledge is a core source of energy for any organization and has been repeatedly highlighted as a critical element for organizational survival in our increasingly dynamic world. This is not only true of the private sector. For example, knowledge sharing is a key factor in maintaining quality education systems (Charband & Jafari Navimipour, 2018). Additionally, changes in the complexity and speed in which we do work, share information, and experience new demands impact the public/governmental and nonprofit/nongovernmental organization (NGO) sectors as well (Hurley & Green, 2005). As a result, knowledge has become as important of a resource for organizational success as any other (Serrat, 2017). With the increased importance of knowledge comes the importance that it be managed effectively for organizational success and innovation (Kremer, Villamor, & Aguinis, 2019). The double-edged sword of knowledge management (KM) is that dynamic knowledge and rapid change are symptoms of a shifting world that can, at the same time, be leveraged toward innovative solutions and impactful outcomes.

The benefit for evolving, knowledge-intensive organizations is that effective utilization of KM systems can lead to productivity increases, enhanced performance, and amplified creativity and innovation (Charband & Jafari Navimipour, 2018; Kremer et al., 2019; Mesmer-Magnus & DeChurch, 2009). Therefore, KM must be counted as an asset that is at least as important as any other organizational resource. Within the aspiration that knowledge be captured for both shared organizational learning and recall are the people engaged in the evolving practice of organizational KM. Because of the latent aspects of KM, managers and employees must recall their personal, interpersonal, and group experiences as well as deal with the tacit nature of knowledge to capture important KM insights. Therefore, the capacity of the organization to incorporate diverse stakeholder perspectives and their related plurality of knowledge is imperative.

In this chapter, we differentiate between explicit knowledge and tacit knowledge and argue for the significance of sharing tacit knowledge throughout organizations. Further, we discuss how human diversity and structural diversity interact with the effectiveness of knowledge management and knowledge sharing practices. Finally, we present communities of practice as a practical solution for leveraging diversity in knowledge management, and we present case studies to illustrate how diversity and knowledge management converge to improve organizational outcomes in a variety of organizational contexts.

2 Knowledge Management in a Knowledge Economy

It is becoming increasingly accepted that knowledge-focused work is the new normal across every sector of the global economy and within each industry and specialization. This evolution has placed every organization in the knowledge business, necessitating each employee become a knowledge worker (Lewis, 2004). Gathering, sharing, analyzing, innovating, and reacting to new knowledge is essential to organizational success and, in most cases, organizational survival. Hislop (2013) defined knowledge management as, "any deliberate efforts to manage the knowledge of an organization's workforce, which can be achieved via a wide range of methods including directly, through the use of particular types of information and communications technology, or more indirectly through the management of social processes, the structuring of organization in particular ways or via the use of particular culture and people management practices" (p. 56). Like many processes and products, knowledge is dynamic but also temporal and perishable if not cared for and managed. But what does knowledge management really mean in present-day organizational contexts?

Beginning in the late 1990s, early research on the notion of KM was linked to information management systems with a primary focus on maintaining data as a form of KM (Wilson, 2002). With the persistent growth of the service economy and the increasing prevalence of knowledge being viewed as a competitive advantage for organizations (Adelstein, 2007; Sen, 2019), the focus of knowledge management has shifted toward leveraging information for knowledge sharing. Knowledge management is no longer just about capturing information and maintaining knowledge. Instead, KM has evolved to include various forms of knowledge generation, storage, representations, and sharing (Ardichvili, Maurer, Li, Wentling, & Stuedemann 2006). "Knowledge sharing is about making valuable knowledge of individual actors available to other actors in the company in a mutual exchange so that it can be used for solving problems in other places of the company" (Andresen, 2007, p. 751). It is this knowledge sharing that supports organizational performance and promotes competitive advantage in a knowledge economy.

2.1 Explicit Knowledge and Tacit Knowledge

As the importance of organizational KM grows, so does the need to frame types of knowledge sharing among individuals, teams, and larger organizational structures. Polanyi (2009), credited with essential work informing the philosophy of social science, has also contributed to core theoretical development now adopted by KM theorists. Polanyi postulated the existence of two types of knowledge—explicit and tacit. Explicit knowledge is more commonly expressed as comprehension associated with intellect and education. A person who can recite how something works or related facts or even trivia may be called knowledgeable. Tacit knowledge, however, is not taught. It is grounded in experience and is an outcome of the knower dwelling in those experiences, requiring emersion in the practice and application of that knowledge (St. Germain & Quinn, 2006). Tacit knowledge sharing commonly involves exchanges related to skills, experiences, contextual narratives, and "know-how" (Taylor, 2007). "Tacit knowledge is *embrained* knowledge and is at the ontological dimension in which its explication requires the use of metaphors and an extensive process of socialization" (Omotayo, 2015, p. 6).

An example of tacit knowledge could involve consideration of how one rides a skateboard. We can see that the process of learning how to do so involves balance and learning how to start, stop, turn, and even jump. Therefore, an individual with demonstrated ability to ride a skateboard should be interpreted to have knowledge on riding a skateboard. However, if asked to explain how to maintain balance while riding, the skateboarder may be unable to provide useful instruction (Tsoukas, 2003). The ability to stand on and steer a rapidly moving skateboard is in part tacit knowledge because it is largely learned by doing, rather than reading a "how-to" manual. Once acquired, tacit knowledge is very difficult to communicate verbally or in writing without loss of meaning. In fact, even though a person is able to perform a task successfully, there may be no conscious awareness that knowledge exists and they are applying it. Polanyi (1967) suggested that while tacit learning of physical ability is easiest to observe and conceptualize, it is similarly related to mental functions such as solving scientific or mathematical equations or recognizing faces and social cues.

Within the establishment of multiple levels of knowledge is the examination of the interrelationship between tacit and explicit knowledge. Although organizations can be successful in developing KM process and systems, it is often complicated. In part, because tacit knowledge is, by definition, not explicit. Tacit knowledge is difficult to imitate; therefore, in competitive environments, it can serve as an advantage. Additionally, tacit knowledge exchange can be both the result of unique features of an organizational culture and a force to further shape organizational culture. Therefore, the benefits of tacit knowledge are most valuable when transformed into explicit knowledge shared throughout the organization. Creating explicit knowledge from tacit knowledge promotes the best likelihood to maximize and expand intellectual capital toward advancing the most critical organizational outcomes and competitive advantage. Professional networking can be used as a tool to exchange, explore, and amplify tacit knowledge among and between groups that are often referred to as communities of practice (Wegner, 2006). These networks allow for the dwelling in the experience of application and practice of tacit knowledge that is required for successful sharing of tacit knowledge (St. Germain & Quinn, 2006).

Moreover, while generally agreed upon to be essential for effective KM development, exchanging and transferring knowledge can be similarly challenging because of the lack of overt frameworks or structures for doing so and barriers that may inhibit tacit knowledge exchange (Joia & Lemos, 2010). If we do not know what we do not know, how is it that we can determine the success of a KM effort? Allee (2001, pp. 1–2) was early in framing the twelve key KM principles listed below, which have been identified to be enduring (Dale, 2015), including:

1. Knowledge is messy. Because knowledge is connected to everything else, you cannot isolate the knowledge aspect of anything neatly. In the knowledge universe, you cannot pay attention to just one factor.
2. Knowledge is self-organizing. The self that knowledge organizes around is organizational or group identity and purpose.
3. Knowledge generally happens in community. Knowledge is propelled, just as life is. Both want to happen as community. The Internet well illustrates this force of community relative to knowledge.
4. Knowledge travels via language. Without a language to describe our experience, we cannot communicate what we know. Expanding organizational knowledge means that we must develop the languages we use to describe our work experience.

5. The more you try to pin knowledge down, the more it slips away. It is tempting to try to tie up knowledge as codified knowledge in documents, patents, libraries, databases, and so forth. But too much rigidity and formality regarding knowledge lead to the stultification of creativity.
6. Looser is probably better. Highly adaptable systems look sloppy. The survival rate of diverse, decentralized systems is higher. That means we can waste resources and energy trying to control knowledge too tightly.
7. There is no one solution. Knowledge is always changing. For the moment, the best approach to managing it is one that keeps things moving along while keeping options open.
8. Knowledge does not grow forever. Eventually, some knowledge is lost or dies, just as things in nature. Unlearning and letting go of old ways of thinking, even retiring whole blocks of knowledge, contribute to the vitality and evolution of knowledge.
9. No one is in charge. Knowledge is a social process. That means no one person can take responsibility for collective knowledge.
10. You cannot impose rules and systems. If knowledge is truly self-organizing, the most important way to advance it is to remove the barriers to self-organization. In a supportive environment, knowledge will take care of itself.
11. There is no silver bullet. There is no single leverage point or best practice to advance knowledge. It must be supported at multiple levels and in a variety of ways.
12. How you define knowledge determines how you manage it. The "knowledge question" can present itself in many ways. For example, concern about the ownership of knowledge leads to acquiring codified knowledge that is protected by copyrights and patents.

Within the twelve principles of KM listed above are several key elements that emphasize interpersonal and interorganizational engagement. The engagement necessary for effective KM is impacted by various dimensions of diversity across the organization.

3 Framing Diversity and Knowledge Management in Organizations

KM is a self-organizing social process that relies on language, interdependency, flexibility, and an inclusive/holistic vantage point. Using a systematic textual analysis research process, Jennex, Smolnik, and Croasdell (2015) derived a collective definition of KM success:

> KM success is a multidimensional concept. It is defined by capturing the right knowledge, getting the right knowledge to the right user, and using this knowledge to improve organizational and/or individual performance. KM success is measured using the dimensions of impact on business processes, strategy, leadership, efficiency and effectiveness of KM processes, efficiency and effectiveness of the KM system, organizational culture, and knowledge content. (p. 8)

At its core, KM and its success is almost entirely people dependent and relies on individual engagement and organizational culture to spawn and advance tacit insights that can be transformed into explicit knowledge.

Because KM is human centered, the ways in which individuals and groups communicate and cooperate are crucial. Knowledge sharing and KM are largely unnecessary in an organizational system where all employees and stakeholders possess very similar knowledge and where there are relatively stable numbers of stakeholders within the organization (e.g., low turnover, stable management structure) and a relatively stable external market environment (e.g., fixed client base, no new competitors). However, organizations cannot survive in a rapidly changing knowledge economy without some diversity of thought and experiences to drive innovation (Kremer et al., 2019). "Competitive advantages can be generated by integrating and using the spectrum of capabilities, experience and knowledge of the staff…in an optimised way" (Andresen, 2007, p. 745). As a result, diversity in conjunction with knowledge management differentiates organizations in the knowledge economy. Attending to the mixtures of people, perceptions, and experiences will lead the organization to reveal tacit knowledge and amplify employee knowledge and abilities.

Diversity exists in many ways in organizations. To examine and understand how KM strategies can leverage diversity to maximize knowledge and organizational impact, a variety of aspects of diversity should be examined. Longtime diversity expert, Roosevelt Thomas (1996), defined diversity broadly as a collective mixture of human similarities and differences linked to the effectiveness of organizational communication and cooperation. Diversity can refer to the many demographic differences that characterize different groups of people. Demographic diversity may include gender, race, ethnicity, nationality, culture, age, sexual orientation, educational background, social class, disability, and a number of other factors. This diversity may impact how knowledge is shared across the organization because members of diverse groups often have different world views, norms, values, goals, and priorities, all of which will impact the knowledge repertoire and knowledge exchange processes (Andresen, 2007; Hajro, Gibson, & Pudelko, 2017). Designing successful KM systems requires understanding of similarities and differences in preferred knowledge sharing strategies among various national and ethnic groups that are represented in an organization (Ardichvili et al., 2006).

3.1 Diversity Within Organizations

In an organization, diversity may also exist with respect to the members' opinions and values, their knowledge and experience, or their pay and status in the organization (Harrison & Klein, 2007). In practice, these three categories of diversity are often confounded in the organizational setting (Edmondson & Harvey, 2018).

However, different affiliations within an organization, divisions, departments, and teams can expose the organization to unique and diverse sources of knowledge.

There is growing empirical support for the idea that diversity within teams and between teams across the organization makes for better performance outcomes (Egan, 2005; Luanglath, Ali & Mohannak, 2019). Egan's (2005) qualitative investigation determined that managers who reported diverse membership within their teams experienced better team outcomes. The rationale is that along with different backgrounds and individual worldviews, diverse workgroups have a broader collective of stakeholders involved in knowledge sharing. Such workgroups experience increased performance because of active knowledge exchange with unique external sources.

Cummings (2004) validated a model supporting the relevance of intragroup team diversity, broader information sharing, and performance outcomes that lead to positive outcomes for knowledge management. A heterogeneous group will have broader perspectives, because there are collectively broader connections between group members and the larger systems to which the group is connected. A homogenous group is more likely to come from the same network(s) and therefore have access to information and perspectives often limited to a shared set of sources and experiences. Team members with different networks will expand the information available and, when exchanged within and between teams, have a higher potential for better decision making and performance. While within group heterogeneity expands the breadth of team knowledge, between group heterogeneity makes for a more informed and realistic organizational picture which, in turn, creates a greater likelihood that KM is captured more clearly and accurately. Part of the diversity on which Cummings is focused included both the aforementioned demographic diversity along with "structural diversity," including geographical differences (e.g., different buildings within the same organizations), different roles/assignments, different managerial support structures, and different business units. Combining these elements of structural diversity along with demographic diversity broadens the information available and expands the potential of a group to access broad perspectives creating a greater likelihood for a well-developed KM system.

Based on their systematic review of KM literature, Asrar-ul-Haq and Anwar (2016) determined that organizational structure impacts KM. "If the relationship network of the professionals is designed to facilitate individuals to locate those who know what, then transfer of knowledge becomes easy in the organization" (p. 6). It is important to note the importance of relationship networks for knowledge transfer in the development of KM. Effective communication, cooperation, and service to colleagues are essential to effective KM development (Hajro et al., 2017), and diversity and inclusion play a key role. The demographic and structural diversity inherent in organizations can either be leveraged cooperatively as a KM asset or serve as a barrier between organization members. Cooperation is especially important because KM often involves tacit knowledge, which is difficult to access without engaged dialogue between organization members.

3.2 Four Layers of Diversity

A holistic model of diversity of people in organizations consists of four layers of diversity: organizational dimensions, external dimensions, internal dimensions, and personality dimensions (Gardenswartz, Cherbosque, & Rowe, 2010). Organizational dimensions of diversity are related to the position of the employees in the organization. These diversity dimensions can include the functional level or classification of the employees, department/unit/division, seniority, or work location. The external dimensions of diversity include fluid characteristics of individual employees that could potentially change over time. For instance, income, religion, educational background, work experience, and parental/marital status are examples of external dimensions of diversity that are dynamic. Internal dimensions of diversity include the fixed characteristics of the employees, such as race, gender, and ethnicity. It is these internal dimensions of diversity that are often identified with the generic use of the term "diversity." The fourth layer of diversity is personality. Personality traits, including agreeableness, conscientiousness, and openness, can impact knowledge sharing (Matzler, Renzl, Müller, Herting, & Mooradian, 2008).

An organization's approach to diversity at each of these levels will dictate how knowledge is managed and shared among members of the organization (Andresen, 2007). For instance, in organizations where the culture is more resistant to diversity, there is typically little support for inclusion of diverse knowledge. Therefore, members of diverse groups are not encouraged or invited to share their tacit knowledge through networking, which will ultimately put that organization at a disadvantage in a knowledge economy. On the other end of the spectrum, organizations that have adopted a learning approach to diversity will leverage diversity for innovation, efficiency, and customer satisfaction (Dass & Parker, 1999) through the sharing of tacit knowledge. In this paradigm of learning through diversity, organizational learning is encouraged through employees' different perspectives, and diversity is viewed as a strategic asset to the organization.

It is also possible that organizations may differ in their approach to diversity, based on which the four levels of diversity are being examined. For instance, multinational corporations may particularly value diverse nationalities as a competitive advantage in which employees "exchange their unique knowledge in order to capture market share in new locations, exceed competitors' customer service, secure local resources, or implement successful distribution in emerging economies" (Hajro et al., 2017, p. 345). Using this strategy, these corporations are demonstrating inclusivity regarding nationality, an external dimension of diversity. Unfortunately, embracing nationality does not necessarily equate to embracing internal dimensions of diversity such as gender or sexual orientation. Likewise, there may not be effective inclusion and knowledge sharing across different divisions in the organization or work locations, suggesting less diversity in knowledge based on organizational dimensions of diversity or from the diverse individuals within those subunits (especially important in geographically and substantively dispersed subunits).

Ultimately, unless diversity is embraced across the four dimensions, there will exist a lost opportunity to capitalize on the power of diverse knowledge management and knowledge sharing. When organizations are not cognizant and inclusive of all aspects of diversity, diverse employees may be excluded from the formal and informal knowledge sharing networks. Furthermore, when all types of diversity are not embraced and included, artificial boundaries are created which will form multiple groups of employees: those who possess valuable tacit knowledge and those who do not possess this knowledge. These artificial boundaries mirror the lines of diversity and serve to block knowledge flow throughout the organization, reducing the positive organizational impacts of KM and knowledge sharing.

The absence of knowledge sharing can be detrimental to organizational effectiveness as it blocks information exchange and the ability of an organization to respond effectively to its environment. For example, "in hierarchical cultures, top managers' need for control over the information flow, and the desire to restrict access to critical information by lower-level employees, could lead to significant organizational barriers to knowledge sharing" (Ardichvili, 2008, p. 547). It behooves organizations to eradicate barriers to knowledge flow that exist merely as a result of not fully embracing the organizational, external, internal, and personality dimensions of diversity (Gardenswartz et al., 2010). This is particularly true when it comes to tacit knowledge. For internal organizational stakeholders to exchange relevant knowledge, there must be active communication and cooperation between them. Ideally, employee diversity should serve as a catalyst for knowledge exchange and a leverage point for explicating tacit knowledge.

4 Theorizing Diversity and Knowledge Management in Organizations

"Knowledge-intensive companies require new learning paradigms such as 'diversity learning', that is learning through diversity" (Andresen, 2007, p. 743). We argue that for organizations to learn through diversity, they must first know how to recognize, honor, value, and cultivate diversity within the organization. As such, diversity contributes to knowledge management efforts through the input of diverse perspectives and the sharing of tacit knowledge. Accordingly, knowledge of how to value and cultivate diverse employees should propagate the organization through knowledge management and sharing strategies. If organizations do not have the know-how to manage a diverse workforce to drive organizational learning, the diverse knowledge cannot be effectively leveraged for improved performance outcomes (Hajro et al., 2017).

With respect to enhancing knowledge management and sharing tacit knowledge throughout the organization, the critical aspects of diversity management are to create networks and orient mindsets toward diversity and inclusion. We, therefore, propose diversity management as a knowledge capability that enhances knowledge pooling. Knowledge pooling is a result of utilizing organizational networks to interactively share and exchange knowledge, "often in nonroutine, personal, and unstructured ways" (Earl, 2001, p. 223). Designating diversity management as a knowledge capability places diversity management at the center of an organization's competitive strategy (Earl, 2001), suggesting that diversity management is valued as a key differentiator for the organization.

In Fig. 1, we depict our vision of diversity management as an integral capability by illustrating our perspective on the interconnectedness of diversity dimensions, beneficial knowledge sharing, effective KM systems, and desired organizational outcomes. The relationships among these ideas are reciprocal in that they influence each other in multiple directions. Ultimately, when done correctly, diversity management has the potential to maximize organizational outcomes. However, to realize these organizational outcomes, organizations must develop diversity capabilities and be adaptable in response to changing environments.

5 Practical Applications of Diversity and Knowledge Management in Organizations

Knowledge of how to promote and sustain diversity and inclusion in an organization is a knowledge capability that can help organizations achieve competitive advantage and increase profitability. However, to capitalize on this knowledge, it should be managed as a core knowledge asset (Li & Tsai, 2009; Li, Tsai, & Lin, 2010) and effectively shared through the organization using knowledge sharing strategies that transcend structures and lines of diversity in the organization.

5.1 Communities of Practice

To encourage and support the knowledge sharing necessary for diversity learning, all employees need to feel a sense of belonging to the community. This can be achieved by "promoting conditions for an open, uninhibited exchange of ideas and information, by creating time and space for exchanging stories and expertise, and by teaching community members about the value of storytelling and how to develop and share stories" (Ardichvili, 2008, p. 550). Communities of practice (COPs) provide a platform for generating and disseminating tacit knowledge through interpersonal interactions, including storytelling (Ardichvili, 2008). COPs are social structures formed within the organization that allow for collective learning through knowledge management (Wenger, 2004). They can be formed intentionally or incidentally based on the members' interactions in the workplace. Members of COPs usually share common interests and regularly interact with each other to improve their knowledge and skills.

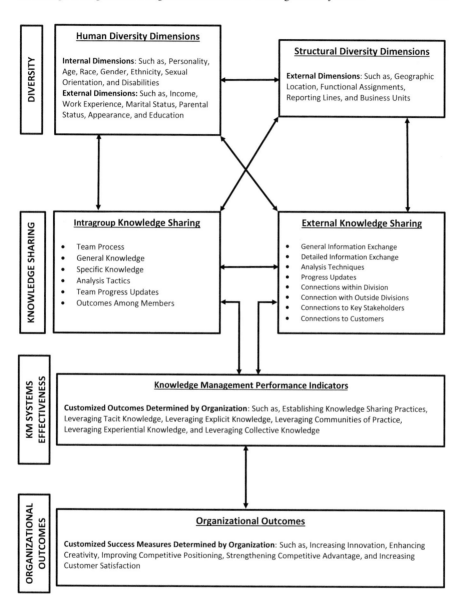

Fig. 1 Theoretical connections between diversity, knowledge sharing, and outcomes

Communities of practice can form the foundation for effectively sharing tacit knowledge among diverse groups of employees. Wenger (2004) identified three characteristics common to all communities of practice: domain, community, and practice. The domain of a COP refers to the shared area of competence among the members of the group. Members of a COP are committed to that domain even if others outside of the COP do not value their domain as an area of expertise. The domain provides a common focus for the COP. The community aspect of a COP requires the members to engage in joint activities, discussions, and knowledge sharing. Members do not necessarily have to work together daily to form a COP, but they should interact and learn from each other. The community involves relationship building and supports collective learning. Members of a COP implement their shared knowledge and collective learning in practice. They are practitioners who share their resources to improve their practice.

Thriving COPs can be formed by organizations that recognize a need to form COPs or by individual employees who are interested in learning from each other related to a particular domain. "The most successful communities have always combined bottom-up enthusiasm and initiative from members with top-down encouragement from the organization. On the one hand, communities are energized by producing value for both their members and the organization. On the other hand, it is crucial that communities set their own agenda and govern themselves because they are the ones with the knowledge to do so" (Wenger, 2004). Critical to the ability for COPs to govern themselves are the interpersonal connections and interactions among the members. Because previous research has explored ethnic and cultural diversity as potential challenges and barriers to effective knowledge sharing in COPs (Ardichvili, 2008), critical aspects of diversity management also apply to the development of effective and generative COPs.

5.2 Knowledge Management Cases

The following vignettes reflect on the use of KM in a variety of organization types. We include these examples to illustrate how embracing diversity as a component of organization KM can improve organizational performance.

5.2.1 Valuing Knowledge Across Structural Barriers in an NGO

Within a broader mission to serve children through supportive housing, foster care, and related supportive services, an NGO became aware of the special needs of children with disabilities, particularly children with severe autism. In the early days of its work in this area, the NGO partnered with a large and well-established psychology practice known for its pathbreaking innovation and well-regarded expertise supporting families and people affected by autism. The initial model used a typical outpatient clinical model, with thorough client assessment and ongoing therapeutic sessions with individual children. While this program was somewhat effective, the NGO recognized that the knowledge gained in the individual client interactions was largely decoupled from the organizational context of the NGOs' ongoing supportive housing—clinical insights were not being translated into the daily lives of the clients and the organizational setting of the NGOs' supportive housing program.

The NGO sought to develop a more holistic model akin to that described by Gardenswartz et al. (2010), which primarily involved utilizing experts from the psychology practice to train supportive housing services staff and counselors about autism. Initially, the approach was largely knowledge transfer oriented, with a focus on dyadic staff and client relationships. This approach had significant traction and was helpful. But as the staff gained and implemented this new knowledge, staff began to further experiment with organizational adaptations and apply the knowledge on autism with the lived experience of their staff roles. They sought physical changes in some group homes to facilitate quiet spaces, which they learned could be helpful for some clients. They also began to document and discuss what worked for individual clients both for their own well-being and relative to the well-being of other children living in the group homes.

But like Ardichvili's (2008) observation about hierarchical organizational cultures and information flow, staff advocated for formal mechanisms to share and integrate their knowledge within the organization more broadly. These staff members, as frontline workers, were structurally lowest in the organization: below in-house counseling staff, program managers, top management, and the contracted experts from the psychology firm. Yet, they possessed the most tacit knowledge regarding how to support autistic children in their day-to-day lives. Because of the advocacy efforts by these frontline workers, the NGO first experimented with implementation of some of the ideas raised by the frontline staff. The organization also created a cluster of staff at multiple levels to discuss and document successful and unsuccessful adaptations, which functioned as a Community of Practice around serving children with autism. In doing so, the organizational lines of diversity began to break down among the internal staff stakeholders and the external stakeholders. Over time, the NGO and the psychology firm began to work collectively to document effective practices, to disseminate this knowledge to other children's services and educational and disability advocacy organizations, and to seek policy changes.

In this example, the diversity dimensions centered somewhat on perceived notions of expertise, with some privileging initially of formal expertise from title/role or educational background. By valuing individual dimensions and diversity of types of knowledge, the NGO effectively leveraged its knowledge management practices. The inclusivity across vertical positions in the organizations and the communities of practice led to greater explication of tacit and then explicit knowledge. The frontline KM participants' intersectional diversity identities also helped to clarify new issues and resulted in greater overall awareness and inclusion across stakeholders and communities of practice.

5.2.2 Government Collaboration Grounded in KM

In recent years in the United States, military families have faced great pressure with multiple and longer deployments and related effects of service, such as family alienation, financial hardship, physical injuries, and mental health problems, including service disabilities and posttraumatic stress disorder. Military families relocate frequently, a problem made more complex by the prevalence of families in which both spouses are members of the military and the trauma that is often the outcome of modern military service. One aspect of this phenomenon resulted in high levels of divorce and problems with child support payments. In the civilian population, child support problems are largely treated as legal problems. And increasingly in many states, the legal mechanisms are increasingly swift and narrow, seeking remedies to address the needs of children. At the same time, recognizing the complexity of child support, many states' Attorney General have supportive family services programs, with missions that augment increasingly punitive legal remedies with social services.

In one such family services division, investigators determined that rates of child support arrears were much higher in military families. The leadership of this division sought to partner with legal personnel in the military Judge Advocates (JAGs) and nonprofit social work organizations serving the military. They first attempted to understand the phenomenon, studying it across racial and gender perspectives. They then added medical and clinical perspectives. They identified critical mechanisms to identify and intervene with supportive services within both the state and military processes. The trained JAG personnel and deployed specific legal personnel to military bases to support military personnel experiencing divorce and child support problems. They held legal regular specialized legal clinics and trainings. JAG staff worked closely with social workers to tailor and streamline services.

The joint initiative of civilian and military personnel helped to greater capitalize on knowledge and to manage it as a core knowledge asset, as described by Li and Tsai (2009). And while this public sector example does not center on profitability in the way that the bottom line is framed in for-profit organizations, the approach to knowledge management is characterized by the qualities of durability and positive outcomes brought forth by Tsai, Li, and Lin (2012).

5.2.3 Leveraging Team Diversity to Enhance Knowledge Management

This chapter's second author engaged in research on for-profit organization leaders and their use of team diversity to catalyze creativity. In this case example, the empirical evidence is focused on individual leaders across a diversity of corporate settings. A key finding of the study was that managers intentionally formed diverse teams to meet the organization's need for creative, impactful ideas (Egan, 2005).

More recently, two of the managers from the study were promoted to company-wide KM roles whereby the previous KM leaders had been ineffective. The leaders applied a team diversity approach to dramatically advance their organization's knowledge management system. In both cases, diversity was framed broadly in a manner that synthesized Gardenswartz et al.'s (2010) framework along with structural, role, departmental, geographic, experience, and knowledge diversity. Similar to the findings in the 2005 study, these KM leaders also identified team diversity as a key element in the success of their KM approach, much as it had been relative to creativity and innovation in the earlier study (Egan, 2005).

In querying the KM leaders about their strategies relative to developing diverse teams in support of organizational KM processes and outcomes, the leaders first described the approach to the composition of teams by a broad and open set of demographic characteristics and job roles with the explicit goal to maximize the diversity of backgrounds and perspectives. Secondary aspects centered on more professional and individual characteristics, centered on prior demonstration of such things as commitment to problem-solving, information sharing, reflection, creativity, and unique training or experience that went beyond what might be expected in a job role.

An important aspect of the team formation was the leaders' efforts to include individuals with a demonstrated track record of valuing diversity and inclusion and seeing it as part and parcel of the corporation's overall success. The KM leaders both noted that they were trying to capture explicit and tacit knowledge and build a team culture that was oriented toward the corporation's knowledge management goals and related strategies and processes. They felt strongly an effective culture for KM was based on a concomitant commitment to diversity and inclusion by team members. They both also reported that their approach to the formation of the KM teams was motivated by their prior experiences with diversity and inclusion being elemental to their successful innovation and creativity efforts in earlier leadership roles. These leaders also emphasized the importance of first intentionally leveraging the collective expertise of the diverse team in helping to establish core aspects of the KM vision. As importantly, the KM leaders noted that this approach also helps bridge and maximize the plurality of perspectives because the KM vision and the explicit commitment to diversity and inclusion are explicit and shared. This reinforces the notion of KM as a multidimensional concept (Jennex et al., 2015). It also emphasizes that KM is a multidimensional process.

Finally, these KM managers reported that a key effort will relate to measuring KM success over time. By having a full complement of organizational roles, diverse functional expertise, diverse perspectives, and individual traits represented on the team, the KM managers feel that they are able to capture a more complex understanding of the KM processes, so that they can measure KM performance formatively for learning and improvement purposes, and summatively relative to larger corporate performance metrics. At the heart of this strategy is working to continue to understand and value tacit aspects of knowledge formation and KM through team diversity.

6 Future Perspectives on Diversity and Knowledge Management in Organizations

In a highly competitive knowledge economy, knowledge sharing is critically important for survival, continued innovation, and creativity. "Innovation is not a luxury but a necessity in the hyper-competitive and global context of 21st century organizations" (Kremer et al., 2019, p. 72). Kremer et al. (2019) argued that innovation leaders are needed in organizations to ensure that knowledge sharing occurs to achieve competitive advantage through creativity and innovation. They recommend that these organizational leaders build group norms that respect and encourage knowledge sharing among all members of the group, giving voice and a sense of inclusion to the diversity of the group. Furthermore, according to Kremer et al. (2019), to drive innovation, creativity, and competitive advantage, knowledge sharing needs to occur across organizational boundaries to increase diversity of thought and perspectives.

KM and knowledge sharing will remain critical enablers for organizational success through innovation across a variety of societal systems, including the organizations featured in the vignettes presented previously in this chapter and the field of education (Charband & Jafari Navimipour, 2018). Indeed, the foundation of education is the transfer and generation of information, knowledge, and skills. Accordingly, leaders of educational institutions should leverage knowledge sharing strategies to innovate educational products and services (Charband & Jafari Navimipour, 2018) and long-term organizational success in educational settings (Jones & Sallis, 2013). Ultimately, realization of these desired organizational outcomes will inevitably require that tacit knowledge be managed and made more explicit across the lines of diversity in the workplace.

References

Adelstein, J. (2007). Disconnecting knowledge from the knower: The knowledge worker as Icarus. *Equal Opportunities International, 26*(8), 853–871.

Allee, V. (2001) The new business and knowledge management fundamentals. Adapted from New Business Fundamentals Perspectives newsletter. ASTD Mt. Diablo Chapter, August 2001.

Andresen, M. (2007). Diversity learning, knowledge diversity and inclusion: Theory and practice as exemplified by corporate universities. *Equal Opportunities International, 26*(8), 743–760.

Ardichvili, A. (2008). Learning and knowledge sharing in virtual communities of practice: Motivators, barriers, and enablers. *Advances in Developing Human Resources, 10*(4), 541–554.

Ardichvili, A., Maurer, M., Li, W., Wentling, T., & Stuedemann, R. (2006). Cultural influences on knowledge sharing through online communities of practice. *Journal of Knowledge Management, 10*(1), 94–107.

Asrar-ul-Haq, M., & Anwar, S. (2016). A systematic review of knowledge management and knowledge sharing: Trends, issues, and challenges. *Cogent Business & Management, 3*(1), 1127744.

Charband, Y., & Jafari Navimipour, N. (2018). Knowledge sharing mechanisms in the education: A systematic review of the state of the art literature and recommendations for future research. *Kybernetes, 47*(7), 1456–1490.

Cummings, J. N. (2004). Work groups, structural diversity, and knowledge sharing in a global organization. *Management Science, 50*(3), 352–364.

Dale, S. (2015). Principles of knowledge management (online). http://www.stephendale.com/2015/09/05/12-principles-of-knowledge-management/

Dass, P., & Parker, B. (1999). Strategies for managing human resource diversity: From resistance to learning. *Academy of Management Executive, 13*(2), 68–80.

Earl, M. (2001). Knowledge management strategies: Toward a taxonomy. *Journal of Management Information Systems, 18*(1), 215–233.

Edmondson, A. C., & Harvey, J. F. (2018). Cross-boundary teaming for innovation: Integrating research on teams and knowledge in organizations. *Human Resource Management Review, 28* (4), 347–360.

Egan, T. M. (2005). Creativity in the context of team diversity: Team leader perspectives. *Advances in Developing Human Resources, 7*(2), 207–225.

Gardenswartz, L., Cherbosque, J., & Rowe, A. (2010). Emotional intelligence and diversity: A model for differences in the workplace. *Journal of Psychological Issues in Organizational Culture, 1*(1), 74–84.

Hajro, A., Gibson, C. B., & Pudelko, M. (2017). Knowledge exchange processes in multicultural teams: Linking organizational diversity climates to teams' effectiveness. *Academy of Management Journal, 60*(1), 345–372.

Harrison, D. A., & Klein, K. J. (2007). What's the difference? Diversity constructs as separation, variety, or disparity in organizations. *Academy of Management Review, 32*(4), 1199–1228.

Hislop, D. (2013). *Knowledge management in organisations: A critical introduction* (3rd ed.). London: Oxford University Press.

Hurley, T. A., & Green, C. W. (2005). Knowledge management and the nonprofit industry: A within and between approach. *Journal of Knowledge Management Practice, 6*(1), 1–10.

Jennex, M. E., Smolnik, S., & Croasdell, D. (2015). Towards a consensus knowledge management success definition. In M. E. Jennex & S. Smolnik (Eds.), *Strategies for knowledge management success* (pp. 1–13). Hershey, PA: IGI.

Joia, L. A., & Lemos, B. (2010). Relevant factors for tacit knowledge transfer within organisations. *Journal of Knowledge Management, 14*(3), 410–427.

Jones, G., & Sallis, E. (2013). *Knowledge management in education: Enhancing learning & education*. London: Routledge.

Kremer, H., Villamor, I., & Aguinis, H. (2019). Innovation leadership: Best-practice recommendations for promoting employee creativity, voice, and knowledge sharing. *Business Horizons, 62*(1), 65–74.

Lewis, K. (2004). Knowledge and performance in knowledge-worker teams: A longitudinal study of transactive memory systems. *Management Science, 50*(11), 1519–1533.

Li, S. T., & Tsai, M. H. (2009). A dynamic taxonomy for managing knowledge assets. *Technovation, 29*(4), 284–298.

Li, S. T., Tsai, M. H., & Lin, C. (2010). Building a taxonomy of a firm's knowledge assets: A perspective of durability and profitability. *Journal of Information Science, 36*(1), 36–56.

Luanglath, N., Ali, M., & Mohannak, K. (2019). Top management team gender diversity and productivity: The role of board gender diversity. *Equality, Diversity and Inclusion: An International Journal, 38*(1), 71–86.

Matzler, K., Renzl, B., Müller, J., Herting, S., & Mooradian, T. A. (2008). Personality traits and knowledge sharing. *Journal of Economic Psychology, 29*(3), 301–313.

Mesmer-Magnus, J. R., & DeChurch, L. A. (2009). Information sharing and team performance: A meta-analysis. *Journal of Applied Psychology, 94*(2), 535–546.

Omotayo, F. O. (2015). Knowledge management as an important tool in organisational management: A review of literature. *Library Philosophy and Practice, 1*(2015), 1–23.

Polanyi, M. (1967). *The tacit dimension*. New York: Anchor Books.

Polanyi, M. (2009). *The tacit dimension*. Chicago: University of Chicago Press.

Sen, Y. (2019). Knowledge as a valuable asset of organizations: Taxonomy, management and implications. In C. Machado & J. P. Davim (Eds.), *Management science* (pp. 29–48). Cham: Springer.

Serrat, O. (2017). *Knowledge solutions*. Singapore: Springer.

St. Germain, L., & Quinn, D. (2006). Investigation of tacit knowledge in principal leadership. *The Educational Forum, 70*(1), 75–90.

Taylor, H. (2007). Tacit knowledge: Conceptualizations and operationalizations. *International Journal of Knowledge Management, 3*(3), 60–73.

Thomas, R. R. (1996). *Redefining diversity*. New York: American Management Association.

Tsai, M. H., Li, S. T., & Lin, C. (2012). An examination of knowledge asset dynamics for competitive advantage in a manufacturing R&D department. *Asia Pacific Management Review, 17*(4), 343–360.

Tsoukas, H. (2003). Forms of knowledge and forms of life in organized contexts. In R. C. H. Chia (Ed.), *In the realm of organization* (pp. 52–76). New York: Routledge.

Wenger, E. (2004). Knowledge management as a doughnut: Shaping your knowledge strategy through communities of practice. *Ivey Business Journal, 68*(3). Retrieved from https://iveybusinessjournal.com/publication/knowledge-management-as-a-doughnut/.

Wegner, E. (2006). *Communities of practice: Learning, meaning, and identity*. London: Cambridge University Press.

Wilson, T. D. (2002). The nonsense of 'knowledge management'. *Information Research, 8*(1), paper no. 144.

Part II
Knowledge Management in Education

Knowledge Management: Theories and Practices

John S. Edwards

Abstract Knowledge management is an age-old activity, yet it has only been identified and named for just over 30 years. This chapter will review the theories and practices that have developed under that name. Although the majority of knowledge management work has been done in a corporate context, its theories cover the whole range from the individual level to that of nations or even the entire human race. As the theme of this book is connecting adult learning and knowledge management, this chapter will place its emphasis on the links between knowledge management and learning and on the area known as personal knowledge management. These emphases mean the chapter will concentrate on theories from the "knowledge as knowing" or "knowledge as process" stream of literature, as opposed to the "knowledge as object" school.

Turning to knowledge management practices, these will be discussed using the three aspects of people, process, and technology. These go together to make up any particular knowledge management initiative, although typically one of them leads. Thus, in a learning initiative within an organization, we might see a focus on mentoring (leading on the people aspect), or support for further external study/ qualifications (process) or e-learning (technology).

One aspect we observe in the literature where knowledge management meets education is that there is more often an emphasis on the supply side (teachers, professors, and trainers) rather than on the demand side (learners, students).

1 Knowledge Management History and Development

This section traces knowledge management throughout its history, beginning in the late twentieth century. It considers the challenges of defining the concept from its early beginnings to the twenty-first century. This section closes by considering the dilemma of: knowledge as object or knowledge as knowing?

J. S. Edwards (✉)
Aston University, Birmingham, UK
e-mail: j.s.edwards@aston.ac.uk

© Springer Nature Switzerland AG 2019
M. Fedeli, L. L. Bierema (eds.), *Connecting Adult Learning and Knowledge Management*, Knowledge Management and Organizational Learning 8,
https://doi.org/10.1007/978-3-030-29872-2_8

1.1 From the Beginnings to the 1990s

The ability to share knowledge—to learn from other people—is central to human development, whether as individuals or at the level of the whole human race. Despite this, or perhaps because of it, knowledge management and knowledge itself are both hard to define precisely. This goes some way toward explaining why the term knowledge management was only coined in the 1980s, even though the activities that make up knowledge management have been going on for millennia. Taking knowledge sharing as an example, the individual teacher–apprentice relationship is documented at least as far back as the Christian Bible's Old Testament; schools were common in ancient China, Greece, India, and Rome; and even universities are known to have existed for almost a thousand years, since the founding of the University of Bologna in 1088.

Henry (1974, p. 189) was probably the first to use the term knowledge management with something approaching its current meaning. He defined it as "public policy for the production, dissemination, accessibility and use of information as it applies to public policy formulation"(p. 189). Henry was applying the concept at a national level, if not even more broadly, but its usage in this specific sense died away after the mid-1970s.

The credit for introducing the term knowledge management (KM) with its current meaning is thus generally given to Karl Wiig, from the 1986 keynote address he gave at a conference entitled "Management of Knowledge: Perspectives of a new opportunity" sponsored by the International Labour Organization. His focus was very much at the level of the organization, and this was where both academic and practical KM attention remained for the rest of the twentieth century.

KM took off rapidly during the mid-1990s. Figure 1 shows the number of KM articles on Web of Science by publication year from 1985 onward. As may be seen, the numbers follow a classic growth curve through the 1990s and indeed for most of the

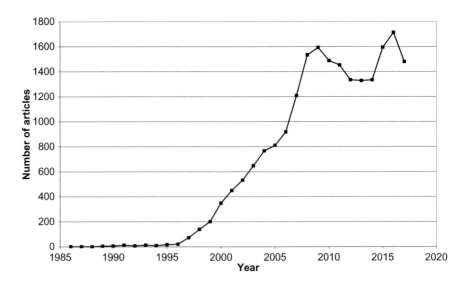

Fig. 1 Number of KM articles published on Web of Science 1986–2017

Knowledge Management: Theories and Practices

2000s. Impetus came from all around the world. Ikujiro Nonaka's work on knowledge creation (beginning with Nonaka, 1991) sparked interest in both Japan and the USA. The best-selling books *The Knowledge-Creating Company* (Nonaka & Takeuchi, 1995) and *Working Knowledge* (Davenport & Prusak, 1998) helped bring the concepts of KM to the attention of many managers. From Europe, centered on Scandinavia, came the growth of the intellectual capital movement, especially the work of Sveiby (e.g., Sveiby & Lloyd, 1987) and Edvinsson (e.g., Edvinsson & Malone, 1997).

2 The Thorny Issue of Definitions

Before going on to describe the development of KM in the twenty-first century, it will be helpful to spend some time considering definitions, and to begin that process in the late 1990s. Interestingly, Wiig himself has never spent much time trying to tie down a single definition of KM. Often he effectively uses the definition that an activity is KM if the people doing it say that it is KM. However, he did give a strong hint when reviewing the past and future of the field himself, some 10 years after coining the term KM (Wiig, 1997). In that paper, published at the height of the original "boom" in KM, Wiig observed that there were three "notions" of KM:

1. The management of explicit knowledge, generally using information technology (IT).
2. The management of intellectual capital.
3. The management of "all relevant knowledge-related aspects that affect the enterprise's viability and success" (Wiig, 1997, p. 1).

He continued by stating that the third notion encompassed the other two, so that it gives us an effective definition of KM at the enterprise (organizational) level as "the management of all relevant knowledge-related aspects that affect the enterprise's viability and success" (p. 1). Nevertheless, this does raise a few questions. Which aspects are knowledge-related? What is relevant? Who decides? Arguably these remain unanswered more than 20 years later.

One of the differences between notions 1 and 3 is the inclusion in notion 3 of tacit knowledge as well as explicit knowledge. The distinction between these two categories, based on the work of Polanyi (1966), was popularized by Nonaka's work, and in this case there is for once a reasonable consensus on definitions. "Explicit or codified knowledge refers to knowledge that is transmittable in formal, systematic language. On the other hand, tacit knowledge has a personal quality, which makes it hard to formalize and communicate." (Nonaka, 1994, p. 16) This means that explicit knowledge can straightforwardly be stored in written documents or a computer system, whereas tacit knowledge is difficult (usually impossible) to store in this way.

A much misunderstood related point, however, is that knowledge cannot be simply classified as tacit or explicit. Knowledge about anything includes both explicit and tacit elements. It is the balance between tacit and explicit that varies from one topic to another. Talking of balance, knowledge of how to ride a bicycle is mostly tacit; knowledge of how a manager should claim back travel expenses from her company is mostly explicit (Edwards, 2005). Tacit–explicit is best thought of as a continuum or a spectrum, not a binary either/or distinction.

Much research in KM has been devoted to trying to make tacit knowledge explicit. See Marshall and Brady (2001) for examples that also consider the limitations of this approach. If we accept Polanyi's (1966) work, then it is never going to be completely possible to make tacit knowledge explicit, because "we can know more than we can tell" (Polanyi, 1966, p. 4). Crucially, that is "we *can* tell" not just "we tell." A person has knowledge that she or he cannot fully explain because she or he does not understand it themselves in a way that can be put into words. Polanyi gave the example of recognizing faces. The perspective of a further half-century shows how good a choice of example this was. Most people cannot explain at all how they recognize someone whose face they know. Work done by police forces from the 1950s onward, on producing facial images from witness statements, led to "kits" of facial features such as noses and mouths. So a little tacit knowledge has been made explicit: that we recognize faces by recognizing facial features, but that is as far as the tacit knowledge can be "told." The technology the police use has improved from the identikit (using sketches of features) to the photofit (using photos of features) and now the e-fit (using features on computer), but our understanding of how humans recognize faces has not advanced. Not surprisingly therefore, machine learning systems for facial recognition do not use the recognition methods of humans at all. Ironically, they typically use so-called deep learning approaches that cannot be explained to humans either.

Thus, we see that it may be possible to make some tacit knowledge explicit, but not all of it. A few authors have tried to introduce the term implicit knowledge for knowledge that could in principle be made explicit but has not yet been. However, as rather more authors use implicit knowledge as a synonym for what we are calling tacit knowledge, this only causes confusion. See Day (2005) for more discussion of the relationship between explicit and tacit/implicit knowledge.

Another term for which we need a definition is knowledge management system (KMS). As with KM itself, there is no general agreement on the definition of a KMS, but at least there are basically just two schools of thought. The "narrow" school sees a KMS only as a technological artifact. For example, "[KMSs are] IT-based systems developed to support and enhance the organizational processes of knowledge creation, storage/retrieval, transfer, and application" (Alavi & Leidner, 2001, p. 114). Despite the Alavi and Leidner paper being the most cited in the history of KM, we prefer a definition from the "broad" or "wide" school, which typically also includes processes and people: "A combination of people, processes and technology whose purpose is to perform knowledge management in an organization" (Edwards, 2005, p. 355). We will pick up the idea of knowledge management systems as a combination of the three elements people, process, and technology in more detail in the next main section.

2.1 From the Late 1990s into the 2000s

Returning to the history of KM, as we saw from Fig. 1, the near-exponential growth in the number of published KM articles continued for most of the 2000s, but the growth then tailed off in 2009, although the number still exceeded previous years, for a peak of 1592. The numbers then fell back to a plateau some 16% short of that peak for the period 2012–2014, before rising again to new peaks in 2015 and 2016 (1713 articles). The year 2017 showed a slight decrease, while full figures for 2018 were not yet available at the time this chapter was written.

As with many topics, some authors are tempted to try to identify "generations," usually to emphasize the novelty of the new generation work, as we see with concepts such as Web 2.0 (or indeed 3.0) and Industry 4.0. KM is no exception, but a curious feature is how closely proposals for third-generation KM followed on the heels of those for second-generation KM, both within 2 or 3 years around the turn of the century. Sometimes the two proposals even appeared in the same article!

Vorakulpipat and Rezgui (2006) identify three different types of attempt to define second-generation KM. The most common type revolved around identifying first-generation KM with Wiig's notion 1, covering only explicit knowledge. Second-generation KM, however, was not identified with Wiig's notion 3, as might have been expected, but almost exclusively with managing tacit knowledge; it was also usually described as a people-centered approach in contrast to the technology-centered approach associated with notion 1. This attempt to define a second generation originally dated from late in the 1990s; the author can recall it being discussed at conferences then, but it is surprisingly hard to find printed references. The description by Koenig (2002) is typical of this view. Replacing one restricted view of KM with another view restricted in a different way has obvious limitations, and as a result, this never fully caught on, although it is often still referred to (see, e.g., Handzic & Durmic, 2014).

A second attempt was by McElroy (Firestone & McElroy, 2003; McElroy, 1999). Firestone and McElroy were both central figures in the Knowledge Management Consortium International (KMCI). KMCI began life as a professional association for KM and went on to offer training, certification, and publications. However, judging by its website, which has not been updated for at least 6 years, KMCI no longer exists. McElroy's definition of the second generation embraced both people and technology. "Unlike first-generation KM, in which technology always seemed to provide the answer, second-generation thinking is more inclusive of people, technology and social initiatives" (McElroy, 2002, p. 4). A review of McElroy's 2002 book by Connell (2003, p. 64) observes that "the focus is upon an organisation's capacity to produce knowledge, rather than an emphasis on its capture and distribution." At the heart of McElroy's arguments is the notion of organizational learning, particularly double-loop learning (Argyris & Schön, 1978, 1996).

The third attempt, by Snowden, took a more nuanced view (Snowden, 2002). He equated the first "age" of KM as being what happened before KM became a widely recognized activity, the second as a concentration on knowledge as a "thing" (akin to Wiig's notion 1), and the third as a more complex activity matching Wiig's notion 3.

Both McElroy and Snowden were motivated in different ways by ideas of complexity—McElroy with complex adaptive systems (Stacey, 2001) and Snowden in the form of his *Cynefin* framework, which includes four different types of context: simple, complicated, complex, and chaotic. Simple and complicated contexts assume that it is possible to perceive cause-and-effect relationships: in a simple context, these relationships are already known, so all that is needed is to act on that knowledge, whereas in a complicated context analysis is needed to discover the necessary relationships and knowledge first. Complex and chaotic contexts do not possess apparent cause-and-effect relationships, and actions must be based on emerging patterns. In a complex context, the patterns are reasonably stable, but in a chaotic context even the patterns constantly change. In knowledge terms, a complex context is unknown and perhaps outside past experience, but a chaotic context is unknowable, and requires action—the only way to find out what works. This was first presented around the turn of the century (e.g., Snowden, 2000) and refined some years later (Snowden & Boone, 2007). Snowden's ideas had more of a lasting influence on KM, but his later work moved into decision-making more broadly, as the title of the 2007 article demonstrates.

A parallel development at this time was the identification by Hansen, Nohria, and Tierney (1999) of what they termed the two fundamental KM strategies used in organizations: codification and personalization. Codification places more weight on explicit knowledge and involves heavy investment in IT; the intention is to connect people with reusable explicit knowledge. Personalization emphasizes tacit knowledge and linking people with each other. Investment in IT is much more modest and aimed at helping people to network. The two strategies are not intended to be exclusive, but rather applied in an 80-20 manner. These different strategies exist even within one industry sector. Hansen et al. gave the examples from management consultancy of Ernst & Young, who offered modular solutions based on a codification KM strategy, and McKinsey & Company, who offered custom-built solutions based on a personalization KM strategy. This work has probably had more influence on the practice of KM in organizations than any other concept or paper; certainly, far more than attempts to define second- or third-generation KM!

2.2 From the Mid-2000s to the Present Day

KM has continued to progress over this period, but agreement, even on the most central concepts and definitions, has been elusive. A study by Heisig (2009), bravely entitled "harmonisation of knowledge management" identified and compared no fewer than 160 KM frameworks from the literature. His most important overall conclusion was that KM needs a holistic effort, not what he calls a "one-sided emphasis" (p. 12) on a single activity or factor. This is the difference between Wiig's notion 3 and notion 1 again.

Despite Heisig's worthy call, KM progress in the last decade has tended to be in the detail, rather than in any major new concepts or understanding. The review of the state of the field in Dulipovici and Baskerville (2015), even though KM is only used as an exemplar, is still one of the best available. The two areas of development that perhaps have the potential to be "major" both address the strategic level of KM in organizations. They are KM maturity models and the impact of KM on organizational performance.

Knowledge Management: Theories and Practices 145

The intention of a KM maturity model is to identify the stage that KM has reached in an organization. Similar models have proved very useful in software engineering. Several different KM maturity models were developed during the 2000s, with some large organizations, such as Siemens AG and Infosys Technologies, producing their own to guide their own KM efforts. The model in most common use now is the one produced by the APQC (American Productivity & Quality Center) (Trees, 2016). It has five levels:

1. Initiate (growing awareness)
2. Develop (localized and repeatable practices)
3. Standardize (common processes and approaches)
4. Optimize (measured and adaptive)
5. Innovate (continuously improving practices)

The APQC offers considerable resources to organizations to help with their journey up these levels.

The connection between KM activities and an organization's "bottom line," or any other measures of organizational performance, has been explored for more than two decades. The results are mixed, with one notable exception: the relationship between successful knowledge transfer from one business unit to another and better performance has long been established (Argote & Ingram, 2000; Krylova, Vera, & Crossan, 2016). The more general relationship is still identified as needing further research. This was the top priority in a study by Heisig et al. (2016) on future research needs in KM. We do not have space here to cover all of the other 28 needs that they listed under the headings of business strategy, intellectual capital, decision-making, knowledge sharing, organizational learning, innovation performance, and productivity, but we will mention just one: risk and KM is identified as requiring deeper exploration (see Durst & Zieba, 2019).

One of the continuing divisions in the KM field is the question of whether knowledge should be thought of as an object or as knowing. We explore this in more detail in the next section.

3   Knowledge as Object or Knowledge as Knowing?

The simple answer to this question is that it all depends on how you look at it. Physicists have known for many decades that light can be thought of as either a wave or a particle and seem to cope with this apparent contradiction. Crucially, the physicists' different ways of thinking are each useful for different purposes, and the same is true in KM. Given the concentration of this book on connecting adult and organizational learning with KM, a focus on thinking in terms of knowledge as knowing is more appropriate. It is instructive that Polanyi himself chose to refer to "tacit knowing" rather than "tacit knowledge." That does not mean the perspective of knowledge as an object is of no use: if it were, there would be no point in writing this chapter, since one function of any written document is as a repository of explicit knowledge.

Thinking of knowledge as knowing forces an emphasis on the people involved in working with knowledge, whether (for example) using it, managing those who use it,

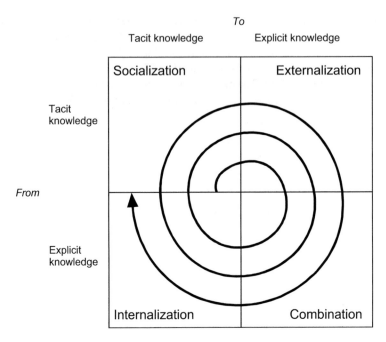

Fig. 2 The knowledge spiral/SECI model, modified from Nonaka (1994) and Nonaka and Takeuchi (1995)

learning it, or creating it. It is hard to give a complete list of knowledge-related activities, because the lists of KM activities found in the literature are typically tied to knowledge life cycles. Even if not intended, such lists encourage thinking of knowledge as an object, so we will not pursue them further in this chapter.

Much more appropriate are theories and models that concentrate on what people *do* by way of KM. We will mention three here: Nonaka's knowledge spiral/SECI (socialization, externalization, combination, and internalization) model of knowledge creation; communities of practice; and the use of narrative/storytelling.

Nonaka and his coworkers were actually concerned principally with knowledge creation, rather than the whole of knowledge management. They theorized knowledge creation as composed of four activities: socialization, externalization, combination, and internalization. These four activities take place in turn, following a spiral running up from the level of the individual to the level of the whole organization, as shown in Fig. 2. The model demonstrates the interplay between explicit and tacit knowledge that we were discussing earlier.

Their model has two other key elements. One is the concept of *ba* (Nonaka & Konno, 1998), an environment in which the SECI activities can take place. This might be a physical place, or in cyberspace, or even a cultural shift that enables knowledge creation to happen. Snowden's *Cynefin* is somewhat similar. Supposedly neither the Japanese *ba* nor the Welsh *Cynefin* has a direct equivalent in English. A recent paper by Canonico, Consiglio, De Nito, Esposito, and Pezzillo Iacono (2018) examines how the *obeya* (team room) concept from the theory of lean product development might serve as *ba* in KM, using an example from Fiat Chrysler Automobiles in Italy. The final element is the presence of dialectic thinking (Nonaka & Toyama, 2003), a process whereby contradictions are addressed through dynamic interactions between individuals, resulting in the creation of knowledge. The process sometimes referred to as constructive disagreement is one form of this thinking.

The concept of a community of practice (CoP), a "group of people informally bound together by shared expertise and passion for a joint enterprise" (Wenger & Snyder, 2000, p. 139), was first identified in the early 1990s (Brown & Duguid, 1991; Lave & Wenger, 1991). There has been extensive research into CoPs ever since, especially by Wenger (Coakes & Clarke, 2006; Inkpen, 1996; Oluikpe, 2012; Wenger, 1998; Wenger, McDermott, & Snyder, 2002). A key finding is that while it is possible to encourage the formation and continuation of CoPs, it is not possible to mandate or enforce them. People must choose to participate in a CoP.

Narrative/storytelling is surely the oldest form of KM, being one of the very few that was possible before the invention of writing, and relevant work predates the KM "boom" (e.g., Polkinghorne, 1988). Those interested in knowing and in tacit knowledge soon realized its importance to the newly named KM (Hannabuss, 2000). Julian Orr's study of stories told by Xerox photocopier engineers was such a milestone study that it has arguably taken on a life of its own (Cox, 2007; Orr, 1996). Considerable interest continues: Burnett, Grinnall, and Williams (2015) offer a recent attempt to devise a method for developing learning narratives in organizations, illustrated by an example case involving a multinational energy company. We now move on to look at knowledge management systems (KMSs) in more detail.

4 Knowledge Management Systems: People, Process, and Technology

As stated earlier, we find the broad definition of a KM system to be the most helpful. From this perspective, it takes the implementation of some form of KM system to achieve anything in KM. We have found a useful lens to consider KM systems in terms of the three aspects of people, process, and technology. This idea was crystallized by several people more or less simultaneously, for example by Edwards (2000) and Malhotra (2000), and at Nortel Networks (Massey, Montoya-Weiss, & O'Driscoll, 2002). Figure 3 shows the interactions between the three aspects.

While KM systems nearly always include all three elements identified by this lens, the balance between the three is specific to each implementation, as the following examples demonstrate.

Gamo-Sanchez and Cegarra-Navarro (2015) discussed a KM program in the engineering and maintenance department of a small airport in Spain. It is strongly focused on the *people* element, paying particular attention to team leadership and supporting and rewarding knowledge sharing behavior.

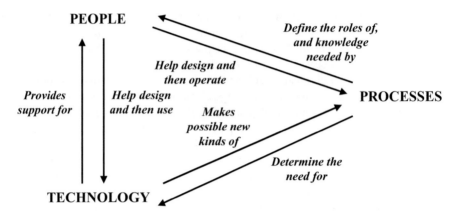

Fig. 3 People, processes, and technology in a KM system (modified from Edwards, 2005)

McCracken and Edwards (2017) described the implementation of a KM system in a large public hospital, centered on a new Electronic Patient Record system. Implementation was based around a *process* view of the patient's journey along the care pathways (a central concept in managing healthcare in the UK) in the system. The need for this to be done with a fluid, flexible approach was identified as important for system success.

Ying, Pee, and Jia (2018) examined the development of KuteSmart, a system in use at RCG, a Chinese manufacturer of customized suits, which includes a rule-based automatic pattern-making system. This is a KM system with a strong *technology* focus.

Oluikpe (2012), by contrast, ascribed the success of the KM program at the Central Bank of Nigeria to a two-pronged approach: both the development of communities of practice (*people*-focused) and the installation of a portal (*technology*-focused).

The lens can be very revealing. Azan, Bootz, and Rolland (2017) examined the implementation of an Enterprise Resource Planning (ERP) system in the French operations of the European cosmetics and wellness product company Paluda. This might therefore be thought of as *technology*-focused, but the thrust of the paper is how important the *people* aspect was, particularly in the early stages of the project, thus enabling the ERP system to connect different communities of practice.

Others continue to use variants of the people–process–technology framework. The APQC's Knowledge Flow Process comprises people, process, technology, and the content of the knowledge (see APQC, 2018). Sedziuviene and Vveinhardt (2009), looking at KM in higher education, took this view even further, using people, processes, and technology as a lens to describe the whole organization, not just a KM system. The recent paper by Durst and Zieba (2019) classified knowledge risks in organizations into three categories: human, operational, and technological; these can of course be mapped straightforwardly to people, process, and technology.

Knowledge Management: Theories and Practices 149

5 Personal KM

One obvious direction for KM to take was to consider a focus on the individual rather than the organization. This led to the idea of personal knowledge management (PKM). There seems to be general agreement that the term itself was coined by Jason Frand and Carol Hixon as part of the MBA program at UCLA's Anderson School of Management (Frand & Hixon, 1999), though the original version of what they proposed seems to have vanished even from web archives. A similar fate has befallen other early work by Paul Dorsey and coworkers in 2000 and 2001, though one archive version survives (see Dorsey, 2001). Frand and Hixon came from a librarianship perspective, and Dorsey's work similarly emphasized information skills. Dorsey identified seven elements: retrieving information; evaluating information; organizing information; collaborating around information; analyzing information; presenting information; and securing information.

The difference between such a conception of PKM and some form of personal information management is far from clear; its focus does appear somewhat narrow. However, chapter 5 of a KM book published slightly earlier the same year (Skyrme, 1999) gave a broader perspective, although it never used the phrase personal KM. Instead, it was entitled the knowledge networker's toolkit. The aspects this toolkit comprises include knowing your thinking style; managing the information glut; communicating effectively; developing your network; being techno-wise (using technology effectively); managing your workspace; engaging in personal development; and leveraging your intellectual capital. As may be seen, it includes all three of people, process, and technology aspects, as well as self-reflection.

Further work on PKM includes that of Truch (2001), Wright (2005), and Smedley (2009), plus a complete Special Issue of *Online Information Review* (Volume 33, Issue 2). Not surprisingly, as with KM itself, there remains no generally agreed definition.

6 Theories Linking KM and Learning

While it is clear that organizational learning (OL) and KM arose from different roots, the overlap between them is considerable, even if McElroy's OL-influenced approach to KM did not outlive the decade of the 2000s. Earlier work characterized one difference as being that KM was top-down whereas OL was bottom-up (Kidd & Edwards, 2000), but this difference has faded away over time. Indeed, Castaneda, Manrique, and Cuellar (2018) went as far as to argue that "OL has been gradually absorbed within KM" (p. 322). As an example of this change, research into communities of practice was certainly situated within the OL literature at first, but by the time Wenger et al. (2002) published *"Cultivating Communities of Practice: A guide to managing knowledge,"* the title definitely placed it within KM.

Definitions of OL seem to command more general agreement than those of KM. An early definition that is still frequently cited is "Organizational learning means the process of improving actions through better knowledge and understanding" (Fiol & Lyles, 1985, p. 803), the mention of knowledge immediately making a potential link to KM. Argote and Miron-Spektor (2011, p. 1124) observe that "Most researchers would agree with defining organizational learning as a change in the organization's knowledge that occurs as a function of experience." They go on to identify the subprocesses of organizational learning as creating, retaining, and transferring knowledge. Almost any KM researcher would regard these as all being within the province of KM: indeed, central to its study.

The best-known theory of knowledge creation is the knowledge spiral/SECI model discussed above, which is "claimed" by both KM and OL. The majority of KM work on knowledge retention is about explicit knowledge, and so not within our scope here. Nevertheless, it is worth noting that both OL and KM have a small stream of work on the opposite of retention, i.e., forgetting (Fernandez & Sune, 2009; Lopez & Sune, 2013; Rao & Argote, 2006). This tends to focus on understanding and mitigating the effects of staff turnover.

The most important work on transferring knowledge arises from the identification of the concept of stickiness: the "difficulty of transferring knowledge within the organization" (Szulanski, 1996, p. 29). Szulanski and coworkers have done much to develop this area (most recently in Szulanski, Ringov, & Jensen, 2016). Many studies find that the two most significant predictors of stickiness are causal ambiguity, which is closely related to the tacitness of the knowledge, and the absorptive capacity of the recipient, which is essentially their ability to learn. The wording of the definition again shows that the original work was at the level of the organization, specifically transfer between organizational units, but the concept of stickiness has been expanded to cover all levels, including that of the individual. An example of the latter is the article by Zaghab, Maldonado, Whitehead, Bartlett, and de Bittner (2015) on the design of online pharmacy training for healthcare professionals.

That particular article focused on the learners, but it is a salutary lesson that there generally seems to be more research into KM for teachers/lecturers/instructors than for students/learners. A search on Web of Science for relevant "KM and learning" papers yielded a total of 95. Of these, 44 were concerned exclusively with the staff, against only 29 concerned exclusively with students. A further 18 either covered both, or concentrated on the relationship between the two parties, while the remaining four were review papers that spanned all aspects.

Like the Zaghab et al. (2015) article, the majority of recent KM references on adult learning examine features of learning online. Fini (2009) studied users of an early MOOC (Massive Open Online Course). The course topic was Connectivism and Connective Knowledge, so the learners were themselves people interested in the online learning process. A Special Issue of *Behaviour and Information Technology* concentrated on informal learning in the workplace (Garcia-Penalvo, Colomo-Palacios, & Lytras, 2012). Manasia (2013) looked at the use of social software to aid a small online community of practice (in Second Life) comprising architecture

Knowledge Management: Theories and Practices 151

professionals. Petrillo (2015) extensively discussed technology-enabled changes in the process of adult learning.

Another example of the overlap between OL and KM is the discussion of exploration and exploitation. This distinction, with its implied trade-off between the future and the present, has long been a key concept in organizational strategy. March (1991) was the first to bring this into the context of OL. His short description (p. 71) contrasts "the exploration of new possibilities and the exploitation of old certainties." However, by the end of that decade his longer explanation of the two concepts brought in the word knowledge: "By exploration is meant things such as search, discovery, novelty and innovation...By exploitation is meant refinement, routinization, production, and implementation of knowledge" (March, 1999, p. 5). Brown and Duguid (2001) pointed out that the trade-off is a dynamic, constantly changing one, but Oshri, Pan, and Newell (2005), in the KM literature, explained that exploration and exploitation should properly be regarded as the ends of a continuum, not a binary choice. The author (Edwards, 2016) found that, in supply chain management, more KM systems support exploitation than support exploration. Even if we do not accept that OL has been absorbed within KM, we can definitely expect the overlap between them to strengthen in future.

7 Implications for KM Research and Practice

Clearly a lack of emphasis on learning is a valid criticism of some KM research, as the numerical analysis in the previous section demonstrates. A counter-argument, however, is that this may simply be a question of semantics. If OL and KM are overlapping and perhaps converging, then work on learning is more likely to be labeled OL than KM.

The relationship between individual and collective knowledge continues to be an important area of study, although the knowledge spiral/SECI model remains the most central, especially for knowledge creation. Some authors have even doubted if collective knowledge exists, except as an aggregation of individual people's knowing.

Rewarding people for knowledge sharing has turned out to be a complex issue. Both intrinsic rewards (such as praise) and extrinsic rewards (such as money) have been tried, with successes and failures. Osterloh and Frey (2000) pointed out that the two types cannot simply be added together; they may in fact cancel each other out. Kankanhalli, Tan, and Wei (2005) studied the topic extensively, but only in public sector organizations. Overall, designing an effective reward system needs to be specific to the particular context of the organization concerned. It is possible that this may also change over time, although this has not been established by research as far as we know. Trying to encourage other forms of knowledge-related behavior, such as learning, is likely to prove at least as difficult.

An important recent proposition by Krylova et al. (2016) is that improvisation by knowledge workers, such as storytelling, may be more important for the success of knowledge transfer than formal processes. This resonates with an earlier point in this chapter, that KM is for volunteers, not conscripts. Their focus on the right-hand part of Fig. 3 may be an interesting counterpoint to the distinction between the two main KM strategies identified by Hansen et al. (1999), which concentrate on the left-hand part, personalization being people-focused while codification is technology-focused. There is surely scope for more emphasis on process when thinking about KM in future.

References

Alavi, M., & Leidner, D. E. (2001). Review: Knowledge management and knowledge management systems: Conceptual foundations and research issues. *MIS Quarterly, 25*(1), 107–136. https://doi.org/10.2307/3250961.

APQC. (2018). APQC's knowledge flow process framework. Retrieved from https://www.apqc.org/knowledge-base/download/277408

Argote, L., & Ingram, P. (2000). Knowledge transfer: A basis for competitive advantage in firms. *Organizational Behavior and Human Decision Processes, 82*(1), 150–169. https://doi.org/10.1006/obhd.2000.2893.

Argote, L., & Miron-Spektor, E. (2011). Organizational learning: From experience to knowledge. *Organization Science, 22*(5), 1123–1137. https://doi.org/10.1287/orsc.1100.0621.

Argyris, C., & Schön, D. A. (1978). *Organizational learning: A theory of action perspective.* Reading, MA: Addison-Wesley.

Argyris, C., & Schön, D. A. (1996). *Organizational learning II.* Reading, MA: Addison-Wesley.

Azan, W., Bootz, J.-P., & Rolland, O. (2017). Community of practices, knowledge transfer, and ERP project (ERPP). *Knowledge Management Research & Practice, 15*(2), 238–256. https://doi.org/10.1057/s41275-017-0047-9.

Brown, J. S., & Duguid, P. (1991). Organizational learning and communities-of practice: Toward a unified view of working, learning and innovation. *Organization Science, 2*(1), 40–57.

Brown, J. S., & Duguid, P. (2001). Knowledge and organization: A social-practice perspective. *Organization Science, 12*(2), 198–213.

Burnett, S., Grinnall, A., & Williams, D. (2015). What have we learned so far? The development and application of an organisational learning narrative. *Knowledge Management Research & Practice, 13*(2), 160–167. https://doi.org/10.1057/kmrp.2013.38.

Canonico, P., Consiglio, S., De Nito, E., Esposito, V., & Pezzillo Iacono, M. (2018). Dealing with knowledge in a product development setting: An empirical analysis in the automotive industry. *Knowledge Management Research & Practice, 16*(1), 126–133. https://doi.org/10.1080/14778238.2018.1428068.

Castaneda, D. I., Manrique, L. F., & Cuellar, S. (2018). Is organizational learning being absorbed by knowledge management? A systematic review. *Journal of Knowledge Management, 22*(2), 299–325. https://doi.org/10.1108/JKM-01-2017-0041.

Coakes, E., & Clarke, S. (Eds.). (2006). *Encyclopedia of communities of practice in information and knowledge management.* Hershey, PA: Idea Group Reference.

Connell, N. A. D. (2003). Book review: The new knowledge management—Complexity, learning and sustainable innovation. *Knowledge Management Research & Practice, 1*(1), 64–66.

Cox, A. (2007). Reproducing knowledge: Xerox and the story of knowledge management. *Knowledge Management Research & Practice, 5*(1), 3–12. https://doi.org/10.1057/palgrave.kmrp.8500118.

Davenport, T. H., & Prusak, L. (1998). *Working knowledge: How organizations manage what they know.* Boston: Harvard Business School Press.

Day, R. E. (2005). Clearing up "implicit knowledge": Implications for knowledge management, information science, psychology, and social epistemology. *Journal of the American Society for Information Science and Technology, 56*(6), 630–635.

Dorsey, P. A. (2001). Personal knowledge management: Educational framework for global business. Retrieved from https://web.archive.org/web/20080906190602/http://www.millikin.edu/pkm/pkm_istanbul.html

Dulipovici, A., & Baskerville, R. (2015). An education model of disciplinary emergence: The ripples of knowledge management. *Knowledge Management Research & Practice, 13*(2), 115–133.

Durst, S., & Zieba, M. (2019). Mapping knowledge risks: Towards a better understanding of knowledge management. *Knowledge Management Research & Practice, 17*(1), 1–13. https://doi.org/10.1080/14778238.2018.1538603.

Edvinsson, L., & Malone, M. S. (1997). *Intellectual capital.* New York: Harper Business.

Edwards, J. S. (2000). *Artificial intelligence and knowledge management: How much difference can it really make?* Paper presented at the KMAC2000. Knowledge management beyond the hype: Looking towards the new millennium, Aston University, Birmingham, UK.

Edwards, J. S. (2005). Business processes and knowledge management. In M. Khosrow-Pour (Ed.), *Encyclopedia of information science and technology* (Vol. I, pp. 350–355). Hershey, PA: Idea.

Edwards, J. S. (2016). Systems for knowledge management along the supply chain. In S. Joshi & R. Joshi (Eds.), *Designing and implementing global supply chain management* (pp. 92–104). Hershey, PA: IGI.

Fernandez, V., & Sune, A. (2009). Organizational forgetting and its causes: An empirical research. *Journal of Organizational Change Management, 22*(6), 620–634. https://doi.org/10.1108/09534810910997032.

Fini, A. (2009). The technological dimension of a massive open online course: The case of the CCK08 course tools. *International Review of Research in Open and Distance Learning, 10*(5).

Fiol, C. M., & Lyles, M. A. (1985). Organizational learning. *Academy of Management Review, 10*(4), 803–813.

Firestone, J. M., & McElroy, M. W. (2003). *Key issues in the new knowledge management.* Amsterdam: Butterworth-Heinemann.

Frand, J., & Hixon, C. (1999). *Personal knowledge management : Who, what, why, when, where, how?* (Working paper). Los Angeles: Anderson School of Management, UCLA.

Gamo-Sanchez, A.-L., & Cegarra-Navarro, J.-G. (2015). Factors that influence the success of a KM-program in a small-sized airport. *Journal of Knowledge Management, 19*(3), 593–610. https://doi.org/10.1108/jkm-02-2015-0052.

Garcia-Penalvo, F. J., Colomo-Palacios, R., & Lytras, M. D. (2012). Informal learning in work environments: Training with the Social Web in the workplace. *Behaviour & Information Technology, 31*(8), 753–755. https://doi.org/10.1080/0144929x.2012.661548.

Handzic, M., & Durmic, N. (2014). Merging knowledge management with project management. In C. Vivas & P. Sequeira (Eds.), *Proceedings of the 15th European conference on knowledge management* (pp. 402–409).

Hannabuss, S. (2000). Narrative knowledge: Eliciting organisational knowledge from storytelling. *Aslib Proceedings, 52*(10), 402–413.

Hansen, M. T., Nohria, N., & Tierney, T. (1999). What's your strategy for managing knowledge? *Harvard Business Review, 77*(2), 106–116.

Heisig, P. (2009). Harmonisation of knowledge management. *Journal of Knowledge Management, 13*(4), 4–31. https://doi.org/10.1108/13673270910971798.

Heisig, P., Adekunle, S. O., Kianto, A., Kemboi, C., Perez-Arrau, G., & Easa, N. (2016). Knowledge management and business performance: Global experts' views on future research needs. *Journal of Knowledge Management, 20*(6), 1169–1198.

Henry, N. L. (1974). Knowledge management: A new concern for public administration. *Public Administration Review, 34*(3), 189–196.

Inkpen, A. (1996). Creating knowledge through collaboration. *California Management Review, 39* (1), 123–140.

Kankanhalli, A., Tan, B. C. Y., & Wei, K. K. (2005). Contributing knowledge to electronic knowledge repositories: An empirical investigation. *MIS Quarterly, 29*(1), 113–143.

Kidd, J. B., & Edwards, J. S. (2000, October 26–27). *Fast moving global demand led supply chains: How organisational learning may offer bridges in crossing cultures.* Paper presented at the first European conference on knowledge management, Bled, Slovenia.

Koenig, M. E. D. (2002). The third stage of KM emerges. *KMWorld, 11*, 20–21.

Krylova, K., Vera, D., & Crossan, M. (2016). Knowledge transfer in knowledge-intensive organizations: The crucial role of improvisation in transferring and protecting knowledge. *Journal of Knowledge Management, 20*(5), 1045–1064. https://doi.org/10.1108/JKM-10-2015-0385.

Lave, J., & Wenger, E. C. (1991). *Situated learning: Legitimate peripheral participation.* New York: Cambridge University Press.

Lopez, L., & Sune, A. (2013). Turnover-induced forgetting and its impact on productivity. *British Journal of Management, 24*(1), 38–53. https://doi.org/10.1111/j.1467-8551.2011.00785.x.

Malhotra, Y. (2000). From information management to knowledge management: Beyond the 'Hi-tech hidebound' systems. In K. Srikantaiah & M. E. D. Koenig (Eds.), *Knowledge management for the information professional* (pp. 37–61). Medford, NJ: Information Today.

Manasia, L. (2013). The impact of social software on developing communities of practice to enhance adult learning. In I. Roceanu, I. Stanescu, & D. Barbieru (Eds.), *Quality and efficiency in E-learning, Vol 2* (pp. 598–603). Bucharest: Carol I National Defence University Publishing House.

March, J. G. (1991). Exploration and exploitation in organizational learning. *Organization Science, 2*(1), 71–87.

March, J. G. (1999). *The pursuit of organizational intelligence.* Malden, MA: Blackwell.

Marshall, N., & Brady, T. (2001). Knowledge management and the politics of knowledge: Illustrations from complex products and systems. *European Journal of Information Systems, 10*(2), 99–112.

Massey, A. P., Montoya-Weiss, M. M., & O'Driscoll, T. M. (2002). Knowledge management in pursuit of performance: Insights from Nortel Networks. *MIS Quarterly, 26*(3), 269–289.

McCracken, S., & Edwards, J. S. (2017). Implementing a knowledge management system within an NHS Hospital: A case study exploring the roll-out of an Electronic Patient Record (EPR). *Knowledge Management Research & Practice, 15*(1), 1–11. https://doi.org/10.1057/kmrp.2015.7.

McElroy, M. W. (1999). The second generation of knowledge management. *Knowledge Management*, 86–88.

McElroy, M. W. (2002). *The new knowledge management: Complexity, learning, and sustainable innovation.* Amsterdam: KMCI/Butterworth Heinemann.

Nonaka, I. (1991). The knowledge creating company. *Harvard Business Review, 69*(6), 96–104.

Nonaka, I. (1994). A dynamic theory of organizational knowledge creation. *Organization Science, 5*(1), 14–37.

Nonaka, I., & Konno, N. (1998). The concept of "ba": Building a foundation for knowledge creation. *California Management Review, 40*(3), 40–54.

Nonaka, I., & Takeuchi, H. (1995). *The knowledge-creating company: How Japanese companies create the dynamics of innovation.* New York: Oxford University Press.

Nonaka, I., & Toyama, R. (2003). The knowledge-creating theory revisited: Knowledge creation as a synthesizing process. *Knowledge Management Research & Practice, 1*(1), 2–10.

Oluikpe, P. (2012). Developing a corporate knowledge management strategy. *Journal of Knowledge Management, 16*(6), 862–878. https://doi.org/10.1108/13673271211276164.

Orr, J. E. (1996). *Talking about machines: An ethnography of a modern job.* Ithaca, NY: ILR Press/ Cornell University Press.

Oshri, I., Pan, S. L., & Newell, S. (2005). Trade-offs between knowledge exploitation and exploration activities. *Knowledge Management Research & Practice, 3*(1), 10–23.

Osterloh, M., & Frey, B. S. (2000). Motivation, knowledge transfer, and organizational forms. *Organization Science, 11*(5), 538–550.

Petrillo, T. (2015). Disruptive trends in adult learning and knowledge management: An exploration into the value of micro-credentialing and digital badging. In L. Gomez Chova, A. Lopez Martinez & I. Candel Torres (Eds.), *Edulearn15: 7th international conference on education and new learning technologies* (pp. 6755–6760).

Polanyi, M. (1966). *The tacit dimension*. Garden City, NY: Doubleday.

Polkinghorne, D. E. (1988). *Narrative knowing and the human sciences*. Albany, NY: State of New York University Press.

Rao, R. D., & Argote, L. (2006). Organizational learning and forgetting: The effects of turnover and structure. *European Management Review, 3*(2), 77–85. https://doi.org/10.1057/palgrave.emr.1500057.

Sedziuviene, N., & Vveinhardt, J. (2009). The paradigm of knowledge management in higher educational institutions. *Inzinerine Ekonomika-Engineering Economics, 65*, 79–89.

Skyrme, D. J. (1999). *Knowledge networking: Creating the collaborative enterprise*. Oxford: Butterworth-Heinemann.

Smedley, J. (2009). Modelling personal knowledge management. *OR Insight, 22*(4), 221–233. https://doi.org/10.1057/ori.2009.11.

Snowden, D. J. (2000). *Cynefin, a sense of time and place: An ecological approach to sense making and learning in formal and informal communities*. Paper presented at the KMAC2000. Knowledge management beyond the hype: Looking towards the new millennium, Aston University, Birmingham, UK.

Snowden, D. J. (2002). Complex acts of knowing: Paradox and descriptive self-awareness. *Journal of Knowledge Management, 6*(2), 100–111. https://doi.org/10.1108/13673270210424639.

Snowden, D. J., & Boone, M. E. (2007). A leader's framework for decision making. *Harvard Business Review, 85*(11), 68–76.

Stacey, R. D. (2001). *Complex responsive processes in organisations: Learning and knowledge creation*. London: Routledge.

Sveiby, K., & Lloyd, T. (1987). *Managing know-how*. London: Bloomsbury.

Szulanski, G. (1996). Exploring internal stickiness: Impediments to the transfer of best practice within the firm. *Strategic Management Journal, 17*(Winter Special Issue), 27–43.

Szulanski, G., Ringov, D., & Jensen, R. J. (2016). Overcoming stickiness: How the timing of knowledge transfer methods affects transfer difficulty. *Organization Science, 27*(2), 304–322. https://doi.org/10.1287/orsc.2016.1049.

Trees, L. (2016). *Accelerators of knowledge management maturity: Insights from APQC's KM capability assessment tool* (pp. 58). Houston, TX: APQC.

Truch, E. (2001). Managing personal knowledge: The key to tomorrow's employability. *Journal of Change Management, 2*(2), 102–105.

Vorakulpipat, C., & Rezgui, Y. (2006). *From knowledge sharing to value creation: Three generations of knowledge management*. Paper presented at the 2006 IEEE international engineering management conference, Salvador, Brazil.

Wenger, E. C. (1998). *Communities of practice: Learning, meaning and identity*. Cambridge: Cambridge University Press.

Wenger, E. C., McDermott, R., & Snyder, W. M. (2002). *Cultivating communities of practice: A guide to managing knowledge*. Boston: Harvard Business School Press.

Wenger, E. C., & Snyder, W. M. (2000). Communities of practice: The organizational frontier. *Harvard Business Review, 78*(1), 139–145.

Wiig, K. M. (1997). Knowledge management: Where did it come from and where will it go? *Expert Systems with Applications, 13*(1), 1–14.

Wright, K. (2005). Personal knowledge management: Supporting individual knowledge worker performance. *Knowledge Management Research & Practice, 3*(3), 156–165.

Ying, W., Pee, L. G., & Jia, S. (2018). Social informatics of intelligent manufacturing ecosystems: A case study of KuteSmart. *International Journal of Information Management, 42*, 102–105. https://doi.org/10.1016/j.ijinfomgt.2018.05.002.

Zaghab, R. W., Maldonado, C., Whitehead, D., Bartlett, F., & de Bittner, M. R. (2015). Online continuing education for health professionals: Does sticky design promote practice-relevance? *Electronic Journal of E-Learning, 13*(6), 466–474.

Using Social Networks and Communities of Practice to Promote Staff Collaboration in Higher Education

Niall Corcoran and Aidan Duane

Abstract A lack of community at the heart of higher education institutions (HEIs) has led to a breakdown of collaboration and knowledge sharing amongst staff. There are a number of contributory factors, including the culture and structure of these organizations, and a divide between academic and other staff. The use of community-based knowledge management (KM) techniques, such as communities of practice (CoP), appears to have some potential in addressing this problem, and particularly when coupled with enterprise social networks (ESN) to create online communities. A case study of the implementation of an ESN and virtual CoP (vCoP) in a public HEI in Ireland is presented. The project involved an action research (AR) study conducted over a 12-month period and used qualitative data from focus groups and interviews to investigate a number of themes based on a conceptual model. The findings indicate that the barriers to staff participation are influenced by the prevalent organizational structure and culture, and a divide between faculty and other staff. However, individual benefits that accrue may influence greater participation, and organizational benefits that accrue may influence organizational strategies that drive change in structure and culture to promote the development of the knowledge sharing environment. A number of strategies for practice and specific tactical approaches for organizations to use are presented. In general, HEIs need to move towards a transformational culture for staff to be suitably motivated to participate in online communities and share knowledge freely.

An idealised higher education environment would display the following characteristics: students attend in order to seek knowledge and learn from the academic instructors; the academic instructors impart their knowledge to the students and seek to expand their own knowledge through research activities; student support

---

N. Corcoran (✉)
Department of Information Technology, Limerick Institute of Technology, Limerick, Ireland
e-mail: niall.corcoran@lit.ie

A. Duane
School of Business, Waterford Institute of Technology, Waterford, Ireland

© Springer Nature Switzerland AG 2019
M. Fedeli, L. L. Bierema (eds.), *Connecting Adult Learning and Knowledge Management*, Knowledge Management and Organizational Learning 8,
https://doi.org/10.1007/978-3-030-29872-2_9

personnel work to enable both of those groups to achieve their goals; and they are all supported by management who fully understand their purpose in creating an environment where the ultimate goal of higher education can be achieved—the generation and transfer of knowledge. This appears a simple and straightforward depiction of what a higher education institution (HEI) should look like, one that would be widely understood by broader society, and indeed by many students that engage with HEIs. The majority of students are transient members of campus communities, whereas the staff of a HEI are the permanent members of the community, whose collective task is to maximize the learning and social experience for the student group, and this is the primary function of the majority of HEIs. This sense of all of these groups working together towards a common goal should stimulate a picture of community within these institutions, and also perhaps across the wider higher education sector, both nationally and internationally. Indeed, the very reason for the existence of HEIs, the process of facilitating learning, is central to the creation of community, and, according to Palmer (2002), "we have at our disposal one of the greatest vehicles for community building known to humankind—the one called education" (p. xv). If education is at the heart of community, then it is somewhat logical to expect that community would be at the heart of education and education institutions. It is somewhat of a paradox then, that this sense of community is in fact not widespread in many HEIs, although it would seem that a strategic plan for a HEI has yet to be written that does not espouse the goal of building campus community (Taub, 1998).

This chapter examines how social media tools, specifically enterprise social networks, can be used in an organization to enable staff knowledge sharing activity and build community. In determining that the prevalent organization structure and culture in higher education institutions have a negative impact on knowledge management, it looks at ways in which social media tools may help to improve this situation. It describes a case study that involved the implementation of an enterprise social networking tool used to underpin the development of a knowledge sharing environment centred on virtual communities of practice in a HEI. The research findings underpin a discussion that ties in the existing literature, and develops a number of strategies for practice, before concluding with recommendations for future directions.[1]

---

[1]Selected portions of this chapter have been part of Niall Corcoran's DBA Thesis, submitted to Waterford Institute of Technology, Ireland, in August 2017. Further excerpts appear in articles published in the VINE Journal of Information and Knowledge Management Systems, the Australasian Journal of Information Systems, and an IGI Global publication, *Educational and Social Dimensions of Digital Transformations in Organizations*. See the Reference List for full details.

1 Organization Culture and Structure in Higher Education Institutions

The lack of community amongst staff working in HEIs is neither new nor perceived and has been the subject of discussion and research for decades. Indeed, Palmer (2002) stated: "academic culture has no sense of being part of a community" (p. 179). A structurally fragmented community may be rooted in the fact that HEIs were historically, largely founded and run by academics, but as they grew in size and student numbers it became necessary to include a wide range of administrative and support functions such as finance, human resources, information technology (IT) services, facilities, and library. Conway (2012) cited a 1966 speech by the noted botanist and educator Eric Ashby, in which he said "all Professors see all administrators as an evil. (If you are an administrator), say to yourself every morning 'I am an evil, but I am a necessary one'" (p. 43). This sense of disengagement between academic staff and support staff does not seem to have gone away or even dissipated much in the interim. Castleman and Allen (1995) maintained that support staff have been a neglected part of the higher education workforce, with their issues often overlooked by management, and Szekeres (2011) described support staff as being an invisible group. Indeed, much of the literature seems to infer that the main reason for this cultural divide is the attitude of academic staff, who see administrative staff as unnecessary, interfering, and controlling (e.g. Dobson, 2011; Szekeres, 2011). In any case, HEIs simply could not function without the existence of support staff. Leaving the attitude of academics and the sensibilities of support staff aside, it is the manifestation of the structural and cultural divide between the two groups at an operational level that is most problematic for HEIs. A lack of understanding, trust and knowledge sharing between academic and support staff can lead to stifled development, both within an institution itself and of the institution. This position is not peculiar to either group in relation to the other but is very much a two-way street, and is described by Conway and Dobson (2003) as two groups with divergent value systems, and an interface that is less than positive, a situation often exacerbated when academics become full-time executives as academic managers.

Both the organizational structure and the organizational culture of HEIs tend to promote the division of the organization into tribes or silos. Of course, divides exist in any organization where different professional groups interact and where professional groups are managed, with individual workers associating with projects, trades, departments, or functions, increasing the difficulties associated with knowledge sharing, coordination, and interaction between these groups. Shoham and Perry (2009) described the current structure of most academic institutions as characterized by a loose coupling between its faculty and staff units, and Kuo (2009) discussed the sense of disconnection between faculty and staff which makes it difficult for them to work collaboratively. James (2000) stated "an unusual organizational characteristic of universities is the deeply entrenched division in roles and status between academic and administrative staff" (p. 51). Santo (2005) argued that the reasons for this entrenchment lie in the fact that two very different knowledge bases are involved, and the interpretation of events by faculty and staff is different due to different values and priorities. This situation is exacerbated in many newer HEIs in a number of jurisdictions, where those institutions tend to be more bureaucratic in character than traditional universities, with a centralized and hierarchical management structure where all staff report to line managers and have less autonomy (Fullwood, Rowley, & Delbridge, 2013).

Many of these jurisdictions also mandate fee-paying, public HEIs, and coupling this with the ever diversifying makeup of the student population means that it is becoming increasingly important that the quality of the educational experience meets expectations. Service quality has now become a fundamental aspect of educational excellence. Aldridge and Rowley (2001) found that students perceive the quality of an institution's learning environment both in terms of intellectual faculty and appropriate facilities of learning and infrastructure, and this perception will decide if their interest in the institution is retained or not. The students are motivated by both the academic and the administrative efficiency of their institution. Malik, Danish, and Usman (2010) believed that the quality of service delivery is contributed to through the cooperation of academic and support staff and by the interaction of both groups with students, and Bassnett (2005) stated that academic and support staff must work more closely together if this is to be achieved, with a need for a cooperative community based on mutual trust.

2 HEI's Cultural Impact on Knowledge Management/Sharing

Given the cultural reality that lacks community in this dystopian depiction of modern HEIs, there is a consequential lack of knowledge sharing amongst staff. As knowledge management (KM) processes such as acquisition, storing, retrieving and sharing, are seen as crucial and core by knowledge intensive organizations (Nunes, Annansingh, Eaglestone, & Wakefield, 2006), it would seem logical that KM might form a key strategic concern for HEIs through which they could recognize, manage, and use their knowledge assets. Kidwell, Vander Linde, and Johnson (2000) believed that HEIs can derive significant value from developing initiatives to share knowledge for the achievement of business objectives, arguing that, if done effectively, KM can lead to better decision making capabilities, reduced development cycle time for curriculum and research, improved academic and administrative services and reduced costs. Nonaka and Von Krogh (2009) asserted that the outcome of knowledge sharing is the creation of new knowledge and innovation that will improve organizational performance, and a number of studies have shown that promoting knowledge sharing practices results in improved organizational effectiveness (Gupta & Govindarajan, 2000; Olivera, 2000; Petrash, 1996). Although the external transfer of knowledge is effectively managed by most HEIs (Kok, 2007; Pinto, 2012), the management of organizational knowledge and the promotion of staff knowledge sharing is largely neglected, with low levels of KM implementation and knowledge sharing evident in these organizations (Fullwood et al., 2013; Ramachandran, Chong, & Ismail, 2009). A lack of KM implementation and

Using Social Networks and Communities of Practice to Promote Staff... 161

knowledge sharing, therefore, has significant negative impacts on the intellectual capital and the overall performance of HEIs, similar to any type of organization, commercial or otherwise (Fullwood et al., 2013; Sohail & Daud, 2009). According to Ramakrishnan and Yasin (2012), speed of curriculum revision and updating, and quality of administrative and support services, are particularly impacted in HEIs.

3 Improving Knowledge Management in HEIs

In searching for ways in which to improve the overall sense of community with a consequential effect of improved staff knowledge sharing, KM must offer some hope, and the use of a number of community-based KM techniques and tools may present new directions for HEIs to explore. Amongst these are Communities of Practice (CoP) and Enterprise Social Networks (ESN), which can be combined to create virtual communities of practice (vCoP). The idea of CoP was first introduced in 1991 by the cognitive anthropologists Jean Lave and Etienne Wenger and describes a group of people who share crafts or professions or areas of common interest, and they can evolve naturally or can be created specifically (Lave & Wenger, 1991). The rigid bureaucratic organizational structures which are prevalent in many HEIs can serve to stifle any sort of real knowledge sharing (Bannister, 2001; Parker & Bradley, 2000), and CoP can be used to circumvent these structures by creating spaces where both academic and other staff with common interests can come together in informal groups and settings to share knowledge. In order for CoP to work efficiently in the modern workplace, it is necessary to introduce some mechanism for online interaction for community members (Hart, 2015), both to capture ideas and allow collaboration in time and space that suits everybody. According to Lewis and Rush (2013), Web 2.0 tools can be applied to enabling vCoP, which would be particularly useful in multi-campus environments. Web 2.0 tools for KM are essentially social media tools such as social networks, blogs, and wikis. Social media are computer-mediated tools that allow people to create, share, or exchange information, ideas, and media in virtual communities and networks (Kaplan & Haenlein, 2010). The application of these technologies within workplaces to facilitate work-related communication and collaboration is referred to as "enterprise social networks" (Richter & Riemer, 2013). Workers can use ESN software to work closely together on group activities and tasks, helping team members to communicate effectively, and it is particularly useful for geographically dispersed groups or organizations. In the context of vCoP, the ESN presents additional benefits, particularly by presenting a convenient and always-on environment for collaboration, and providing a relatively straightforward means for anyone to establish vCoP According to Laal (2011), the use of corporate social media tools has given somewhat of a new impetus to KM, and Levy (2013) maintains that these tools have the capability to refresh KM practices because they have a special collaborative and sharing emphasis and because people will be expecting to find them and use them in organizations.

3.1 Case Study of an ESN Implementation in a HEI

This section profiles an action research project to implement and develop an ESN for staff collaboration and knowledge sharing in a public HEI. The following discussion describes the study context, action research process, data collection and analysis, and findings.

Higher Education Context The study was undertaken as an action research (AR) project, in a public, multi-campus HEI in Ireland with approximately 6500 students and 600 staff, over a 12-month period from September 2015 to August 2016. As the research focused on staff knowledge sharing, the student population was not part of study. AR involves the active participation of the researcher and seeks to bring about change within the organization in which it is conducted. It is an iterative process normally constructed with a longitudinal design to allow time to examine changes as iterations of the research progress (Baum, MacDougall, & Smith, 2006). Furthermore, while AR involves an intervention by a researcher in an organization with the aim of improving the context and gaining relevant knowledge of the intervention, according to Venters (2010), it also assures the active interest of management and has the advantage of enabling access to situations usually unavailable to other research approaches. The practical aspect of the project involved the implementation of ESN tools in the organization, specifically Microsoft's social networking tool called Yammer, and the promotion and support of these to facilitate the establishment of vCoP. Yammer is a social network that is entirely focused on a business. It facilitates group conversation and collaboration and has many similarities to familiar social media tools such as Facebook and Twitter. The project involved the creation of a Communities Portal and the use of ESN to facilitate the establishment and operation of vCoP. The portal acts as a collection point for all of the vCoP in the organization, and allows users to see what communities are active, join communities, or create new ones (Corcoran & Duane, 2018).

Action Research Process The AR project engaged three cycles that followed a process of Diagnosing, Action Planning, Action Taking, Evaluating and Specifying Learning and was adapted from a model developed by Susman and Evered (1978). The first cycle of the AR project involved the technical implementation of the ESN, and this was used to create a number of vCoP. A Yammer feature called Groups directly facilitates the hosting of communities and provides an online environment for file sharing, conversations, etc. The Groups feature makes it a suitable tool to support vCoP and the primary reason that it was selected for the project. During an exploratory process, a number of staff members had expressed an interest in establishing communities, and these became community leaders for a number of vCoP that were setup as Yammer Groups. Communities were trained in the use of Yammer and the principles of CoP, and specialist training for community leaders was also provided. As the user base and resultant activity on Yammer increased, a number of ESN champions were identified. Social network champions are typically individuals who tend to be immediately comfortable with using systems and will have a higher level of engagement than other users. According to Hart (2015), champions are crucial to stimulate the growth of the network and attract more users. These more active users were engaged in order to create a more formal recognition for their role and to empower them to promote the ESN in the organization (Corcoran & Duane, 2018).

Packages of interventions for the second and third cycles of the AR project were based on the evaluations of the interventions carried out in the previous cycles. These cycles focused on growing the user base on the ESN, nurturing the development of the online communities and promoting the establishment of additional vCoP. A number of initiatives to increase the number of Yammer users were developed, including the provision of additional functionality, such as support groups, working groups, department groups, and information feeds. This led to a number of groups being established on the network with different characteristics from the CoP, such as department groups and academic course groups, and other project groups established for particular purposes, such as organizing events and conferences. These types of groups have the advantage of engaging staff who may not be initially interested in community participation, and their inclusion is an important strategy for the long-term viability of the network. Both cycles included awareness campaigns, comprising of mass emails, advertisements on information portals, and digital signage; Webinars; and live training sessions (Corcoran & Duane, 2019).

Data Collection and Analysis The study itself was qualitative in nature, and the primary data collection methods used were focus groups for Cycle 1 and semi-structured interviews for Cycles 2 and 3. Reflective journaling was used extensively throughout the AR cycles in order to capture interpretations of the interventions for each cycle, and also to capture informal conversations, observations, and anything else to do with the project. The content of a number of conversation threads from the ESN was also analysed to determine the depth of engagement of staff with particular communities (Corcoran & Duane, 2018). According to Miles and Huberman (1984), data analysis is based on segmenting the data into parts, and then reassembling the data into a coherent whole. A thematic analysis was performed on the data and this was achieved by largely followed the methods developed by Bryman and Bell (2011), for analysing transcripts. These methods require an extensive reading of all the transcripts together to try and recognize patterns before any coding process begins. The NVivo 11 application was then used to manage the extensive coding process, and was useful for the combination and reduction of codes to produce categories, from which the findings were derived.

Findings All staff have a perception of the existence of a divide between the two major staff groups, academic staff and support staff. However, this view is more strongly held by support staff, indicating a stronger desire in this group to feel a sense of belonging to community and the organization in general. The widely accepted isolating nature of the academic role, coupled with the siloed organization, help to contribute towards a culture that limits opportunities for staff interaction, collaboration and knowledge sharing. The structure of the organization is generally recognized as being a significant impediment to the development of a collaborative workspace, and its size and geographical dispersion were also highlighted as problematic in this regard. The strongest individual barrier to participation is time, with fear and trust issues also presenting as inhibiting factors. Some interviewees attributed their reluctance to use the ESN to a lack of understanding of the nature of social media tools by their managers. This created a fear that management would not understand why a member of staff would want to participate in a community that was not necessarily part of their area of expertise. A number of subjects felt that social media has no application in the workplace and see it as a frivolous activity with no professional characteristics. The concept that certain people see knowledge as a public good and are very willing to openly share knowledge with others, and look for it in return, was fully supported by the findings. The online activity of these individuals has a positive effect on the development of communities. Staff are also motivated to participate in communities if they either find their engagement to be enjoyable, interesting or stimulating, or can derive other benefits from participation, such as making their working lives easier or gaining some rewards in terms of career progression or other forms of recognition. Another strong motivational factor is the opportunity that participation presents for reducing workloads through acquiring knowledge from other community members. This was particularly applicable to newer academic staff when it came to preparing class materials, and the concept of "not having to reinvent the wheel" arose on a number of occasions (Corcoran & Duane, 2017, p. 563).

All of the participants strongly believed that engagement with the communities' model and general participation in the network would be of considerable benefit, both to themselves in their jobs and personal development, and to the wider organization. Much of the commentary was aspirational in nature and indicated a desire for cultural change that may follow on from the existence of an active and vibrant knowledge sharing environment. However, a number of more tangible organizational benefits were also elucidated, including the possibility for vCoP to break down social divides and help to eliminate siloes. A perceived benefit that was strongly held by support staff was the possibility that community participation would help to bridge the divide between them and the academic staff group, consequently reducing the sense of their group isolation and making them feel more a part of the organization. The benefits of having ready access to knowledge through vCoP and ESN participation also drew some commentary. The ESN presents a significant opportunity to improve communications across the organization, providing pathways to reach staff who would not normally meet on a day-to-day basis, and this is a particular benefit for multi-campus HEIs that may have departments and faculties spread across multiple sites (Corcoran & Duane, 2017).

The perceived organizational and individual benefits indicate that the promotion of collaboration and staff knowledge sharing should be a priority for management and reflected in organizational strategy. Management have a central role to play in shaping the knowledge sharing environment by leading change initiatives and promoting the use of vCoP and ESN as KM strategies, and the existence of vCoP, supported by ESN, is essential to build a successful knowledge sharing environment. Furthermore, community leaders and champions are pivotal to the success of vCoP and ESN because they are instrumental in helping the user base to reach a critical mass, where enough users are producing enough content for the network to become self-sustaining.

4 Discussion

This section outlines the potential benefits of CoP and ESN, and a knowledge sharing environment underpinned by ESN and vCoP. These are tied in with the case study findings and developed under a number of themes, including the role of management, the role of champions and leaders, and organizational structure and culture.

Benefits of CoP Much of the CoP literature describes the benefits to the organization if CoP are adopted as a KM technique, and individual benefits derived from participation are also widely discussed. CoP can also deliver different benefits to different types of organization. For example, Lesser and Storck (2001) suggest that they have the potential to overcome many of the inherent problems for slow-moving, hierarchical organizations that have to exist in a fast-moving, virtual economy. They are also an effective way for organizations to share knowledge outside traditional structural boundaries, suggesting that CoP would be a beneficial KM technique for public sector organizations such as HEIs to adopt. However, because communities do not appear on the organizational charts and balance sheets of organizations, they can only be considered as a hidden asset, and this presents a difficulty in determining how exactly they deliver value. This may also present a problem for highly risk-averse organizations, such as public sector bodies, which generally need to be able to quantify a return before making an investment. Rather than attempting to quantify the benefits of a CoP model, a better approach may be for the organization to develop an understanding of how CoP can create value. Lesser and Storck (2001) suggested that thinking of communities as engines for the development of social capital would be helpful, and argued that the development of social capital in CoP leads to behavioural change, resulting in greater knowledge sharing, and this in turn can positively influence organizational performance. Additional studies across different industries have been carried out that appear to validate this suggestion (Cordery et al., 2015; Paasivaara & Lassenius, 2014).

Benefits of ESN Similar to CoP, the benefits of ESN implementation and use for organizations can be difficult to quantify in terms of specific deliverables and direct value. Various consultancy firms make claims such as "effective use of social technologies can result in 20–25% improvement in knowledge worker productivity", which appears in a 2012 McKinsey report (as cited in Mäntymäki & Riemer, 2016, p. 1042). For organizations that are considering the introduction of an ESN, claims of this nature, which are generally neither scientifically nor empirically tested, are not helpful. More beneficially, there is a growing body of research arguing that ESN can bring many and significant benefits to organizations through increased communication and knowledge sharing and increased social capital (Davison, Ou, Martinsons, Zhao, & Du, 2014; Leonardi & Meyer, 2015). Some recent empirical research furthers this by making positive associations between ESN use and employee performance (Riemer, Finke, & Hovorka, 2015), and finding that ESN can help to overcome some of the barriers to organizational knowledge sharing, such as motivation to share knowledge, and developing and maintaining social ties (Fulk & Yuan, 2013).

For HEIs, the use of ESN is seen to have the potential to promote communication amongst staff and encourage interaction across functional areas, and between academic and support staff (Schneckenberg, 2009; Zhao & Kemp, 2013). Corcoran and Duane (2019) proposed that there is an opportunity to use ESN and vCoP as on-boarding tools to support new staff, where participating in relevant online communities would allow them to assimilate into the organization more efficiently and provide a means to tap into the existing organizational knowledge base. Leidner, Koch, and Gonzalez (2010) investigated the use of ESN in this fashion, and found that participation can immediately increase the sense of cultural belonging to the organization, make the environment exciting for entry-level workers, and increase morale amongst a "Generation Y workforce" (p. 229).

Knowledge Sharing Environment For genuine social interaction to take place in online communities, they need to be relevant, purposeful and appealing in order to engender a real desire or need to engage with them. The network also needs to provide an environment that is similar to what people are already used to on the social web, which embodies the underlying open ethos that people enjoy, rather than be a forced environment for conversations. Therefore, the choice of the network tool itself is important, and it must provide an interface and functionality that people expect from a social media platform. The provision of a familiar tool makes the system more attractive to users, and also reduces the need for extensive training. However, it does not reduce the need for training in CoP, which is essential to provide members with a complete understanding of what communities are, how they operate, and to provide a set of guidelines or a framework to work within (Corcoran & Duane, 2018).

Role of Management The attitudes, actions and behaviours of leaders and managers have an important role to play in the context of knowledge sharing in HEIs. In order to promote and cultivate knowledge sharing behaviours amongst staff, management must provide opportunities and manage the processes for staff to share and transfer their knowledge (Bircham-Connolly, Corner, & Bowden, 2005). According to Wang and Noe (2010), the general perception of the existence of a knowledge sharing culture in the organization is enhanced when management is supportive of knowledge sharing. However, such support will only arise if management recognize the benefits of staff collaboration, knowledge sharing, and the use of modern social media platforms for these purposes. Such an understanding can be difficult to develop in the absence of quantifiable, short-term benefits to the organization. Although a certain number of communities may develop within an organization from the bottom-up, for the long-term success of a CoP-based KM model, management support and participation is absolutely necessary. In general, leaders are aware that they should engage with employees, and particularly through social and digital channels, but they tend not to. There are a number of reasons for this including fear that such engagement would result in a weakening of power relations, reducing their ability to control and command. Li (2015) maintains that collaboration depends on trust and leaders must learn how to trust their staff on platforms such as an ESN, although the tools themselves are not as important as managements' understanding of the purpose and nature of the tools. Using platforms such as ESN requires organizational change, and that change generally needs to be led by management. This requires visionary leadership, defined strategic objectives, and a commitment to lead the organization through the necessary change. Fidelman (2012) describes this change as organizations becoming "social businesses", requiring new strategies, which take "time, persuasion, planning, teamwork, and measurable goals" (p. xiv). However, this process may be quite difficult for bureaucratic and hierarchical organizations, of which HEIs are typical examples. This problem may also be exacerbated in HEIs by the requirement for a different set of leadership skills than needed in business, and Spendlove (2007) concluded that HEIs have no organizational strategies for identifying or developing leadership skills. However, if the value of greater staff collaboration and knowledge sharing can be recognized, a vision for how to develop it, and the expected outcomes, can be provided. The development of a community management plan to support the vision, specifying the people, processes, resources, and technology required, should follow. Lastly, the execution of the plan requires the identification of leaders and champions who will help to promote the vision and the changes associated with it (Corcoran & Duane, 2019).

Leaders and Champions According to Borzillo, Aznar, and Schmitt (2011), community leaders are specific people within a community who undertake organizing roles with the objective of developing and sustaining the community. They are typically the founders of particular communities and are invariably the driving force behind them. The vitality of CoP is very dependent on the interest and commitment of their leaders, and communities that do not have dedicated leaders are bound to fail (Corcoran & Duane, 2018). Another important role in vCoP is that of champions, a role that is increasingly recognized as being central to the growth of an ESN in an organization (Chin, Evans, & Choo, 2015; Oostervink, Agterberg, & Huysman, 2016). During the early growth phase of an ESN, the conversations tend to be dominated by a number of individuals who use the technology freely and enthusiastically, and are generally comfortable with using social media, consistent with Rogers' (1995) diffusion of innovations theory. The identification of these individuals is central to opening up the ESN to everyone in the organization as they, in conjunction with community leaders, keep conversations and activity within communities at levels that are necessary to attract other users and reach a critical mass for sustainability, where enough users are producing enough content for the network to become self-sustaining. According to Geddes (2011), the level of users required for the success of technological adoption and social networks is generally accepted to be 15% of the total population.

Organizational Culture The willingness and motivation of staff to share knowledge and participate in ESN and vCoP is influenced by a number of factors, almost all of which are inexorably linked to the culture of the organization. The majority of public HEIs exhibit strong, hierarchical organizational cultures, which are driven by rigid and bureaucratic organizational structures, largely mandated by national policy. This is in turn is influenced by additional factors over time such as the attitudes and actions of management and the organizational strategy. For example, it is widely recognized in HEIs, and indeed in the wider public sector, that organizational structures encourage the creation of silos and lead to staff isolation (Bannister, 2001; Tippins, 2003). Organizations that can create an open and transparent culture help to make employees feel empowered and have a voice, making them feel more connected and loyal to the organization (Lok & Crawford, 2004; Trice & Beyer, 1993).

Management has an important role to play in helping to change the culture through developing and implementing organizational strategies that stimulate staff collaboration and knowledge sharing. However, a number of authors argue that managing cultural change is difficult and that a natural change of culture is more likely, taking place through the socialization of new staff over time (Ogbonna & Harris, 1998; Pascale, 1985; Sathe, 1983). Sathe (1983) developed a conceptual model of how an organizational culture perpetuates itself, and argued that attempts at culture change should focus on the means of perpetuation such as communications. Indeed, the development of a common understanding of the organization's mission and goals can be achieved by the creation of a robust social, communications and collaboration framework. It is also possible for culture change to be led through a bottom-up approach, where pockets of excellence and influence can have a significant impact on the overall behaviour of the organization, through individuals described by Pascale and Sternin (2005) as "positive deviants" (p. 72), and these can be likened to the roles of community leaders and ESN champions.

Although most staff are motivated to participate in a knowledge sharing environment and recognize both the individual and organizational benefits of doing so, in many cases they are either unable or unwilling to break free of the boundaries that the organizational culture places around them. In the context of HEIs, this is exacerbated by the existence of a divide between academic and other staff in the organization. In some cases, staff will share knowledge freely if a convenient and meaningful environment is available, and they are suitably motivated. The presence of vCoP in this environment is important as a motivator for participation as these can help to break down the structural and cultural boundaries that inhibit knowledge sharing. vCoP must be relevant, purposeful and appealing for staff to participate in them. Although CoP can and do emerge from the bottom-up, their growth is helped by a positive approach from management that fosters a sustaining environment where they can flourish. The ESN presents additional benefits, particularly by presenting a convenient and always-on environment for collaboration, and providing a relatively straightforward means for anyone to establish vCoP.

5 Strategies for Practice

If ESN and vCoP are to be successfully used by HEIs as part of a KM implementation, a number of high-level, strategic objectives will first have to be negotiated and addressed in these organizations.

1. Because a hierarchical organizational culture is a barrier to staff interaction, collaboration and knowledge sharing, organizations require a developed understanding of their culture to inform meaningful and achievable strategic vision and

Using Social Networks and Communities of Practice to Promote Staff... 169

goals in order to change it. Organizations should consider the use of specific models and frameworks to develop this understanding.

2. This culture is prevalent in the majority of public sector HEIs and is largely contributed to by state-mandated organizational structures. Tackling this problem with a view towards implementing alternative organizational structures requires sectoral understanding of the problem and willingness at national level to influence change.
3. The divide between academic and support staff in HEIs further limits the opportunities for staff to collaborate and share knowledge. The existence of this divide must first be recognized and understood by management if it is to be dealt with.
4. Management support is pivotal to the success of KM initiatives, and management must understand their role in KM initiatives from facilitation to participation.
5. Knowledge sharing environments, underpinned by ESN and vCoP, must be adequately designed, resourced and supported. To achieve this, the selection of an ESN platform must be given due consideration. vCoP terms of reference and generic blueprints should be established, and these should be bolstered by structured training.
6. For ESN and vCoP to become established, the roles of community leaders and social media champions are very important. Individuals in the organization, who exhibit the traits of these roles, should be identified, encouraged, and incentivized to participate.
7. The establishment of ESN and vCoP provides opportunities for mentoring and supporting new staff, and these should be examined by Human Resources departments that are interested in the efficient assimilation of new staff into the organization. As many of these staff are likely to be regular social media users, it would also reinforce the resultant practices as part of an everyday work routine, and increase the ESN user base rapidly.
8. The terminology used to describe work-based social media tools can be problematic and inhibit many staff from using them. Those implementing ESN should be cognisant of this and apply community-based terminology instead of social, which can carry connotations of frivolity and is seen by many as having no place in professional work settings.

Once established, a knowledge sharing environment based on ESN and vCoP must be carefully nurtured and managed, not only if it is going to develop, but if it is to survive at all. Many organizations are now developing new roles to help with this, such as an Enterprise Community Manager. These roles have the overall responsibility within the organization for the development and management of the knowledge sharing environment, through providing support for staff who want to participate, creating general awareness, and identifying staff who see knowledge as a public good with a view towards making them ESN ambassadors, as some of their functions. There are also a number of specific, tactical things that organizations can do in order to manage a developing knowledge sharing environment.

1. A communities' model need not be limited to CoP and can be expanded to include communities of interest, communities of place, such as campus communities in multi-campus HEIs, and external communities.

2. Case studies of successful CoP within organizations should be developed in order to learn from their success and to promote the CoP model.
3. Metrics should be established to measure the health and success of communities.
4. Best practice guides for ESN users should be developed to help establish its use as part of daily work routines.
5. Strategies can be devised to increase participation rates in CoP by moving members along the membership life cycle as per Lave and Wenger (1991).
6. The use of ESN as a teaching and learning tool should be promoted, not alone in its usefulness in that regard, but also with a view towards engaging more academic staff with the platform.

6   Conclusion and Future Directions

The main limitations associated with studies in the field of social media implementation and usage, and indeed with the use of KM tools and techniques in general, are related to the time available to carry out the research. The concept of ESN in organizations is relatively new and particularly so in HEIs, who are rarely to the fore in the implementation of information systems for either their teaching or corporate practices, and, according to Leidner and Jarvenpaa (1995), academic institutions typically lag behind businesses by about 10 years in the adoption of new technologies. According to Holtzblatt, Drury, Weiss, Damianos, and Cuomo (2013, p. 1), the adoption of social software in organizations can be very slow, with user interaction, changes to work practices, and, most importantly, the impact on business outcomes, all taking time to emerge. In order for these "long-tail effects" to be realized, social communities must reach a critical mass, and the impacts are only seen in large populations over long periods of time. The problem is further exacerbated in the higher education context by the nature of the academic year, during which there are significant periods when academic staff are largely absent from campus, including a three-to-four-week period in December/January and an eight to twelve-week period from June to August (Corcoran & Duane, 2018). Longer term studies, conducted over a number of academic years, would overcome this limitation and allow for the introduction of more quantitative measures, informing mixed-method approaches to provide greater understanding of the implications of achieving strategic goals for knowledge sharing, both in terms of the derived benefits to both the organization and individuals, and also for the culture of the organization. Comparable studies on the use of CoP in different industries have been carried out and would provide useful comparators for similar studies in HEIs (e.g. Cordery et al., 2015; Paasivaara & Lassenius, 2014).

The existence of a divide between faculty and other staff is not perceived equally by the two groups, and further study is required to examine why this is the case. Much of the research to date into this phenomenon has been from a staff perspective (e.g. Conway & Dobson, 2003; Szekeres, 2004), and a different approach giving equal credence to both perspectives might yield more balanced results. The role of management support for the success of ESN and CoP initiatives is perceived differently by the management group and staff in the wider organization, with staff perceiving management's role as of far greater importance than management do themselves, and this unequal perception warrants further investigation. The importance of the role of transformational leaders in HEIs and their impact on organizational culture change has been investigated in certain jurisdictions (e.g. Basham, 2012; Bryman, 2007). Further studies in the contexts of ESN implementations and the use of CoP would extend the body of knowledge on organizational culture in HEIs.

In summary, organizational culture and structure are major barriers to staff knowledge sharing in HEIs and this is exacerbated by the existence of a divide between academic and other staff. Management have a significant role to play in shaping a knowledge sharing environment, underpinned by modern social media tools, such as ESN, and this can only be achieved through transformational leadership that recognizes the existence of the postulated problems in the first instance, and then sets about changing the organizational culture to one where staff will openly and willingly share knowledge and collaborate with each other. The existence of vCoP is essential to build an active knowledge sharing environment, and community leaders and champions are pivotal to the success of vCoP and the ESN. In addition, staff must be suitably motivated to participate in the knowledge sharing environment, and this will only happen with a change to a transformational culture within the organization.

References

Aldridge, S., & Rowley, J. (2001). Conducting a withdrawal survey. *Quality in Higher Education, 7* (1), 55–63.

Bannister, F. (2001). Dismantling the silos: extracting new value from IT investments in public administration. *Information Systems Journal, 11*(1), 65–84.

Basham, L. M. (2012). Transformational leadership characteristics necessary for today's leaders in higher education. *Journal of International Education Research, 8*(4), 343.

Bassnett, S. (2005). The importance of professional university administration: A perspective from a senior university manager. *Perspectives, 9*(4), 98–102.

Baum, F., MacDougall, C., & Smith, D. (2006). Participatory action research. *Journal of Epidemiology and Community Health, 60*(10), 854–857.

Bircham-Connolly, H., Corner, J., & Bowden, S. (2005). An empirical study of the impact of question structure on recipient attitude during knowledge sharing. *Electronic Journal of Knowledge Management, 32*(1), 1–10.

Borzillo, S., Aznar, S., & Schmitt, A. (2011). A journey through communities of practice: How and why members move from the periphery to the core. *European Management Journal, 29*(1), 25–42.

Bryman, A. (2007). Effective leadership in higher education: A literature review. *Studies in Higher Education, 32*(6), 693–710.

Bryman, A., & Bell, E. (2011). *Business research methods* (3rd ed.). Oxford: Oxford University Press.

Castleman, T., & Allen, M. (1995). The forgotten workforce: Female general staff in higher education. *Australian Universities' Review, 38*(2), 65–69.

Chin, C. P.-Y., Evans, N., & Choo, K.-K. R. (2015). Exploring factors influencing the use of enterprise social networks in multinational professional service firms. *Journal of Organizational Computing Electronic Commerce, 25*(3), 289–315.

Conway, M. (2012). Using causal layered analysis to explore the relationship between academics and administrators in universities. *Journal of Futures Studies, 17*(2), 37–58.

Conway, M., & Dobson, I. (2003). Fear and loathing in university staffing. *Higher Education Management Policy, 15*(3), 123–133.

Corcoran, N., & Duane, A. (2017). Using enterprise social networks as a knowledge management tool in higher education. *VINE Journal of Information and Knowledge Management Systems, 47* (4), 555–570.

Corcoran, N., & Duane, A. (2018). Using social media to enable staff knowledge sharing in higher education institutions. *Australasian Journal of Information Systems, 22*, 1–26.

Corcoran, N., & Duane, A. (2019). Organizational knowledge sharing and enterprise social networks: A higher education context. In *Educational and social dimensions of digital transformation in organizations* (pp. 78–114). Hershey, PA: IGI Global.

Cordery, J. L., Cripps, E., Gibson, C. B., Soo, C., Kirkman, B. L., & Mathieu, J. E. (2015). The operational impact of organizational communities of practice: A Bayesian approach to analyzing organizational change. *Journal of Management, 41*(2), 644–664.

Davison, R. M., Ou, C. X., Martinsons, M. G., Zhao, A. Y., & Du, R. (2014). The communicative ecology of Web 2.0 at work: Social networking in the workspace. *Journal of the Association for Information Science Technology, 65*(10), 2035–2047.

Dobson, I. R. (2011). How the other half lives: university general staff today and tomorrow. *Campus Review, 2012*(3), 1–7.

Fidelman, M. (2012). *Socialized!: How the most successful businesses harness the power of social.* Brookline, MA, USA: Bibliomotion.

Fulk, J., & Yuan, Y. C. (2013). Location, motivation, and social capitalization via enterprise social networking. *Journal of Computer-Mediated Communication, 19*(1), 20–37.

Fullwood, R., Rowley, J., & Delbridge, R. (2013). Knowledge sharing amongst academics in UK universities. *Journal of Knowledge Management, 17*(1), 123–136.

Geddes, C. (2011). Achieving critical mass in social networks. *Journal of Database Marketing & Customer Strategy Management, 18*(2), 123–128.

Gupta, A. K., & Govindarajan, V. (2000). Knowledge management's social dimension: Lessons from Nucor Steel. *MIT Sloan Management Review, 42*(1), 71.

Hart, J. (2015). *Modern workplace learning: A resource book for L&D.* Self-published: Centre for Learning & Performance Technologies.

Holtzblatt, L., Drury, J. L., Weiss, D., Damianos, L. E., & Cuomo, D. (2013). Evaluating the uses and benefits of an enterprise social media platform. *Journal of Social Media for Organizations, 1*(1), 1.

James, R. (2000). Quality assurance and the growing puzzle of managing organisational knowledge in universities. *Journal of the Programme on Institutional Management in Higher Education, 12* (3), 41–59.

Kaplan, A. M., & Haenlein, M. (2010). Users of the world, unite! The challenges and opportunities of social media. *Business Horizons, 53*(1), 59–68.

Kidwell, J. J., Vander Linde, K. M., & Johnson, S. L. (2000). Knowledge management practices applying corporate in higher education. *Educause Quarterly, 4*, 28–33.

Kok, A. (2007). Intellectual capital management as part of knowledge management initiatives at institutions of higher learning. *The Electronic Journal of Knowledge Management, 5*(2), 181–192.

Kuo, H. M. (2009). Understanding relationships between academic staff and administrators: An organisational culture perspective. *Journal of Higher Education Policy and Management, 31*(1), 43–54.

Laal, M. (2011). Knowledge management in higher education. *Procedia computer science, 3*, 544–549.

Lave, J., & Wenger, E. (1991). *Situated learning: Legitimate peripheral participation*. Cambridge: Cambridge University Press.

Leidner, D., & Jarvenpaa, S. L. (1995). The use of information technology to enhance management school education: A theoretical view. *MIS Quarterly, 19*(3), 265–291.

Leidner, D., Koch, H., & Gonzalez, E. (2010). Assimilating generation Y IT new hires into USAA's workforce: The role of an enterprise 2.0 system. *MIS Quarterly Executive, 9*(4), 229–242.

Leonardi, P. M., & Meyer, S. R. (2015). Social media as social lubricant: How ambient awareness eases knowledge transfer. *American Behavioral Scientist, 59*(1), 10–34.

Lesser, E. L., & Storck, J. (2001). Communities of practice and organizational performance. *IBM Systems Journal, 40*(4), 831–841.

Levy, M. (2013). Stairways to heaven: implementing social media in organizations. *Journal of Knowledge Management, 17*(5), 741–754.

Lewis, B., & Rush, D. (2013). Experience of developing Twitter-based communities of practice in higher education. *Research in Learning Technology, 21*(1), 1–13.

Li, C. (2015). *The engaged leader: A strategy for your digital transformation*. Philadelphia, PA: Wharton Digital Press.

Lok, P., & Crawford, J. (2004). The effect of organisational culture and leadership style on job satisfaction and organisational commitment: A cross-national comparison. *Journal of Management Development, 23*(4), 321–338.

Malik, M., Danish, R., & Usman, A. (2010). The impact of service quality on students' satisfaction in higher education Institutes of Punjab. *Journal of Management Research, 2*(2), 1–11.

Mäntymäki, M., & Riemer, K. (2016). Enterprise social networking: A knowledge management perspective. *International Journal of Information Management, 36*(6), 1042–1052.

Miles, M. B., & Huberman, A. M. (1984). Drawing valid meaning from qualitative data: Toward a shared craft. *Educational Researcher, 13*(5), 20–30.

Nonaka, I., & Von Krogh, G. (2009). Perspective—Tacit knowledge and knowledge conversion: Controversy and advancement in organizational knowledge creation theory. *Organization Science, 20*(3), 635–652.

Nunes, M. B., Annansingh, F., Eaglestone, B., & Wakefield, R. (2006). Knowledge management issues in knowledge-intensive SMEs. *Journal of Documentation, 62*(1), 101–119.

Ogbonna, E., & Harris, L. C. (1998). Managing organizational culture: Compliance or genuine change? *British Journal of Management, 9*(4), 273–288.

Olivera, F. (2000). Memory systems in organizations: An empirical investigation of mechanisms for knowledge collection, storage and access. *Journal of Management Studies, 37*(6), 811–832.

Oostervink, N., Agterberg, M., & Huysman, M. (2016). Knowledge sharing on enterprise social media: Practices to cope with institutional complexity. *Journal of Computer-Mediated Communication, 21*(2), 156–176.

Paasivaara, M., & Lassenius, C. (2014). Communities of practice in a large distributed agile software development organization–Case Ericsson. *Information Software Technology, 56*(12), 1556–1577.

Palmer, P. J. (2002). Foreword. In W. M. McDonald (Ed.), *Creating campus community: In search of Ernest Boyer's legacy* (pp. ix–xv). San Francisco: Jossey-Bass.

Parker, R., & Bradley, L. (2000). Organisational culture in the public sector: Evidence from six organisations. *International Journal of Public Sector Management, 13*(2), 125–141.

Pascale, R. (1985). The paradox of "corporate culture": Reconciling ourselves to socialization. *California Management Review, 27*(2), 26–41.

Pascale, R., & Sternin, J. (2005). Your company's secret change agents. *Harvard Business Review, 83*(5), 72–81.

Petrash, G. (1996). Dow's journey to a knowledge value management culture. *European Management Journal, 14*(4), 365–373.

Pinto, M. (2012). *A framework for knowledge managemt systems implementation in higher education.* Paper presented at the Proceedings in ARSA-Advanced Research in Scientific Areas, Virtual.

Ramachandran, S. D., Chong, S. C., & Ismail, H. (2009). The practice of knowledge management processes: A comparative study of public and private higher education institutions in Malaysia. *The Journal of Information and Knowledge Management Systems, 39*(3), 203–222.

Ramakrishnan, K., & Yasin, N. M. (2012). Knowledge management system and higher education institutions. *International Proceedings of Computer Science and Information Technology, 37* (1), 67–71.

Richter, A., & Riemer, K. (2013). *The contextual nature of enterprise social networking: A multi case study comparison.* Paper presented at the ECIS Completed Research.

Riemer, K., Finke, J., & Hovorka, D. (2015). *Bridging or bonding: Do individuals gain social capital from participation in enterprise social networks?* Paper presented at the Thirty Sixth International Conference on Information Systems, Fort Worth, Texas, USA.

Rogers, E. M. (1995). *Diffusion of innovations* (4th ed.). New York: The Free Press.

Santo, S. A. (2005). Knowledge management: An imperative for schools of education. *TechTrends, 49*(6), 42–49.

Sathe, V. (1983). Implications of corporate culture: A manager's guide to action. *Organizational Dynamics, 12*(2), 5–23.

Schneckenberg, D. (2009). Web 2.0 and the empowerment of the knowledge worker. *Journal of Knowledge Management, 13*(6), 509–520. https://doi.org/10.1108/13673270910997150.

Shoham, S., & Perry, M. (2009). Knowledge management as a mechanism for technological and organizational change management in Israeli universities. *Higher Education, 57*(2), 227–246.

Sohail, M. S., & Daud, S. (2009). Knowledge sharing in higher education institutions: Perspectives from Malaysia. *Vine, 39*(2), 125–142.

Spendlove, M. (2007). Competencies for effective leadership in higher education. *International Journal of Educational Management, 21*(5), 407–417.

Susman, G. I., & Evered, R. D. (1978). An assessment of the scientific merits of action research. *Administrative Science Quarterly, 23*(4), 582–603.

Szekeres, J. (2004). The invisible workers. *Journal of Higher Education Policy and Management, 26*(1), 7–22.

Szekeres, J. (2011). Professional staff carve out a new space. *Journal of Higher Education Policy Management, 33*(6), 679–691.

Taub, D. J. (1998). Building community on campus: Student affairs professionals as group workers. *Journal for Specialists in Group Work, 23*(4), 411–427.

Tippins, M. J. (2003). Implementing knowledge management in academia: Teaching the teachers. *International Journal of Educational Management, 17*(7), 339–345.

Trice, H. M., & Beyer, J. M. (1993). *The cultures of work organizations.* Englewood Cliffs, NJ, USA: Prentice-Hall.

Venters, W. (2010). Knowledge management technology-in-practice: A social constructionist analysis of the introduction and use of knowledge management systems. *Knowledge Management Research & Practice, 8*(2), 161–172.

Wang, S., & Noe, R. A. (2010). Knowledge sharing: A review and directions for future research. *Human Resource Management Review, 20*(2), 115–131.

Zhao, F., & Kemp, L. (2013). Exploring individual, social and organisational effects on Web 2.0-based workplace learning: A research agenda for a systematic approach. *Research in Learning Technology, 21*(1), 1–15.

Knowledge Management for Adult and Higher Education: Mapping the Recent Literature

Ettore Bolisani

Abstract The recent literature shows that the field of knowledge management (KM) has a potential importance for the education area. It has been argued that KM concepts, models, and practices may be beneficial to teachers, learners, and university managers. An open issue, however, is whether and how the research and practice in these two distinct fields—education and KM—are really converging. This chapter proposes a systematic analysis of the literature to shed light onto the intersection between the fields of KM and adult and higher education. The main research trends are detected and highlighted. The analysis shows that there are promising applications of KM to higher education and university management. However, there is still the need to carry out more theoretical or applicative research with the purpose to facilitate the effective incorporation of KM notions, concepts, or practices into the education field.

1 Introduction

Knowledge management (KM) holds importance for education. Schools and universities, being knowledge-intensive organizations (Schaller, Allert, & Richter, 2008), are natural candidates of KM applications. Indeed, it is recognized that education is not simply a process of "transferring knowledge" from teachers to learners: therefore, KM models and tools can help to implement new active teaching/learning practices more effectively. Also, in all job environments, "collective learning processes" are needed, where people interact in working groups and take decisions with others. Again, KM can help to understand the mechanisms and technologies that can support these processes. What is more, instructors are not single professionals that "work alone" in their classroom: they have to plan teaching strategies collectively, to integrate elements of knowledge that come from different disciplines, and to share their teaching experience with colleagues. Finally,

E. Bolisani (✉)
University of Padova, Padova, PD, Italy
e-mail: ettore.bolisani@unipd.it

© Springer Nature Switzerland AG 2019
M. Fedeli, L. L. Bierema (eds.), *Connecting Adult Learning and Knowledge Management*, Knowledge Management and Organizational Learning 8,
https://doi.org/10.1007/978-3-030-29872-2_10

universities are complex contexts that require modern and effective management solutions. Since knowledge is the "main input and output" of these organization, KM processes and measurement methods can help to manage higher education institutions and help to assess the "quality" of knowledge production and delivery.

In summary, the KM field can provide insights into the way higher educational processes can be improved. Although KM is a relatively young branch of organizational management, the literature already provides a rich set of concepts, interpretative models, and technical and organizational solutions, for understanding and solving the many issues implied by the management of knowledge. However, an open point is whether and how the research and practice in these two distinct fields—education and KM—are really converging.

The aim of this chapter is to shed light into the intersection between the literatures on KM and Adult education. It proposes a systematic analysis and a mapping of the recent studies, by examining the main scientific journals in the two research areas of Education and KM/IC (Knowledge Management and Intellectual Capital). The main trends in research and practice are detected and highlighted. A brief qualitative analysis of papers is also carried out, to provide reflections into the potential of KM for education, the hot topics, and the key research or practical issues that remain open.

The analysis shows that there are some topics of KM/IC that are increasingly considered important for education research and practice. For example, the notion of community of practice, which is a key topic in KM, is also of particular importance in the recent literature that treats higher or adult education; conversely, it must be noticed that other KM/IC concepts or models are substantially neglected in the education field. Similarly, the application of KM/IC approaches in education generally focuses on specific areas (for instance, KM is often applied to university management, to help knowledge sharing among instructors, or to examine the effective use of technologies in education); but some other key issues (e.g., modeling learning processes) are substantially underexamined. Therefore the convergence between the fields of KM/IC and education appears to be still immature.

2 Basic Terminology and Reference

The purpose of this section is to present the basic concepts of KM, intellectual capital, and related terms that are pertinent to this study. Also, by introducing some essential references to the literature, it is shown that the connection of the KM field with adult and higher education has a potentially high importance for both the scientific areas.

KM essentially means "managing the relationship between knowing and acting in organizational context" (Spender, 2015; p. 3) and, in itself, is not a novelty in the human history. As Spender (2015) argues, wherever there was an organization there was some KM activity, because any human activity implies the necessity of approaches to managing knowing, learning, storing, retrieving, and communicating knowledge in some form with the purpose of pursuing the organization's ends. However, it is in recent times that KM has gained its place in the management literature, as a consequence of three main trends of our societies (Prusak, 2001): globalization (which implies an opportunity and a necessity to scouting or exchanging knowledge wherever it can be found), availability of ubiquitous computing devices and methods (which enable an efficient and effective processing of big amounts of data, seen as the basic element of knowledge), and a knowledge-centric view of organizations (i.e., organizations are seen as structures where knowledge is the core ingredient of activities and processes). What is substantially new with KM is that knowledge is seen as a specific "resource" (Drucker, 2008); therefore, it requires a special management approach.

There is no universally accepted definition of KM (Dalkir, 2013; Girard & Girard, 2015): roughly speaking, KM is intended as a "branch" of management that aims to define and apply methods, tools, processes, technologies, and organizational settings for supporting the creation, sharing, memorization, delivery, etc., of knowledge in an organization. KM has been developing around practical definitions of knowledge like, e.g., that of Davenport and Prusak (1998): knowledge is, substantially, information that is useful to take decisions and actions. Researchers have also worked intensely to classify the basic kinds of knowledge in human activities (like for example the famous distinction between tacit and explicit knowledge that stems from Polanyi's, 1966 works). There is also a flourishing literature about KM processes, organizational settings, technological solutions, and strategic approaches (Edwards, 2015). The promoters of KM have initially proposed its application to the business context. Later, it has been extended to services (Hallin & Marnburg, 2008; Sarvary, 1999), public administration (Wiig, 2002), and, as is also highlighted below, education (Jones & Sallis, 2013).

As regards Intellectual Capital (IC), the origins of this field of research (Stewart, 1997) can be traced back to the 1980s and 1990s in economics and management: there was increasing awareness that companies are worth much more than those "physical or financial assets" that can be easily recorded in the financial statements and balance sheets. So, many economists started considering the necessity of developing concepts, methods, and approaches to identifying, measuring, and managing these "hidden resources" which are essential to any organization. The term "Intellectual Capital" itself refers to that particular category of business assets that are important for value production but, by nature, are intangible and mostly associated to the knowledge of people (e.g., their know-how) or are embedded in artifacts and procedures. The literature on IC has often focused on its nature, characteristics, and components (Bontis, 1998), on the modalities of economic assessment (Dumay, 2009), and on its integration into the classic economic reports (Roos, Edvinsson, & Dragonetti, 1997).

Although the KM and IC fields have initially developed independently from one another, the points of contact and overlapping are several and, in this study, the two fields will be considered together. In addition, we will consider the area of study of the learning organization, which centers on the modalities, structures, and processes that facilitate the learning of people in an organization and its consequent changes (Senge, 1991). Again, this field has a different origin from the KM/IC literature, but they have so many connections that they can be jointly considered.

In this chapter, the focus is on the actual and potential relevance of KM/IC studies to education and, specifically, adult and higher education. As mentioned, KM practices may be beneficial to supporting faculty, instructors, and lecturers in their complex work. Indeed, a classical view of teaching and learning, mostly based on a process of pure transmission of knowledge from a "teacher" to a "learner" (as a passive receiver), has been increasingly questioned. Especially considering the case of adult education (which is the central topic of this chapter), it is now recognized that learning is a multifaceted process that involves many capabilities, requires active participation and contribution by learners, and it is also based on individual and social experience of "what is being learned" (Merriam & Bierema, 2013). Also, new types of jobs appear every day, with new knowledge requests: therefore, especially (but not only) at an adult education level, the challenge is how to switch the focus on learners from purely passive "acquirers" to active "creators" of their personal knowledge. In addition, in our complex societies, very rarely a person has "all the knowledge that is required" to face a situation: improved organizational and interactive skills are needed to activate "collective learning processes," where people work together, develop shared communication languages, and make decisions with others.

For specular reasons, the "job of education" implies complex KM processes (Ratcliffe-Martin, Coakes, & Sugden, 2000; Stevenson, 2000): the role of an instructor is that of helping learners to receive and process knowledge contents, to activate autonomous "learning processes," and to build their own knowledge base that will be helpful in their professional career or life. Indeed, teaching is a complex activity that, to be effective, may need a combination of different perspectives and attitudes (Pratt, 2002). Furthermore, successful educational processes require that instructors be able to plan teaching strategies collectively, integrate elements of knowledge that come from different disciplines, share their teaching experience with colleagues, and "actively learn" themselves in a continuous improvement process. The creation of professional "communities of practice" (Bolisani & Scarso, 2014) of teachers is increasingly considered in schools and universities (Lieberman & Miller, 2008): teachers interact and assist each other in their daily problems, improve collective learning, facilitate consistent teaching methods across various subjects, which, in turn, can favor a positive learning experience by students. Finally, KM can be useful for management purposes (Jones & Sallis, 2013): universities are a place where knowledge is the "main input and output," and their effectiveness should be evaluated taking into consideration the "quality" of knowledge produced and delivered.

All this explains why the KM/IC field can provide essential insights into the way the effectiveness of educational processes can be improved. The point is whether and how these two areas of research and practice are connected.

3   A Systematic Review of KM/IC and Higher Education Literature: Methodology

This study proposes an analysis of the literature that consists of an integration of a "scoping" and "mapping" approach (Grant & Booth, 2009). A mapping review is a process of categorization of existing literature to perform further reviews and/or to carry

Knowledge Management for Adult and Higher Education: Mapping the Recent... 179

out primary research on a topic, identify gaps, and other pertinent information. Scoping is a preliminary assessment of potential size and scope of available literature, to identify nature and extension of the current research. It is based on both a quantitative analysis of papers and a (fast) assessment of their content. Finally, mapping can result in graphic or tabular representations of quantitative or qualitative features of the selected studies.

These methods were used to derive pertinent data for assessing the importance that the scholars ascribe to the KM/IC models for the study of education approaches, and for implementing organizational changes in the delivery of innovative educational services. As mentioned, the main focus is on higher education, especially in the context of universities, colleges, and academic institutions.

Specifically, the analysis had the goals of:

- Examining literature trends (i.e. number of papers and time distribution) and significance of the published papers (by considering citational indexes)
- Classifying the retrieved papers, based on some specific criteria that will be described below
- Mapping topics and research directions, by examining the "keywords," with which papers have been tagged

3.1 Steps of the Literature Review

As mentioned, the method is a combination of a quantitative survey of retrieved papers (e.g., by counting number of publications, citations, keywords) and an essential qualitative assessment of the contents, to better detect pertinence, research topics, and orientation of each surveyed study. The procedural steps that were used are described as follows (Fig. 1).

(a) *Relevant journals.* The analysis was limited to the papers included in the SCOPUS database in the last 10 years (2009–2018—last date considered: 5 November 2018). Two distinct groups of journals were scanned: (1) Education. The journals were selected from the Scopus SJR (Scientific Journal Ranking), based on two criteria: the first 6 journals appearing in the Scopus list of the subject category "Education," provided that they have sufficient pertinence to "higher education," and the subsequent 6 journals in the list that had specifically "higher education" in the title or keywords; (2) KM/IC. The ranking list of KM/IC journals reported in Serenko and Bontis (2013) was used (particularly, the list of Table VII, p. 317): only journals indexed in Scopus were considered (Tables 1 and 2).

(b) *Keywords.* The internal search engine of the Scopus service was used. Specific keywords were researched in the field "Article title abstract or keywords." Keywords were chosen to keep the research range as widest as possible (so that the risk of omitting pertinent papers was limited) but avoiding an excessive number of articles. After some tests the following keywords were used: for Education papers, "KM" and/or "knowledge management"; for KM/IC papers, "higher education."

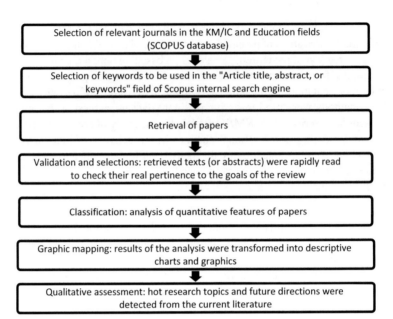

Fig. 1 Steps of literature review

Table 1 Education journals

Journal title	Indexed in Scopus from	Citational index SJR	Position in the SJR list	No. of retrieved papers	No. of selected papers
Review of Educational Research	(1931)	3.719	2	0	0
Educational Researcher	(1972)	3.473	3	0	0
Learning and Instruction	(1991)	3.432	4	0	0
Internet and Higher Education	(1998)	3.347	5	6	5
Sociology of Education	(1996)	3.203	6	0	0
Educational Research Review	(2006)	2.963	12	1	0
Higher Education	(1972)	1.782	43	3	3
Research in Higher Education	(1973)	1.702	45	0	0
Review of Higher Education	(1996)	1.601	53	0	0
Studies in Higher Education	(1976)	1.513	61	0	0
Higher Education Research and Development	(2008)	1.416	69	1	0
Active Learning in Higher Education	(2000)	1.397	70	0	0

Knowledge Management for Adult and Higher Education: Mapping the Recent... 181

Table 2 KM/IC journals

Journal title	Indexed in Scopus from	Citation index SJR	Position in Serenko and Bontis (2013) list	No. of retrieved papers	No. of selected papers
Journal of Knowledge Management	(1997)	0.922	1	8	5
Journal of Intellectual Capital	(2000)	0.701	2	15	11
Learning Organization	(1994)	0.345	3	21	9
Knowledge Management Research and Practice	(2006)	0.445	4	4	1
Knowledge and Process Management	(1997)	0.328	5	0	0
Int. Journal of Knowledge Management	(2005)	0.261	6	7	3
Journal of Information and Knowledge Management	(2002)	0.19	7	8	5
International Journal of Learning and Intellectual Capital	(2004)	0.228	9	3	1
International Journal of Knowledge and Learning	(2005)[a]	0.103	10	11	10
VINE[b]	(1971)	0.32	11	9	6
International Journal of Knowledge Management Studies	(2006)[a]	0.111	12	2	1
Intangible capital	(2009)	0.164	21	22	7

[a]With the exception of year 2013
[b]From 2016 VINE—Journal of Information and Knowledge Management Systems

(c) *Retrieval.* In total, 120 papers were initially collected (10 in the Education journals, 110 in the KM/IC journals—see Tables 1 and 2).

(d) *Validation and selection.* Abstracts and (when necessary) papers were checked, to verify pertinence of contents: only papers that were related to the application of KM/IC concepts and methods to higher education were considered for further analysis. In the end, 8 "Education" papers and 59 "KM/IC" papers were included.

(e) *Classification.* To carry out a mapping of the existing literature, some basic classifications of papers were made (see Sect. 4). In addition, an analysis of keywords was performed, in order to detect the mainstream topics.

(f) *Graphic mapping.* To facilitate an assessment "at a glance," results were also transformed into descriptive charts and graphics.

(g) *Qualitative assessment.* Research topics and future directions were also analyzed by reading the relevant papers in detail.

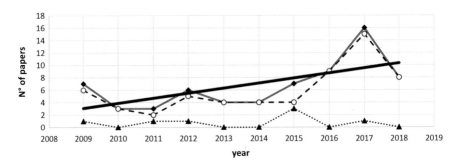

Fig. 2 Quantitative analysis of trends (dotted line: Education journals; dashed line: KM/IC journals; double line: total; thick continuous line: linear regression of total)

Table 3 Citational measurement

	Education journals	KM/IC journals	Total
Average yearly citations per retrieved paper	3.72	1.88	2.07
Relative yearly citations[a]	2.47	4.08	3.89

[a]Calculated as ratio between "average yearly citations per retrieved paper" and "average yearly citations per paper of that journal" (based on Scopus' "CiteScore 2017" index)

3.2 Trend Analysis and Classifications

Figure 2 reports a chart of the temporal distribution of papers that was considered in the analysis. There is a yearly variation in the number of papers, which can also depend on contingent cases (for example, Special Issues). In any case, there is a steady growth, which may signal an increasing interest by the research community.

Papers published in the Education journals are far less numerous than those of the KM/IC field. In addition, only two journals (*Higher Education* and *Internet and Higher Education*) published papers related to KM/IC. This can mean that KM/IC is not yet a fully established "disciplinary field," especially compared to education, where there is a much longer tradition of concepts, research methodologies, and applicative areas. In other words, KM can be, for education, at most just one among the various possible fields "of inspiration" for researchers. While, for the KM/IC community, education represents an interesting field of application of new methods of managing knowledge.

As regards citations, an analysis would require more sophisticated calculations. Roughly speaking, the number of citations is higher for education journals, which, indeed, have a more established reputation and popularity than the KM/IC field. In any case, at a first glance, the average yearly citations of papers are slightly higher than the yearly average of each respective journal (Table 3). This may confirm that papers combining education and KM/IC topics are gaining some interest and momentum in the research community.

Knowledge Management for Adult and Higher Education: Mapping the Recent... 183

Table 4 Classification criteria

Criteria	Classes	Meaning
Type of research	Quantitative	Paper mostly based on statistical quantitative surveys
	Qualitative	Case-study research and similar methods
	Conceptual	Mostly theoretical or speculative
	Applicative/action	Action research or description of projects, applications of systems, methods, etc.
	Literature review	Systematic or qualitative literature review
	Mixed	Mixed paper with qualitative, quantitative, and/or action research methods
Context	General university/ college	Application of KM/IC concepts or methods to generic university context
	Business school/professional HE	Application of KM/IC concepts or methods specifically to business schools or other institutions specializing in professional higher education
Use of KM/IC notions or models	Management of universities	KM/IC is used for managers and for organizational purposes
	Organizing teaching/ teachers	KM/IC applied mainly to teaching or to supporting teachers' work and career
	Helping learners	KM/IC focusing on learning methods and learners' experience
	Understanding or modeling teaching/ learning	KM/IC used to provide fresh understanding of teaching or learning processes

To help understand the directions that the research has been taking in the recent years, the sampled papers were also mapped by using the classification criteria reported in Table 4.

Findings are displayed in Table 5. Firstly, purely research purposes (i.e., studying and modeling impact of KM in education, analyzing experience) tend to prevail largely over "applications" or "system designs." This may mean that many studies still have an "exploratory goal" (i.e., exploring usage of KM concepts to understand or improve education) and less papers have a practical goal of implementing KM solutions to education.

The context is, largely, the generic higher education institution, with few studies specifically focusing on professional education: in substance, the adoption of a KM perspective does not have (yet) any specific orientation. Approximately half of the papers considers KM for management issues (e.g., measuring effectiveness of educational services, administration, staff management): The remaining studies are applied to teaching and learning, with an attention to general interpretative models, or to teaching problems (more than learning issues).

Table 5 Classification of papers

Criteria	Categories	No. of papers in education journals	No. of papers in KM/IC journals	Total	%
Type of research	Quantitative	3	25	28	41.8
	Qualitative	4	12	16	23.9
	Conceptual	0	7	7	10.4
	Applicative/action	1	11	12	17.9
	Literature review	0	1	1	1.5
	Mixed	0	3	3	4.5
Context	General university/ college	8	52	60	89.6
	Business school/professional higher ed.	0	7	7	10.4
Use of KM/IC notions or models	Management of universities	0	31	31	46.3
	Organizing teaching/ teachers	4	12	16	23.9
	Helping learners	1	3	4	6.0
	Understanding or modeling teaching/ learning	3	13	16	23.9

3.3 Maps of Current Research

A graphic analysis of keywords is here provided, with the purpose to highlight the main research issues and directions. A concept map of keywords and their logical connections is reported in Fig. 3. The picture is quite full, but reader can, at least, get a general map of the most important keyword areas. The interest of researchers for KM/IC in education is polarized around four main areas: (a) organizational issues (i.e., how to manage a higher education institution, programming curricula, measuring performances); (b) student career and future jobs (e.g., measuring students' satisfaction and expectations, building competencies for employability, etc.); (c) new approaches to teaching (and, partially, learning); and (d) e-learning methods and technologies.

As regards the typical KM/IC keywords, these can be grouped into some distinct areas, i.e.: (a) some classic KM topics that are of primary interest in education (for instance, knowledge creation or sharing, and communities of practice); (b) intellectual capital measurement and reporting, which are often seen vital for assessing educational services; (c) KM as change management and innovation (KM processes are sometimes intended as carriers of innovation into educational institutions); and (d) learning organizations, which is what universities should be according to many researchers. There are two additional recurring groups: research methodologies (with a prevalence of keywords regarding statistical methods) and geographical location. This latter group denotes that some studies still focus on a specific environment or local context.

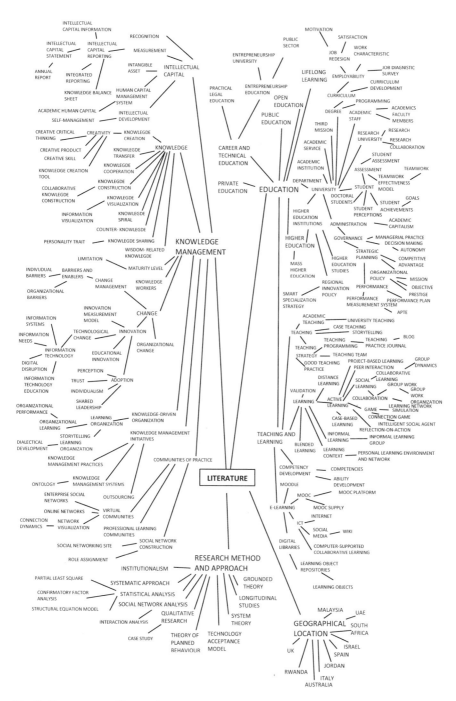

Fig. 3 Concept map of keywords

Fig. 4 Keyword cloud

Figure 4 reports a word cloud, built based on counting the recurrence of keywords. The picture is, again, quite full, but it provides an idea that there are some very frequent keywords and many others appear only marginally. In addition to some obvious instances (like, e.g., "universities," "knowledge management," "intellectual capital," or "higher education"), there are others that signal some important directions of the current research. For example, "e-learning" is a topical subject of the moment; "knowledge sharing" and "knowledge creation" (among the other KM processes) have also a special place. Also, "organizational learning" and "change management" denote that a strict relationship is ascribed between KM and innovations in education. The rest of keywords (regarding specific topics of analysis, methods, or application areas) appear very rarely. This may mean that the existing literature tends to spread on single problems rather than focus on recurring key issues, or it may be the case that each author tends to use different synonyms (instead of common terms) even to classify papers that treat the same subject.

3.4 Qualitative Summary of Research Directions

This section proposes a grouping of the selected papers, with the purpose to highlight hot topics in current research.

Introduction of KM in Universities A significant number of papers analyze whether and how KM principles, concepts, and tools are really and effectively used in universities, and with what purpose. Some treat this issue in general terms: Ramachandran, Chong, and Ismail (2009) studied the centrality of KM in universities and compared public and private environments; Nur, Fauzi, and Sukoco (2017) analyzed KM maturity of universities (specifically in Indonesia); Asma and Abdellatif (2016) explored a model to understand the impact of KM on university performance; Shih and Tsai (2016) correlated adoption of KM methods and "school effectiveness." To sum up, the adoption of KM is (directly or not) associated with improved performances and service quality of universities.

However, different possible roles are ascribed to KM in higher education institutions. Sometimes KM is seen to be important for the management of universities (Dee & Leisyte, 2017; Veer Ramjeawon & Rowley, 2017): for example, facilitating knowledge sharing between staff, improving knowledge exchanges between research and education services, etc. Some other papers focus on the potential of KM for improving teaching and learning: Alexandropoulou, Angelis, and Mavri (2019) examined the literature connecting KM and education processes; and Lam and Chua (2009) illustrated a case study of a KM strategy and its usefulness for improving teaching and learning.

Universities as Learning Organizations Papers that examine universities as learning organizations can be classified into two subgroups. A first group attempts to detect the features of a learning organization in universities. For example, Bak (2012) discussed whether and when universities can be really seen as learning organizations, Bui and Baruch (2010) applied the classic "5 disciplines of Senge's model" to academic institutions, and Hillon and Boje (2017) analyzed various models of universities as learning organizations. A second group examines how universities can be transformed into learning organizations. In short, it is argued that higher education institutions may not be, spontaneously, learning organizations but, rather, may need a process of transformation for facilitating a continuous learning of its staff and management: Shoham and Perry (2009) analyzed possible technological changes that may lead to the transformation of universities into learning institutions, and also put an emphasis on communities of practice (of staff) as a possible catalyst for this innovation; similarly, Lauer and Wilkesmann (2017) focused on the importance of collaboration for turning universities into learning organizations.

Innovations in Teaching and Learning Innovation and change in higher education are often associated with KM and KM capabilities. In some papers, a KM perspective is explicitly adopted to understand how teaching and learning can be innovated and improved. A central topic is how teaching methods can facilitate knowledge creation, development, and exchange and, more generally, active participation of learners and teachers. Fink (2012) examined the case-study methodology and its future as a teaching/learning instrument. Martín and Aznar (2017) investigated KM in the use of simulation games for a business school and their significance for active learning and teaching. Marín-García, Martínez-Gómez, and Giraldo-O'Meara (2014) analyzed work class and related methods and proposed an assessment of student satisfaction. Jørgensen (2018) discussed storytelling as a (new) educational approach. In this "new vision" of education, student–teacher interaction, reciprocal knowledge exchanges, and mutual learning are considered central. As Lueakha, Tongngam, and Phoewhawm (2016) argued, learning from students is also important for a process of continuous improvement of universities and educational services.

Communities of practice and related concepts are also seen as an essential ingredient of innovative teaching and learning. Kagwesage (2014) studied how communities of students can facilitate learning processes and mutual development of knowledge. Tsang and Tsui (2017) illustrated the design and test of a personal learning environment to support peer-based social learning. Cegarra-Sánchez and Cegarra-Navarro (2017) highlighted the potential importance of a learning community to reduce the risk of counter-knowledge in learning. Communitarian collaboration is also seen central for teachers: Angehrn and Maxwell (2010) suggested the use of a collaboration platform with the purpose of enhancing change management capabilities by teachers; Diez, Zárraga-Rodríguez, and García (2013) introduced a method for assessing teamwork performance of instructors.

KM Processes: Knowledge Creation, Sharing, and Collaboration A group of papers directly examines the impact of specific processes (that are central in the KM literature) on education and educational institutions. A first topic is knowledge creation and creativity: these are deemed to be vital processes in universities, and efforts are suggested to improve them (Poce, 2012). Rodríguez-Gómez and Gairín (2015) examined the importance of knowledge creation and management for the general functioning of universities; while Kaba and Ramaiah (2017) analyzed knowledge creation and KM tools used by academics.

A second topic is the process of knowledge sharing and, again, collaboration. Vătămănescu, Andrei, Dumitriu, and Leovaridis (2016) underlined the positive impact of organizational policies for facilitating collaboration and knowledge exchange. Tan (2016) focused on teachers and developed a statistical model to understand knowledge sharing in faculties, and how to improve it. Similarly, Angehrn, Maxwell, Luccini, and Rajola (2009) suggested the use of a collaboration platform for teachers, and Corcoran and Duane (2017) illustrated action research on a virtual community of practice of teachers. Others focused on student collaboration (Mayordomo & Onrubia, 2015) or on student–instructor collaboration (Memon, Nor, & Salleh 2016). Of course, nothing is ever easy, and some authors stressed the potential difficulties or barriers to sharing knowledge (Fullwood & Rowley, 2017; Khalil & Shea, 2012; Sohail & Daud, 2009; Van Ta & Zyngier, 2018).

E-learning and Other ICT Tools for Supporting Teaching and Learning Many papers attempt to use KM concepts and models to understand e-learning tools, which can improve KM processes and knowledge sharing. Some papers treat this topic in general, others with reference to specific geographical or cultural environments: Trevitt, Steed, Du Moulin, and Foley (2017) examined the importance of e-learning platforms for professional higher education; Maabreh (2018) underlined the importance of e-learning for students; Alsmadi, Chen, Prybutok, and Gadgil (2017) examined the maturity level of e-learning in Jordan universities; and Mohorovičič and Tijan (2011) examined its role in Croatian institutions.

Specific tools, projects, or implementations are also examined, from a perspective of students, of teachers, or both. Chu et al. (2017) analyzed wikis for project-based teaching and learning. Pavo and Rodrigo (2015) illustrated the use of blogs in knowledge sharing between teachers. Gu, Shao, Guo, and Lim (2015) discussed a model of computer-based applications for collaborative learning of students. Wodzicki, Schwämmlein, and Moskaliuk (2012) studied the impact of social media on learning processes. Ospina-Delgado, Zorio-Grima, and García-Benau (2016) focused on MOOC (Massive Open Online Courses) in higher education.

Finally, Fidalgo-Blanco, Sein-Echaluce, and García-Peñalvo (2018) studied the design of a "social repository" platform for facilitating teaching innovation; and Xu (2016) investigated the use of a repository of "learning objects" (namely, collections of content items and practice examples that are combined together for addressing a specific learning objective).

Another group of papers investigates the problem of e-learning implementation, acceptance, or use. Dukić, Dukić, and Penny (2012) considered the attitude of students toward KM through e-learning. Martins and Baptista Nunes (2017) discussed the importance of trust for the adoption of e-learning platforms in academics' knowledge exchange. Ramirez-Anormaliza, Sabaté, Llinàs-Audet, and Lordan (2017) analyzed the acceptance of e-learning by students.

Intellectual Capital Measurement Several papers focus on methods for measuring intellectual capital and intellectual capital production in universities. This is often considered a key KM issue for higher institutions, because universities are seen as a special kind of organization, whose main purpose and functional characteristic is the production and delivery of knowledge and, therefore, the improvement of intellectual capital of teachers, students, and all potential stakeholders. Wiedenhofer, Friedl, Billy, and Olejarova (2017) underlined the importance of assessing IC in academies, and its policy implications. Similarly, Martin-Sardesai and Guthrie (2018) underscored the centrality of intellectual capital measurement in managing university staff.

There are many examples of IC measurement methods and their application in universities, in different conditions and for various purposes. Some studies treat the topic at a general level (Jones, Meadow, & Sicilia, 2009) but, more often, specific methods, usage, or application context are examined (e.g., Habersam, Piber, & Skoog, 2018; Secundo, Elena-Perez, Martinaitis, & Leitner, 2015; Ramírez & Gordillo, 2014; Siboni, Nardo, & Sangiorgi, 2013; Córcoles, Peñalver, & Ponce, 2011; Secundo, Margherita, Elia, & Passiante, 2010; Veltri & Silvestri, 2015). This vast literature provides a rich "toolbox" of methods for IC measurement of universities, but also shows that the issue of measuring IC has not a single and generally accepted solution.

Human Capital Development The improvement of human capital (one of the main components of IC) is, again, a central goal of KM in universities. Some papers particularly focus on the idea that institutions should prepare students for their future careers, therefore enhancing human capital means providing educational services for employability. For example, Passaro, Quinto, and Thomas (2018) focused on the essential role of universities in the enhancement of human capital for entrepreneurship. Van De Wiele and Ribière (2014) proposed a tool for facilitating the development of curricula for better description of competencies and improved employability. Fitó, Martínez-Argüelles, and Rimbau-Gilabert (2015) defined a model for evaluating generic skills in transversal university programs. Martínez-Gómez, Marin-Garcia, and Giraldo-O'Meara (2013) proposed an assessment of teaching methods based on a job diagnostic survey. Finally, since the mission of universities is not simply education but also research, Ho, Woods, Aziz, and Sin

(2013) argued that managing knowledge exchanges between research and teaching can be essential for the development of human capital.

4 Conclusion

This study confirmed that the KM/IC field has a potential importance for adult and higher education, and there are promising applications of KM concepts to higher education and universities. The simple statistics provided here show the growing interest for the connection between KM/IC and education. Indeed, in some cases, concepts and methods of KM/IC can potentially enrich the research or practice in higher education, and especially the design or analysis of teaching/learning processes in universities. Some areas appear of particular interest. The use of KM/IC models or concepts to analyze the effective adoption and usage of e-learning applications is a good example. Another typical KM concept—the community of practice—also finds application in education, especially in the organization of teaching activities. In addition, KM approaches are proposed for the organization of universities and colleges (seen as "learning organizations") and for measuring their effectiveness (in terms of the amount and quality of intellectual capital they are able to produce, manage, and deliver).

On the other hand, there is still the need to carry out more theoretical or applicative research to facilitate the incorporation of KM notions, models, and practices into the education field. Especially, the convergence between the two areas sometimes appears to be still incomplete, limited to specific themes, not systematic, or the result of occasional opportunities of study or application. In particular, some topics are still underdeveloped, and especially, there is a lack of focus on learners. At least in principle, the adoption of a KM-based perspective can provide useful insights into the way learners perform their cognitive processes but, as the study shows, there is little research on this, or it is restricted to specific themes such as e-learning and its effectiveness.

4.1 Implications for Research

As recalled, the current direction that the research is taking apparently favors some topics and themes: among these, the application of KM to the management of universities (rather than to the modelization of teaching or learning processes), the measurement of IC in higher education, and the development or use of e-learning. While other topics, that are indeed quite popular in the KM/IC literature (for example, the processes of conversion between tacit and explicit knowledge) are substantially neglected. Conversely, in topics that are quite important for higher education (like, for instance, innovations in teaching and learning methods), the convergence between the fields of KM/IC and education appears to be still immature.

On the one hand, this can depend on the fact that KM is still an emerging area that is not well known by education scholars. Sometimes these scholars, in their studies, adopt terminologies, notions, and concepts that implicitly refer to KM, but they may tend to use them in a purely instrumental way. By examining the education articles that declare to focus (in some way) on KM/IC issues, even the cited literature is often not that typical of the KM/IC area. On the other hand, KM/IC scholars often consider education as a field where to transfer and apply models developed elsewhere (particularly, in the industrial or business context). A recognition that education is a completely different environment that requires peculiar models of KM can be vital.

In short, it may be advisable that researchers working in these distinct (but related) fields may benefit from a more effective reciprocal knowledge. To boost research in the intersection between KM and education, the different scholars can be involved in joint multidisciplinary projects. The foundation of scientific journals or book series directly focusing on "KM and Education" that, in addition, involve authoritative scholars of both fields, can provide an opportunity of discussion and confrontation. Funding multidisciplinary studies involving researchers specializing in the two areas can also be useful. All this may lead to important results, in terms of development of common scientific languages and conceptual grounds, and implementation of research based on actual problems whose solution may need the adoption of multiple perspectives.

4.2 Implications for Practice

The current literature already shows that some concepts, methods, or practices of KM can be really vital in higher education as well. A good example is the notion of the community of practice: this concept originates from the business context, but it is also increasingly applied in the education sector, especially for modeling or designing collaboration methods between teachers and/or learners. A further experimentation of these KM practices can provide fruitful results, and this may require not only the involvement of the single professional but also specific sponsoring at institutional levels: universities and colleges may launch new programs and initiatives with the purpose to help the implementation of KM practices in higher education. The achievements of the past studies in the KM/IC field can be highly beneficial, provided that an effort of transfer of these models to the peculiar context of education is made.

In addition, education professionals (and, especially, instructors at various levels) may benefit from specific training in KM practices, methods, technologies, and processes. So far, KM capabilities have rarely been included in the curriculum of instructors, lecturers, and university professors.

4.3 Limitations and Further Studies

This analysis has been deliberately restricted to a specific subset of the available literature. Therefore, any statistical or qualitative generalization is affected by this limitation. A first possible improvement can be made by extending the range of observed publications (by including other journals, conference papers, or book chapters). A second option is to perform a critical qualitative analysis of selected papers.

In short, this chapter shows that KM/IC concepts and models, which have knowledge and cognitive processes at their very core, are strictly intertwined with the education field. However, the actual connection between these two fields is still underdeveloped, and more efforts not only are required but can also be worthwhile. The good news for researchers and practitioners is that there is a new field—the interconnection between KM and education—that can provide lots of opportunities for innovative studies and practical advancements. The points in common of the two fields are so many that it is even surprising they have not been explored enough so far.

References

Alexandropoulou, D. A., Angelis, V. A., & Mavri, M. (2019). Knowledge management and higher education: Present state and future trends. *International Journal of Knowledge and Learning, 5*(1), 96–106.

Alsmadi, D., Chen, J., Prybutok, V., & Gadgil, G. (2017). E-learning in Jordanian higher education: Cultural perspectives and institutional readiness. *Journal of Information and Knowledge Management, 16*(4), 1750035.

Angehrn, A. A., & Maxwell, K. (2010). Increasing change readiness in higher educational institutions through a simulation-based change management experience. *International Journal of Knowledge and Learning, 6*(2–3), 162–174.

Angehrn, A. A., Maxwell, K., Luccini, M. A., & Rajola, F. (2009). Designing effective collaboration, learning and innovation systems for education professionals. *International Journal of Knowledge and Learning, 5*(3–4), 193–206.

Asma, K., & Abdellatif, M. A. (2016). A new model for the impact of knowledge management on university performance. *Journal of Information and Knowledge Management, 15*(4), 1650041.

Bak, O. (2012). Universities: Can they be considered as learning organizations? A preliminary micro-level perspective. *Learning Organization, 19*(2), 163–172.

Bolisani, E., & Scarso, E. (2014). The place of communities of practice in knowledge management studies: A critical review. *Journal of Knowledge Management, 18*(2), 366–381.

Bontis, N. (1998). Intellectual capital: An exploratory study that develops measures and models. *Management Decision, 36*(2), 63–76.

Bui, H., & Baruch, Y. (2010). Creating learning organizations in higher education: Applying a systems perspective. *Learning Organization, 17*(3), 228–242.

Cegarra-Sánchez, J., & Cegarra-Navarro, J. G. (2017). Making meaning out of noise: A knowledge management core competence for higher education students. *VINE Journal of Information and Knowledge Management Systems, 47*(4), 506–521.

Chu, S. K. W., Zhang, Y., Chen, K., Chan, C. K., Lee, C. W. Y., Zou, E., & Lau, W. (2017). The effectiveness of wikis for project-based learning in different disciplines in higher education. *Internet and Higher Education, 22*, 49–60.

Córcoles, Y. R., Peñalver, J. F. S., & Ponce, A. T. (2011). Intellectual capital in Spanish public universities: Stakeholders' information needs. *Journal of Intellectual Capital, 12*(3), 356–376.

Corcoran, N., & Duane, A. (2017). Using enterprise social networks as a knowledge management tool in higher education. *VINE Journal of Information and Knowledge Management Systems, 47*(4), 555–570.

Dalkir, K. (2013). *Knowledge management in theory and practice*. Abingdon-on-Thames: Routledge.

Davenport, T. H., & Prusak, L. (1998). *Working knowledge: How organizations manage what they know*. Cambridge: Harvard Business Press.

Dee, J., & Leisyte, L. (2017). Knowledge sharing and organizational change in higher education. *Learning Organization, 24*(5), 355–365.

Diez, E. V., Zárraga-Rodríguez, M., & García, C. J. (2013). A tool to assess teamwork performance in higher education. *Intangible Capital, 9*(1), 281–304.

Drucker, P. F. (2008). *The age of discontinuity: Guidelines to our changing society*. New Brunswick: Transaction Publishers.

Dukić, D., Dukić, G., & Penny, K. I. (2012). Knowledge management and e-learning in higher education: A research study based on students' perceptions. *International Journal of Knowledge and Learning, 8*(3–4), 313–327.

Dumay, J. C. (2009). Intellectual capital measurement: A critical approach. *Journal of Intellectual Capital, 10*(2), 190–210.

Edwards, J. S. (2015). Knowledge management concepts and models. In E. Bolisani & M. Handzic (Eds.), *Advances in knowledge management* (pp. 25–44). Berlin: Springer.

Fidalgo-Blanco, Á., Sein-Echaluce, M. L., & García-Peñalvo, F. J. (2018). Knowledge spirals in higher education teaching innovation. *International Journal of Knowledge Management, 10*(4), 16–37.

Fink, D. (2012). The future of case teaching: Applying strategies for enhancing student knowledge with wisdom. *International Journal of Knowledge Management Studies, 5*(1–2), 154–170.

Fitó, À., Martínez-Argüelles, M.-J., & Rimbau-Gilabert, E. (2015). Comprehensive implementation of generic skills in transversal university programs: The experience of the UOC's faculty of economics and business. *Intangible Capital, 11*(4), 589–611.

Fullwood, R., & Rowley, J. (2017). An investigation of factors affecting knowledge sharing amongst UK academics. *Journal of Knowledge Management, 21*(5), 1254–1271.

Girard, J., & Girard, J. (2015). Defining knowledge management: Toward an applied compendium. *Online Journal of Applied Knowledge Management, 3*(1), 1–20.

Grant, M. J., & Booth, A. (2009). A typology of reviews: An analysis of 14 review types and associated methodologies. *Health Information & Libraries Journal, 26*(2), 91–108.

Gu, X., Shao, Y., Guo, X., & Lim, C. P. (2015). Designing a role structure to engage students in computer-supported collaborative learning. *Internet and Higher Education, 24*, 13–20.

Habersam, M., Piber, M., & Skoog, M. (2018). Ten years of using knowledge balance sheets in Austrian public universities: A retrospective and prospective view. *Journal of Intellectual Capital, 19*(1), 34–52.

Hallin, C. A., & Marnburg, E. (2008). Knowledge management in the hospitality industry: A review of empirical research. *Tourism Management, 29*(2), 366–381.

Hillon, Y. C., & Boje, D. M. (2017). The dialectical development of "storytelling" learning organizations: A case study of a public research university. *Learning Organization, 24*(4), 226–235.

Ho, A. P. C., Woods, P. C., Aziz, A. A., & Sin, N. M. (2013). Lecturers as knowledge workers and the self-management of their intellectual capital growth and development from a teaching to a research-teaching fusion - A Malaysian case study. *International Journal of Learning and Intellectual Capital, 10*(1), 88–105.

Jones, N., Meadow, C., & Sicilia, M. A. (2009). Measuring intellectual capital in higher education. *Journal of Information and Knowledge Management, 8*(2), 113–136.

Jones, G., & Sallis, E. (2013). *Knowledge management in education: Enhancing learning & education.* Abingdon-on-Thames: Routledge.

Jørgensen, K. M. (2018). Spaces of performance: A storytelling approach to learning in higher education. *Learning Organization, 25*(6), 410–421.

Kaba, A., & Ramaiah, C. K. (2017). Demographic differences in using knowledge creation tools among faculty members. *Journal of Knowledge Management, 21*(4), 857–871.

Kagwesage, A. M. (2014). Peer interaction and learning: A study of higher education students initiated group work activity. *International Journal of Knowledge and Learning, 9*(3), 179–193.

Khalil, O. E. M., & Shea, T. (2012). Knowledge sharing barriers and effectiveness at a higher education institution. *International Journal of Knowledge Management, 8*(2), 43–64.

Lam, W., & Chua, A. Y. K. (2009). Knowledge outsourcing: An alternative strategy for knowledge management. *Journal of Knowledge Management, 13*(3), 28–43.

Lauer, S., & Wilkesmann, U. (2017). The governance of organizational learning: Empirical evidence from best-practice universities in Germany. *Learning Organization, 24*(5), 266–277.

Lieberman, A., & Miller, L. (2008). *Teachers in professional communities: Improving teaching and learning.* New York: Teachers College Press.

Lueakha, J., Tongngam, P., & Phoewhawm, R. (2016). Relearning the practice of managing an undergraduate program: A learning lesson from a Thai institution. *International Journal of Knowledge and Learning, 11*(4), 221–231.

Maabreh, K. S. (2018). The impact of e-learning usage on students' achievements: A case study. *International Journal of Knowledge and Learning, 12*(3), 193–203.

Marín-García, J. A., Martínez-Gómez, M., & Giraldo-O'Meara, M. (2014). Redesigning work in university classrooms: Factors related to satisfaction in engineering and business administration students. *Intangible Capital, 10*(5), 1026–1051.

Martín, A. C. U., & Aznar, C. T. (2017). Meaningful learning in business through serious games. *Intangible Capital, 13*(4), 805–823.

Martínez-Gómez, M., Marin-Garcia, J. A., & Giraldo-O'Meara, M. (2013). Validation of the work characteristics scales applied to educational university environments. *Intangible Capital, 9*(4), 1170–1193.

Martins, J. T., & Baptista Nunes, M. (2017). Academics' e-learning adoption in higher education institutions: A matter of trust. *Learning Organization, 23*(5), 299–331.

Martin-Sardesai, A., & Guthrie, J. (2018). Human capital loss in an academic performance measurement system. *Journal of Intellectual Capital, 19*(1), 53–70.

Mayordomo, R. M., & Onrubia, J. (2015). Work coordination and collaborative knowledge construction in a small group collaborative virtual task. *Internet and Higher Education, 25*, 96–104.

Memon, M. A., Nor, K. M., & Salleh, R. (2016). Personality traits influencing knowledge sharing in student-supervisor relationship: A structural equation modelling analysis. *Journal of Information and Knowledge Management, 15*(2), 1650015.

Merriam, S. B., & Bierema, L. L. (2013). *Adult learning: Linking theory and practice.* San Francisco: John Wiley & Sons.

Mohorovičič, S., & Tijan, E. (2011). Blended learning model of teaching programming in higher education. *International Journal of Knowledge and Learning, 7*(1–2), 86–99.

Nur, R. N. N., Fauzi, A. M., & Sukoco, H. (2017). Strategies of knowledge management implementation for academic services improvement of Indonesian higher education. *Journal of Information and Knowledge Management, 16*(4), 1750032.

Ospina-Delgado, J. E., Zorio-Grima, A., & García-Benau, M. A. (2016). Massive open online courses in higher education: A data analysis of the MOOC supply. *Intangible Capital, 12*(5), 1401–1450.

Passaro, R., Quinto, I., & Thomas, A. (2018). The impact of higher education on entrepreneurial intention and human capital. *Journal of Intellectual Capital, 19*(1), 135–156.

Pavo, M. Á. H., & Rodrigo, J. C. (2015). Interaction analysis of a blog/journal of teaching practice. *The Internet and Higher Education, 27*(October), 32–43.

Poce, A. (2012). Fostering creativity through assessment and the use of IT: A feasibility study carried out in higher education. *International Journal of Knowledge and Learning, 8*(1–2), 6–19.

Polanyi, M. (1966). *The tacit dimension.* Garden City: Doubleday Anchor.

Pratt, D. D. (2002). Good teaching: One size fits all? *New directions for adult and continuing education, 93*, 5–16.

Prusak, L. (2001). Where did knowledge management come from? *IBM Systems Journal, 40*(4), 1002–1006.

Ramachandran, S. D., Chong, S. C., & Ismail, H. (2009). The practice of knowledge management processes: A comparative study of public and private higher education institutions in Malaysia. *Vine, 39*(3), 203–222.

Ramírez, Y., & Gordillo, S. (2014). Recognition and measurement of intellectual capital in Spanish universities. *Journal of Intellectual Capital, 15*(1), 173–188.

Ramirez-Anormaliza, R., Sabaté, F., Llinàs-Audet, X., & Lordan, O. (2017). Acceptance and use of e-learning systems by undergraduate students of Ecuador: The case of a state university. *Intangible Capital, 13*(3), 548–581.

Ratcliffe-Martin, V., Coakes, E., & Sugden, G. (2000). Knowledge management issues in universities. *VINE Journal of Information and Knowlegde Management Systems, 30*(4), 14–18.

Rodríguez-Gómez, D., & Gairín, J. (2015). Unravelling knowledge creation and management in educational organisations: Barriers and enablers. *Knowledge Management Research and Practice, 13*(2), 149–159.

Roos, J., Edvinsson, L., & Dragonetti, N. C. (1997). *Intellectual capital: Navigating the new business landscape.* Berlin: Springer.

Sarvary, M. (1999). Knowledge management and competition in the consulting industry. *California Management Review, 41*(2), 95–107.

Schaller, R., Allert, H., & Richter, C. (2008, June). *Knowledge management in universities.* Paper presented at EdMedia: World Conference on Educational Media and Technology, Vienna.

Secundo, G., Elena-Perez, S., Martinaitis, Ž., & Leitner, K.-H. (2015). An intellectual capital maturity model (ICMM) to improve strategic management in European universities: A dynamic approach. *Journal of Intellectual Capital, 16*(2), 419–442.

Secundo, G., Margherita, A., Elia, G., & Passiante, G. (2010). Intangible assets in higher education and research: Mission, performance or both? *Journal of Intellectual Capital, 11*(2), 140–157.

Senge, P. M. (1991). The fifth discipline, the art and practice of the learning organization. *Performance+ Instruction, 30*(5), 37–37.

Serenko, A., & Bontis, N. (2013). Global ranking of knowledge management and intellectual capital academic journals: 2013 update. *Journal of Knowledge Management, 17*(2), 307–326.

Shih, W.-L., & Tsai, C.-Y. (2016). The effects of knowledge management capabilities on perceived school effectiveness in career and technical education. *Journal of Knowledge Management, 20* (6), 1373–1392.

Shoham, S., & Perry, M. (2009). Knowledge management as a mechanism for technological and organizational change management in Israeli universities. *Higher Education, 57*(2), 227–246.

Siboni, B., Nardo, M. T., & Sangiorgi, D. (2013). Italian state university contemporary performance plans: An intellectual capital focus? *Journal of Intellectual Capital, 14*(3), 414–430.

Sohail, M. S., & Daud, S. (2009). Knowledge sharing in higher education institutions: Perspectives from Malaysia. *Vine, 39*(2), 125–142.

Spender, J. C. (2015). Knowledge management: Origins, history, and development (pp. 3–23). In E. Bolisani & M. Handzic (Eds.), *Advances in knowledge management.* Berlin: Springer.

Stevenson, J. M. (2000). A new epistemological context for education: Knowledge management in public schools. *Journal of Instructional Psychology, 27*(3), 198–198.

Stewart, T. A. (1997). *Intellectual capital: The new wealth of organizations.* New York: Doubleday.

Tan, C. N.-L. (2016). Enhancing knowledge sharing and research collaboration among academics: The role of knowledge management. *Higher Education, 71*(4), 525–556.

Trevitt, C., Steed, A., Du Moulin, L., & Foley, T. (2017). Leading entrepreneurial e-learning development in legal education: A longitudinal case study of universities as learning organisations. *Learning Organization, 24*(5), 298–311.

Tsang, H. W. C., & Tsui, E. (2017). Conceptual design and empirical study of a personal learning environment and network (PLE&N) to support peer-based social and lifelong learning. *VINE Journal of Information and Knowledge Management Systems, 47*(2), 228–249.

Van De Wiele, P., & Ribière, V. (2014). Using knowledge visualisation techniques to support the development of curriculum for employability: Exploring the capability tree representation. *International Journal of Knowledge and Learning, 9*(1–2), 43–62.

Van Ta, C., & Zyngier, S. (2018). Knowledge sharing barriers in Vietnamese higher education institutions (HEIS). *International Journal of Knowledge Management, 14*(1), 51–70.

Vătămănescu, E.-M., Andrei, A. G., Dumitriu, D. L., & Leovaridis, C. (2016). Harnessing network-based intellectual capital in online academic networks. From the organizational policies and practices towards competitiveness. *Journal of Knowledge Management, 20*(3), 594–619.

Veer Ramjeawon, P., & Rowley, J. (2017). Knowledge management in higher education institutions: Enablers and barriers in Mauritius. *Learning Organization, 24*(5), 366–377.

Veltri, S., & Silvestri, A. (2015). The Free State University integrated reporting: A critical consideration. *Journal of Intellectual Capital, 16*(2), 443–462.

Wiedenhofer, R., Friedl, C., Billy, L., & Olejarova, D. (2017). Application of IC-models in a combined public-private sector setting for regional innovation in Slovakia. *Journal of Intellectual Capital, 18*(3), 588–606.

Wiig, K. M. (2002). Knowledge management in public administration. *Journal of Knowledge Management, 6*(3), 224–239.

Wodzicki, K., Schwämmlein, E., & Moskaliuk, J. (2012). Actually, I wanted to learn: Study-related knowledge exchange on social networking sites. *Internet and Higher Education, 15*(1), 9–14.

Xu, H. (2016). Faculty use of a learning object repository in higher education. *VINE Journal of Information and Knowledge Management Systems, 46*(4), 469–478.

Part III
Case Studies and Best Practices That Consider Classroom Learning, Higher Education Change, and Organization Development

Sharing Active Learning Practices to Improve Teaching: Peer Observation of Active Teaching in a School of Engineering

Stefano Ghidoni, Monica Fedeli, and Massimiliano Barolo

Abstract Promoting faculty development in a School of Engineering is quite unusual within the Italian academic context. Engineering education is strongly content-oriented, and the assumption that—in essence—effective teaching amounts to delivering maximum content is deeply rooted in most engineering instructors. Stated differently, one common assumption among instructors is that whenever one educator masters the content of a course, no need for improvement in teaching is needed or even possible. Under this perspective, a class is seen as the way to feed the students with new content, thus making learning an almost entirely self-guided process to be activated by each student individually outside the classroom.

To overcome this instructor-centered educational model and promote modernization of the teaching practice, in 2016 the School of Engineering of the University of Padova (UniPD) pioneered for Italy a faculty development program named *Teaching for Learning* (T4L). The program kicked off with a two-and-a-half-day retreat workshop for engineering instructors recruited on a voluntary basis. The principles of active learning were introduced and practiced during the workshop under the guidance of national and international experts in adult learning and teaching in higher education. The retreat involved thirty instructors and was extremely successful, to the point that the T4L workshop experience rapidly spread across UniPD, engaging a tenfold greater number of instructors across all disciplines in the subsequent 2 years.

The T4L@Engineering program continued in the two following years with the objective of sharing active teaching/learning practices both among the retreat participants and among other engineering instructors who did not participate in the residential retreat. Several half-day workshops were organized, including some dealing with the use of digital technologies to promote active learning. Paralleling these activities was a "peer observation of active teaching" (POAT) process, which was conceptualized, designed, and tested in a small group, and finally proposed to the entire community of engineering instructors through a call for volunteers.

S. Ghidoni (✉) · M. Fedeli · M. Barolo
University of Padova, Padova, PD, Italy
e-mail: stefano.ghidoni@unipd.it; monica.fedeli@unipd.it; max.barolo@unipd.it

© Springer Nature Switzerland AG 2019
M. Fedeli, L. L. Bierema (eds.), *Connecting Adult Learning and Knowledge Management*, Knowledge Management and Organizational Learning 8,
https://doi.org/10.1007/978-3-030-29872-2_11

This chapter presents how the POAT process was developed and put into practice, and discusses some lessons that were learnt after 1 year of experimentation.

1 Setting the Context

In this chapter, we discuss the context within which the Peer Observation of Active Teaching (POAT) process was developed. First, a short introduction about the organization of the engineering education programs at the University of Padova is presented. Then, the active learning and peer observation are framed into a theoretical background.

1.1 Engineering Education at the University of Padova

Founded in 1222, the University of Padova (UniPD) is one of the oldest universities in the world and one of the largest in Italy. Nearly 60,000 students are currently enrolled, with ~12,000 involved in engineering degree programs at the bachelor's or master's level (PhD degree programs are not considered in this chapter). A schematic of the network of academic departments concurring to the engineering educational offer at UniPD is shown in Fig. 1: the School comprises four engineering departments and two science departments. Each degree program is designed and managed by a single engineering department, and each department can manage several programs. The four engineering departments offer over 30 degree programs in the three major areas of engineering, namely industrial engineering, information engineering, and civil and environmental engineering. Whereas the instructors for the core and elective engineering courses are affiliated with the engineering departments, the mathematics and physics courses are typically taught by instructors affiliated with the science departments.

The main role of the School of Engineering is to coordinate the degree programs offered across the departments involved in engineering education. The School has no role with respect to either instructor recruitment or academic research: both activities are entirely managed at the departmental level. Typical tasks assigned to the School are evaluation of new degree program proposals, evaluation of the effectiveness and efficiency of the existing ones, solution of conflicts among departments in relation to instructor allocation in the degree programs, promotion of continual improvement of the programs, interaction with the stakeholders, development of orientation material for high-school students, interfacing to the higher academic bodies.

The overall number of instructors involved in engineering education at UniPD is nearly 400. By law, each instructor is required to teach 120 class hours (also called "frontal" hours in Italy) each academic year. However, despite this apparent emphasis on teaching, whether one instructor is a freshly recruited scholar or an experienced professor, teaching was meant as an entirely self-guided activity when the T4L program was started. In fact, on the one side, training in teaching was not provided in any form to

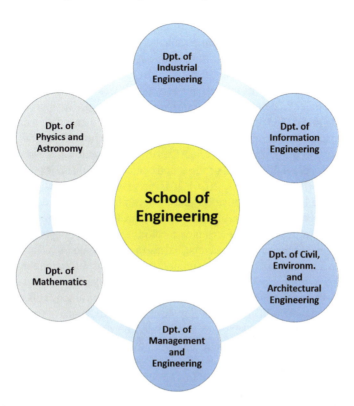

Fig. 1 The network of departments concurring to the engineering educational offer at the University of Padova. The School of Engineering coordinates the departmental educational activities

any instructor at any academic level; on the other side, formal interaction among fellow instructors was not promoted or even fostered. Each class was considered a very private relation between the instructor and his or her students, and instructors received feedback on teaching only by means of an end-of-the-course satisfaction questionnaire to be filled in by each student anonymously. The responses were made (and currently are) available to the instructor and to the degree program chair.

1.2 Active Learning and Peer Observation: The Theoretical Framework

Active learning is based on a learner-centered teaching approach (Weimer, 2013) and consists of a broad range of methods and pedagogical approaches that put the student in the center of the learning process with an active role. It consists of group work, research-based/problem-based learning, and diverse assessment practices, thus developing the students' critical thinking and interpersonal skills. Active learning foresees the involvement of different stakeholders in the teaching and learning process like businesses, professional communities, teachers, students, and administrators to promote a holistic dimension of learning that aims to the promotion of transformative learning (Taylor, 2007).

Active learning is an intentional process that needs to be well designed and scaffolded in order to be effective. An instructor using an active approach functions more as a facilitator (Fedeli, 2016; Fedeli & Taylor, 2016), than a sage lecturer, who is promoting change and designing learning in collaboration with the students to create an authentic climate for learning and critical reflection. Research indicates that active learning works across disciplines, genders, and contexts, and that it is transformational and long term (Felder & Brent, 2016). It is necessary for instructors using active learning to take the risk and move beyond their comfort zone in order to reflect and try to find ways to move the attention from teaching to learning outcome. This innovative way of teaching involves new methods and different approaches ("active teaching") from the side of the instructors, and also a new awareness and involvement of the students. This process of active learning can be promoted through the peer observation of active teaching. This is a practice that aims to deprivatize (Adams & Mix, 2014) teaching, promoting sharing of practices and discussion among colleagues. Some of the faculty at the UniPD School of Engineering started the active teaching process and decided to take the challenge to observe and be observed among peers in this activity. Gosling (2014) stated: "There are many advantages to using the observation of teaching sessions as a basis for a dialogue about teaching" (p. 14). Consistent with the literature, we have found peer observations are a very important way to promote "good teaching" among faculties (Gosling, 2014; Jensen & Aiyegbayo, 2011; Kahut, Burnap, & Yon, 2007; McGrath & Monsen, 2015). We are aware of the need to invest more time in this process and to involve more faculty members, leading to greater sharing and enriching perspectives. The theoretical achievements in the field of education detailed so far were translated into a real set of best practices, agreed among an engineering learning community, as detailed in the remainder of this chapter.

2 The Peer Observation of Active Learning and Teaching Process

The POAT process typically involves one instructor and two fellow observers (the "triad"), who meet in order to analyze and discuss one learning activity proposed by the instructor—each member of the triad will take the role of instructor, alternately. The term "learning activity" is general and suggests that this process is not restricted to lectures only, but can be effectively applied to other activities like laboratory experiences, open discussions, and flipped classrooms. The peer observation process goes beyond the specific activity being observed, as it also involves the course syllabus as well as the teaching material used.

Triad creation is a semi-spontaneous process, which follows a call for volunteers typically issued right after the start of the semester within which the POAT process is

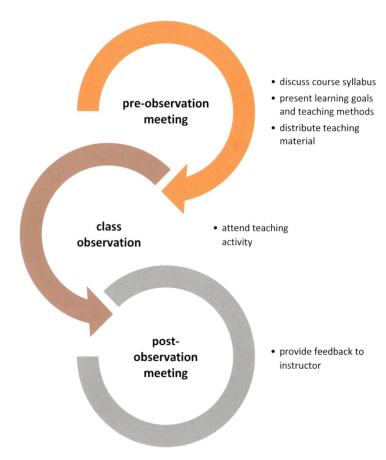

Fig. 2 The peer observation of active teaching process at the School of Engineering of the University of Padova

proposed. The volunteers responding to the call are then collectively met up in one single occasion, where they are informed about the process (also using the witness of one or two fellow instructors who already practiced it), and receive a short on-the-spot training on how to carry out the observation. At that point, the volunteers cluster in triads according to their preferences, and then they proceed independently with the POAT activities. A meeting of the triads may be scheduled after the end of the semester to receive feedback on the whole process according to a continual improvement framework. The POAT process is structured in three phases (Fig. 2):

1. *A pre-observation meeting*, i.e., a meeting of the triad to be carried out before the proper class observation takes place. The aim of the meeting is: (a) to discuss the course syllabus (to be made available to the observers in advance); (b) to let the instructor illustrate the learning goals and the teaching methods he or she plans to use in the observed class; and (c) to provide the observer with the same teaching material the students are provided with. Typically, the meeting is carried out right before the class observation.

2. *The proper class observation*, when the observers take part in the teaching activity organized by the instructor. A typical class subject to observation lasts 1.5 clock hours, possibly spaced by a 15-minute break.
3. *A post-observation meeting*, where the observers provide feedback to the instructor.

At the beginning of the class observation step, the instructor presents the observers to the students, in order to make them aware of the continual improvement process he or she is involved in. However, the observers will not participate in the class activities: their role is solely to observe both the instructor and the students.

Whereas the class observation is obviously carried out in a formal setting (e.g., a classroom or a laboratory), both the pre-observation meeting and the post-observation meeting are better carried out in an informal setting (e.g., coffee and drinks help creating a relaxed and non-judging atmosphere within the triad). An appropriate time to do the pre-observation meeting is right before class observation; with respect to the post-observation meeting, we recommend doing it right after the class or within a few days, to avoid losing the momentum generated by the observation.

The documentation developed to support the triad is illustrated at the end of this chapter (Fig. 3). Namely, class observation is guided by a checklist summarizing a set of elements to be observed. The checklist is circulated among the triad in advance, because it can help drive the discussion in the pre- and post-observation meetings, as well as assessment during the class observation. As the checklist is very general, some elements might not be applicable to all teaching activities. On the other hand, some other elements might be added, following the specific needs of the instructor and of the learning community.

With reference to the actual class observation, the checklist includes the following statements:

1. The use of the lecture room facilities (e.g., projector, board, space for students to take note, etc.) is appropriate.
2. Instructor clearly communicates the purpose of the class and teaching activities.
3. Instructor uses practical examples and illustrations that clarify the material.
4. Instructor explicitly links new material to previously learned concepts.
5. Instructor uses visuals and handouts where appropriate to accompany verbal presentation.
6. Instructor proposes interactive activities (e.g., completing a task, applying concepts, or engaging in a discussion).
7. Students are comfortable in asking questions.
8. Students actively participate in class activities and discussion.
9. Instructor asks for feedback on proposed activities and teaching methods, checks students' comprehension and their capability of identifying key concepts.
10. Instructor welcomes students' questions/remarks/enquiries.
11. Instructor proposes independent study activities.
12. At the end of the class, instructor summarizes some key concepts (conclusions/ wrap-up/take-home messages).

SCHOOL OF ENGINEERING

Guidelines for Peer Observation of Active Teaching

Peer observation of the lecturing activity should be carried out following an assigned protocol to ensure the feedback is provided properly. This document outlines the protocol and can be used as a checklist. The peer observation process involves one **instructor** and one or more **observers**; it is composed of three steps: i) **pre-observation meeting**; ii) **class observation**; iii) **post-observation meeting**. The expected output is a report prepared according to a form that is part of the process itself; it can be found in the companion document "Peer Observation of Active Teaching". The blank form should be shared by the instructor and the observer(s) before starting the process. Classes need to be observed as a whole from beginning to end.

In the following, details of the three phases are given.

Pre-observation Meeting

The observer should start by getting some information about the class. The instructor needs to:

- list the teaching methods (including active learning techniques, if any) that will be used during the class;
- outline the goals of the class;
- provide the documents and resources already made available (e.g., via Moodle) to the students.

The observer should also read the syllabus as it appears on the official course website.

This information should be put in the context of the course and its learning outcomes, i.e. the skills students are supposed to develop within the course – beyond simple knowledge of the technical content. The choice of the class to be observed is made by the instructor, ensuring that it is representative of the teaching methods and strategies usually employed. The observation of two classes is also highly desirable.

Once it is agreed that a specific class is going to be observed, a ten-minute meeting will be organized before the class. Such meeting may be arranged in presence, via Skype or as a phone call. The observers show the feedback form to the instructor, who summarizes the class and discusses any deviation with respect to what has been previously planned.

The instructor should make the students aware of the peer observation activity, and inform them in advance when it is going to take place.

Class Observation

The second step requires observers to attend the whole class. The feedback form should be filled in *during* the class; therefore, the observers need to become familiar with the form *before* the class is given to be able to easily cover all the required elements. Filling in the

v.1.1 © 2017 Stefano Ghidoni, Massimiliano Barolo and Monica Fedeli (University of Padova, Italy)

Fig. 3 Accompanying documents to be used by the triads for the peer observation process

form should not be intended as *grading* the instructor. Rather, it should be meant as a concise way to provide feedback on the teaching activity.

If only one observer is present, it is advisable that he/she seats in the rear rows of the classroom, in order to better observe the students' reactions to the instructor. If two observers are present, they should sit in two different areas of the classroom (e.g., one in the front and one in the back), in order to have different perspectives on the classroom.

Post-observation Meeting

A meeting shall be scheduled after the observation. It can take place right after the class or after some (ideally 2-3) days, but no later than a week after the observation. Observers give their feedback on the class, based on the forms they filled in; a discussion at this point would be extremely beneficial to the instructor.

Fig. 3 (continued)

SCHOOL OF ENGINEERING

Peer Observation of Active Teaching

This document may be used in a classroom peer observation situation and includes questions and guidelines to facilitate the practice of peer observation of active teaching. It is meant to assist faculty members who are observing a class and provides suggestions for the pre-observation meeting, the class observation, and the post-observation meeting. The companion document "Guidelines for Peer Observation of Active Teaching" clarifies how to develop the peer observation protocol.

Course title	
Instructor	Observer
Topic	Class time
Observation date and lecture room	Number of students

Pre-observation Meeting

During the pre-observation meeting, the instructor and the observer(s) shall discuss the following points:
- **Aim of the course:** *What is the purpose of this course?*
- **Objectives of the class:** *What is the purpose of the class that is going to be observed?*
- **Learning outcomes:** *What does the instructor expect the students will learn in the class observed?*
- **Teaching methods:** *What shall the observer expect to see?*
- **Link to previous learning:** *What pre-class work will the students have done for this class?*

During the pre-observation meeting the syllabus should also be reviewed. Please rate your opinion: 1 (disagree); 2 (partially disagree); 3 (partially agree); 4 (agree).

			Observations and suggestions
1	The syllabus includes clear indications on the learning outcomes of the course	☐ 1 ☐ 2 ☐ 3 ☐ 4	
2	The assessment criteria are clearly stated in the syllabus	☐ 1 ☐ 2 ☐ 3 ☐ 4	

v.1.1 © 2017 Stefano Ghidoni, Massimiliano Barolo and Monica Fedeli (University of Padova, Italy)

Fig. 3 (continued)

Class Observation Checklist

Please express your opinion: 1 (disagree); 2 (partially disagree); 3 (partially agree); 4 (agree). Please use the blank space to include your observations and suggestions.

1	The use of the lecture room facilities (e.g. projector, board, space for students to take note, etc.) is appropriate	☐1 ☐2 ☐3 ☐4
2	Instructor clearly communicates the purpose of the class and teaching activities	☐1 ☐2 ☐3 ☐4
3	Instructor uses practical examples and illustrations that clarify the material	☐1 ☐2 ☐3 ☐4
4	Instructor explicitly links new material to previously learned concepts	☐1 ☐2 ☐3 ☐4
5	Instructor uses visuals and handouts where appropriate to accompany verbal presentation	☐1 ☐2 ☐3 ☐4
6	Instructor proposes interactive activities (o.g., completing a task, applying concepts, or engaging in a discussion)	☐1 ☐2 ☐3 ☐4
7	Students are comfortable in asking questions	☐1 ☐2 ☐3 ☐4
8	Students actively participate in class activities and discussion	☐1 ☐2 ☐3 ☐4
9	Instructor asks for feedback on proposed activities and teaching methods, checks students' comprehension and their capability of identifying key concepts	☐1 ☐2 ☐3 ☐4
10	Instructor welcomes students' questions/remarks/enquiries	☐1 ☐2 ☐3 ☐4
11	Instructor proposes independent study activities	☐1 ☐2 ☐3 ☐4
12	At the end of the class, instructor summarizes some key concepts (conclusions/wrap-up/take-home messages)	☐1 ☐2 ☐3 ☐4

v. 1.1 © 2017 Monica Fedeli and School of Engineering, University of Padova

Fig. 3 (continued)

Sharing Active Learning Practices to Improve Teaching: Peer Observation... 209

TEACHING FOR LEARNING – SCHOOL OF ENGINEERING ◆ UNIVERSITY OF PADOVA

Post-observation Meeting

The following is meant to help the post-observation discussion. The instructor reflects on these points:

- What went well?
- What challenges were there?
- What might be changed for the next time?
- Discuss any additional points that were raised in the pre-observation meeting.

Observers are requested to provide a score from 1 to 4 (disagree/partially disagree/partially agree/agree) to describe how, after observing the class, they agree with each statement. The score is accompanied by a short textual narrative, which can be discussed during the post-observation meeting. It is important to note that the scores shall not be considered a marking, grading, or ranking; rather, they represent how much every specific statement was present in the activity proposed to the students. This shall be pointed out very clearly during the pre- and post-observation meetings, as instructors must not feel under examination: rather, they should feel as a part of a learning community that offers the chance to discuss about teaching as it develops in one's daily practice.

3 Implementation of the Peer Observation Process and Discussion

The POAT process outlined in the previous section was conceived, designed, and initially tested by a small group of instructors/observers. While the arrangement into pre-observation meeting, class observation, and post-observation meeting was agreed upon from the very beginning and never required changes, the definition of the statements to be included in the checklist, as well as their exact formulation and way of scoring, all underwent several revisions. The first observations involved a group of 12 "pioneers," who agreed to test the process. Later, a larger group of ~40 instructors was involved to further test the process.

Our experimentation led to the definition of the optimal size of the observation group, namely two observers plus one observed instructor (a larger size would require facing slightly greater organizational problems). It was also reported that observers benefit from sitting in different areas of the lecturing room (front and rear seats), in such a way as to observe the lecture from different perspectives. Almost all instructors pointed out that peer observation was useful not only to the observed instructor but also (and perhaps mainly) to the observers. This is related to the fact that, while participating in a class, an observer can truly experience the students' perspective and is much more attentive to details that go beyond the pure disciplinary content.

Related to observation logistics is the issue of disciplinary expertise of the observers. The peer observation involved instructors of very different disciplines, spread across bachelor's and master's degree programs, including pure science (mathematics and physics) as well as specialized engineering disciplines. This disciplinary diversity did not create problems: for example, a professor of physics was perfectly able to act as an observer in a chemical engineering lecture. Besides discipline diversity not being a problem, no substantial advantage was found in having discipline-homogeneous triads. This happens because the POAT process is focused on providing feedback on active teaching, which is unrelated to the specific subject being taught. An advantage of interdisciplinary triads is that they favor the sharing of best practices across the entire learning community. An additional, more subtle point in favor of interdisciplinary triads is the lack of disciplinary expertise. If the observer is not an expert of the discipline, he or she is placed within the same learning process as the students. In this way, the observer can directly experience to what extent the instructor's teaching practice favors learning. Interestingly, some observers reported that it was not easy to stay focused on the observation process (namely, on filling the checklist and adding comments), because their attitude was to pay attention to the lecture content instead. In other words, it was experienced that *observing* a lecture is very different from *participating in* a lecture.

Discussion among the learning community raised a number of important points that are worth being mentioned here. A major point was about the nature of the feedback provided. Instructors often misleadingly associate feedback to evaluation and marking; this is probably the reason why some instructors reported they felt "under evaluation" while being observed in a class (interestingly, this possibly reveals how *the students* may feel when a discussion is engaged in a class). Such attitudes prevented some observed instructors from being natural with their classes and sometimes led the instructors to modify their teaching method. To reduce this effect, we think that the POAT process needs to be clearly presented as a method for fostering discussion about teaching, but not as a way to evaluate the performance of each instructor. Such a constructive attitude starts from the name itself: "Peer *observation*" was selected, suggesting the idea that observed instructors and observers are peers who discuss what was observed. We preferred this name to "Peer review" to highlight that there is no review (a reviewer is typically associated with a judgment). This point was stressed whenever the POAT process was presented. The triads were also recommended to discuss this point explicitly during the pre-observation meetings. Another important discussion was about the meaning of the scores in the checklist: as discussed earlier, the scores 1, 2, 3, and 4 are not marks, but rather four agree/disagree levels about the presence of a given statement. To reinforce this aspect, we agreed that the scores and notes on the checklist, as well as any other written comments, shall be provided only to the instructor and not to authorities in charge of evaluation (e.g., the head of department).

Even though, on the one hand, instructors should not feel under evaluation, on the other hand it is important that the observers frankly express their thoughts to the instructor. Positive comments are very pleasant, although constructive critiques are much more useful for continual improvement of the instructor's teaching. The absence of judgment should leave the observer free to make comments on any aspect of the teaching activity, highlighting both strong and weak points. This is also a key element of the process that needs to be stressed when presenting the activities to the instructors who are starting their first peer observations.

Another point of discussion was about how to express feedback on the statements listed in the checklist. Several options were discussed, and eventually the aforementioned scale between 1 and 4 was chosen. The number of choices is even in order to force observers not to be balanced (the middle-of-range option is not available). For the same reason, the "not available" option was removed, because tests demonstrated that it was often used as a way to avoid expressing feedback. Alternatives that were eventually discarded are: (a) a scale from A to D, essentially identical to the one used but without numbers (it was considered less clear); (b) a continuous line ranging from "do not agree" to "totally agree" where observers would put a mark in any position (this could have caused troubles comparing the opinions of the observers, and offered the middle-of-range option); (c) a choice between two options only (that was not expressive enough). In any of the options considered, it was always clear that the scale is a method for providing a very quick feedback, but written comments should also be provided by the observers and serve as drivers of the post-observation meeting discussion.

We received a lot of feedback also on the number of items in the checklist and on their formulation. The final list provided in Sect. 2 has little overlap among statements and pushes observers to consider teaching from similar yet different perspectives. For example, consider statement #7 ("Students are comfortable in asking questions") and statement #8 ("Students actively participate in class activities and discussion"): even though they may seem the same, the former considers interactions from students' initiative, while the latter consider how students respond to the instructor's stimulation. Similarly, statement #9 ("Instructor asks for feedback on proposed activities and teaching methods, checks students' comprehension and their capability of identifying key concepts") and statement #10 ("Instructor welcomes students' questions/remarks/ enquiries") also seemed very similar to some instructors involved in the first phase of the project. However, they consider two different elements: #9 relates to how students react to the instructor's initiative, while #10 relates to the instructor's reaction to students' initiative. Again, statement #10 was considered similar to item #7, but they differ in a detail: #7 is related to students' attitude, while #10 refers to the instructor's attitude. Even though these are often connected, we decided to leave them as distinct items in order to foster the discussion about this in the post-observation meeting.

We found that it is important to stress such differences and subtleties while presenting the peer observation activity and during the pre-observation meeting. Recall that this process was meant to work for learning communities outside the education disciplines (engineering instructors in the study at hand), who may require a while to reflect about the differences just highlighted, especially if they are new to the process.

4 Conclusions

This chapter has shared the description of how the practice of peer observation of active teaching was first developed and then spread across the faculty learning community of the School of Engineering at the University of Padova, Italy. Activities began in 2016 when a small group of instructors was strongly motivated to improve their teaching and to investigate new teaching methods. Among other initiatives, peer observation was established in the community as a method for discussing teaching with fellow instructors, sharing ideas, and providing suggestions. Involving an increasing number of instructors in the initiative pushed the learning community to formalize a method for guiding the peer observation process. The final process was the focus of this chapter. This was the result of several discussions that took place while fine-tuning the process. We propose our process as a successful way to promote discussion about teaching among colleagues who share the focus on continual improvement or may want to reconsider their teaching activity from a different perspective.

The process of peer observation of active teaching can be framed in the theories and practices of knowledge management as a way to share knowledge, processes, and practices. Sharing knowledge for promoting better teaching and better learning is central to human development and change (Anderson, 2016).

One of the aims of knowledge management theory is to make knowledge explicit (Polanyi, 1966). This process encourages self-disclosure of the instructors and awareness related to teaching and learning. The peer observation can be also considered an organizational and individual intervention to generate, share, and promote new knowledge in teaching and learning in a context where individuals are acting as isolated silos, and the practices of sharing for improving teaching are not common at all. Peer observation concentrates on what instructors do and how they decide and want to share their knowledge with colleagues driven by the desire of improving their teaching and creating community of practices (Wenger, 2002).

References

Adams, S. R., & Mix, E. K. (2014). Taking the lead in faculty development: Teacher educators changing the culture of university faculty development through collaboration. *AILACTE, 11*, 37–56.

Anderson, D. L. (2016). *Organization development. The process of leading organizational change.* Thousand Oaks, CA: SAGE.

Fedeli, M. (2016). Coinvolgere gli studenti nelle pratiche didattiche: potere, dialogo e partecipazione. In M. Fedeli, V. Grion, & D. Frison (Eds.), *Coinvolgere per apprendere. Metodi e tecniche partecipative per la formazione* (pp. 113–142). Lecce: Pensa Multimedia.

Fedeli, M., & Taylor, E. W. (2016). Exploring the impact of a teacher study group in an Italian University. *Formazione & Insegnamento, XIV*(3), 2279–7505.

Felder, R. M., & Brent, R. (2016). *Teaching and learning STEM. A practical guide.* San Francisco, CA: Jossey Bass.

Gosling, D. (2014). Collaborative peer-supported review of teaching. In J. Sachs & M. Parsell (Eds.), *Peer review of learning and teaching in higher education* (Professional learning and development in schools and higher education 9). Dordrecht: Springer Science+Business Media.

Jensen, K., & Aiyegbayo, O. (2011). *Peer observation of teaching: Exploring the experiences of academic staff at the University of Huddersfiel.* Working paper. University of Huddersfield, Huddersfield.

Kahut, G. F., Burnap, C., & Yon, M. G. (2007). Peer observation of teaching: Perception of the observer and the observed. *College Teaching, 55*(1), 19–25.

McGrath, D., & Monsen, S. (2015). *Peer observation of teaching.* A discussion paper prepared for the peer observation of teaching colloquium 27 March 2015. Institute for teaching and learning innovation.

Polanyi, M. (1966). *The tacit dimension.* Garden City, NY: Doubleday.

Taylor, E. W. (2007). An update of transformative learning theory: A critical review of the empirical research (1999–2005). *International Journal of Lifelong Education, 26*(2), 173–191.

Weimer, M. (2013). *Learner-centered teaching: Five key changes to practice.* San Francisco, CA: Jossey-Bass.

Wenger, E. C., McDermott, R., & Snyder, W. M. (2002). *Cultivating communities of practice: A guide to managing knowledge.* Boston, MA: Harvard Business School Press.

Comparative Studies, the Experience of COMPALL Winter School

Monika Staab and Regina Egetenmeyer

Abstract International comparative research enables ways of imparting encoded and culturally embedded knowledge and ways of generating new knowledge. Comparison allows for disclosing cultural practices and structures in other countries and in one's own. It can grant access to previously unavailable or hidden knowledge, and it can shape new knowledge for theory and practice. In the field of adult education, where theory and practice often remain national, comparison allows for understanding, sharing, and creating theoretical frameworks, structures, and practices. To that end, the project Erasmus+ Strategic Partnership "Comparative Studies in Adult Education and Lifelong Learning—COMPALL" developed a joint module in study programmes related to adult education and lifelong learning. Through its innovative teaching and study programme, which is based on blended learning mobility, COMPALL became a forum for knowledge sharing and creation. Over 3 years, seven European universities designed innovative learning and teaching strategies that foster the exchange of knowledge, cultural understanding, and knowledge creation by conducting comparative research. The study programme consistently received a positive response from participants and produced three books presenting the results.

1 International Comparative Research

Over the last decades, several developments on the international level have challenged the field of adult education. The concept of lifelong learning and the European Education and Training 2020 goals also emphasise the role of adult education in the increasingly globalised world. In these documents, adult learning is understood as a key element for improving employability on the changing labour market, responding to demographic change and counteracting economic crises (European Commission, 2011). Moreover, migration in Europe has created new

---

M. Staab (✉) · R. Egetenmeyer
University of Würzburg, Würzburg, Germany
e-mail: monika.staab@uni-wuerzburg.de; regina.egetenmeyer@uni-wuerzburg.de

© Springer Nature Switzerland AG 2019
M. Fedeli, L. L. Bierema (eds.), *Connecting Adult Learning and Knowledge Management*, Knowledge Management and Organizational Learning 8,
https://doi.org/10.1007/978-3-030-29872-2_12

target groups for adult learning, posing a challenge for equal education and training as well as social integration in many European countries (Research voor Beleid, 2008, p. 61). The new demands and developments on the transnational level have led to a dynamic structure in the field. The internationalisation of adult education is seen as an ongoing process that asks for greater international cooperation among researchers and practitioners (Schmidt-Lauff & Egetenmeyer, 2015). Therefore, international comparative research can provide opportunities to strengthen cooperation and research in adult education. By reflecting on current theory and practice, it can offer valuable guidance for the future. In the academic sector, international comparison, by identifying and analysing similarities and differences between different countries, contributes to a better understanding, improvement, and adaptation of adult education (Reischmann, 2008, p. 20). The comparative approach is used for enhancing and adapting policies on the national level (Bray, 2008, p. 34). In this context, transnational actors have conducted comparative studies with the aim of policy formulation and policy intervention. Driven by the policy objectives, however, this research can be seen as politically motivated rather than academic (Singh, 2017). Aside from transnational comparative research, which created a world of big data, benchmarking, and rankings, the scientific community in adult education has used comparative methods to a smaller extent (Egetenmeyer, 2016, p. 93). This is why the project ERASMUS+ Strategic Partnership *Comparative Studies in Adult Education and Lifelong Learning (COMPALL)* has made the adaptation and dissemination of international comparative research its strategic objective. It aims to promote comparative studies in adult education and lifelong learning to foster mutual understanding, knowledge sharing, and knowledge generation among (future) professionals in the field. The project is situated in the higher education sector and applies the following definition of international comparative research.

The primary objective of methods in international comparative adult education is disclosing and understanding the differences and similarities of phenomena in adult education. According to the definition of Charters and Hilton (1989), country perspectives form the basis of comparative study:

> A study in comparative international adult education must include one or more aspects of adult education in two or more countries or regions. Comparative study is not the mere placing side by side of data concerning one or more aspects of adult education in two or more countries. Such juxtaposition is only a prerequisite for comparison. At the next stages one attempts to identify the similarities and differences between the aspects under study and to assess the degree of similarities or differences. Even at this point the work of comparisons is not complete. The real value of comparative study emerges only from stage three—the attempt to understand why the differences and similarities occur and what their significance is for adult education in the countries under examination and in other countries where the finding of the study may have relevance. (p. 3)

However, in today's world, a merely state-based comparison will not work for adult education. The provision of adult education is highly influenced by societal, cultural, economic, and international contexts that necessitates a contextual rather than national perspective in comparative research (Egetenmeyer, 2016, p. 81). Besides the fast and complex developments on the global level, the diverse nature of adult education makes it difficult to define research categories. Comparative categories need to be identified according to the research objectives and the richness of comparison. Targets or measurements of policies, programmes, or target groups of providers can constitute possible categories. As a consequence, doing research means considering specifics in adult education practice on the one hand and transnational developments on the other. To meet this requirement, Egetenmeyer (2016) developed a relationship model for comparative research in adult education that includes different dimensions of comparison: time, societal sectors (state, market, and civil society), (non) participants and learners, provision and effects of adult education, and transnational contexts. This holistic approach looks not only at *what* to compare (comparative categories) but also considers the *who, when, where, and why* of phenomena (context). It helps to examine and understand various issues in adult education. For each focus, new knowledge can be generated and made applicable for practice. The understanding arising from this kind of comparison cannot only benefit adult education research and practice—more generally speaking, the quality of the adult education discipline—but also transform the personal values of the researchers. According to Reischmann (2008), international comparison creates tolerance towards others and their living environments (p. 22). It can make an important contribution to a better intercultural understanding in society, promoting peace in the world (Charters, 1999, p. 55).

Based on this holistic understanding of international comparative research, the COMPALL team developed a didactical concept designed to raise the quality of adult education in academia and practice and to transform researchers' and practitioners' personal values. In the following sections, the authors analyse the joint international learning environment of COMPALL by reflecting on the implemented learning and teaching methods in relation to the project's objectives. The evaluation and academic results demonstrate the successful implementation of the project. The notes on lessons learnt provide answers on the outcomes of the project and its contribution to comparative studies in adult education and lifelong learning. Several aspects can be identified that are part of organisational learning and change in the Strategic Partnership and exemplify the unique teaching and learning practice.

2 Joint International Learning Environment

As outlined above, international comparison can be used to explore and understand different phenomena in adult education. It can promote intercultural understanding and mutual respect in society. In teaching and learning research, sharing information, methods, and experiences between different countries can notably help improve learning and teaching worldwide (Charters, 1999, p. 55). The ERASMUS+ Strategic Partnership COMPALL (2015–2018) used this approach of sharing experiences to develop a joint module in comparative studies in adult education and lifelong learning. Seven universities from Denmark, Germany, Italy, Portugal, and Hungary brought together their expertise to build a joint international learning environment for master's and PhD students working on related topics. The joint module is embedded in an intensive programme and builds on blended learning mobility. The joint module can be understood "as a strategy combining different educational steps and didactic approaches based on shared aims and directed at specific groups of students" (Tino, Guimarães, Frison, & Fedeli, 2017, p. 160). It is developed "by multiple higher education institutions in order to involve a diverse range of academic staff and students coming from various countries and sharing several academic and research traditions" (p. 160). To implement the joint module successfully, challenges concerning sustainability and a reasonable adaptation to participants' skills and needs must be overcome. Consequently, the COMPALL joint module evolved over a three-year period of drafting, piloting, revising, and implementing. After concluding the project in September 2018, it was possible to reflect on the outcomes of the joint international learning approach.

3 The COMPALL Joint Module

The joint module of the COMPALL Strategic Partnership is designed as a blended learning module and in a way that responds to the individual pathways of master's and doctoral students. Various teaching and learning methods were implemented that nurture comparative analytical competences and the integration of national and international perspectives in adult education and lifelong learning. The joint module is structured in two parts: (1) an online preparatory phase and (2) a 2-week intensive programme on the campus of the University of Würzburg, Germany. Programme follow-up is provided by a professional online network on the LinkedIn platform and by publication opportunities for PhD students (Fig. 1).

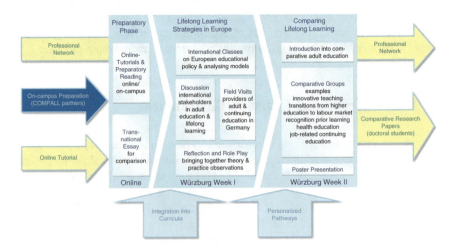

Fig. 1 Structure of the COMPALL joint module. Reprinted from *Joint Module in Comparative Studies in Adult Education and Lifelong Learning*, by COMPALL, n.d.-b, retrieved 10 May 2019 from https://www.hw.uni-wuerzburg.de/compall/joint-module/. Reprinted with permission

Comparative Studies, the Experience of COMPALL Winter School

The joint module is centred on students' learning. Given the highly diverse target group, the Strategic Partnership implemented personalised pathways that respond to participants' individual needs and knowledge. The module integrates students from various study programmes and academic levels regardless of their prior knowledge and experiences concerning international comparative adult education. English language skills, ECTS recognition, and support structures at students' home universities intensified the prevailing heterogeneity. Occasionally, students participated in the programme more than once and therefore had deeper knowledge on the topic (Tino et al., 2017, p. 161 f.).

As a consequence, the organisers carefully designed a preparatory phase within the blended learning approach to facilitate equal preparation. In this phase, an online tutorial introduces students to European and international policies in adult education and lifelong learning, providing first insights into comparative analysis. The tutorial was created by multiple partners and includes videos, readings, and tasks, as well as two online discussions. The online tutorial is embedded in the Moodle platform, which offers space for exchanging experiences, questions, and concerns during the process.

After following the online tutorial in a self-directed way, students are asked to write a transnational essay on a selected topic to finalise their preparation. The essay is used for later comparisons during the intensive phase. The participants are guided through the self-directed learning path by an extensive participant guide and on-campus sessions at COMPALL partner universities. Moreover, students have the option to receive guidance via the Moodle platform. Besides, a professional online network on the LinkedIn platform offers the opportunity to get in touch with future participants and professionals in the field. The didactical and methodical approach of the preparatory phase forms the basis for the intensive phase. It introduces students to comparative studies in adult education and promotes exchanges, knowledge sharing, and intercultural encounters via various online forums.

The intensive programme is split into two parts. In the first week, students become familiar with different lifelong learning strategies in Europe. The theoretical sessions are done in smaller groups of no more than 30 students. These groups are mixed in a way to enable students get in touch with participants from other universities, study levels, and cultural backgrounds. The teaching and learning interactions include discussions with international stakeholders in adult education and lifelong learning, field visits to selective providers of adult and continuing education in Germany, and reflections and role plays. Theory and practice are interlinked throughout the programme. On the first day of the second week, students take a joint introductory class on comparative methods in international adult education. Afterwards, students are assigned to their comparative groups to conduct their own comparative research on a selected topic. These comparative groups, consisting of five to eight students, are arranged prior to the programme and always mix students from different countries and study levels. Group members have the chance to get in touch during the online preparation phase and can intensify their exchanges during group work. Each group is jointly guided by an expert in the field (moderator) and a young research fellow (co-moderator). At the end of the second week, students present their own international comparative study to the other groups in a final session. The comparative group work can be considered the heart of the joint module. The comparisons result in exchanging knowledge and creating new knowledge about various phenomena in adult education and lifelong learning. Intercultural understanding is promoted among students and teachers in relation to their professional and personal views.

To disseminate the results of the comparative analysis, PhD students are invited to publish a paper in a joint volume on different comparative studies in adult education and lifelong learning. Furthermore, various dissemination events and activities are used to share the knowledge and experiences of the programme. All developed products are available on open access terms on the project website (https://www.hw.uni-wuerzburg.de/compall/). The professional online network on LinkedIn sustains students' and teachers' professional and intercultural exchange, strengthening cooperation with other professionals in the field. Efforts of the partner universities have led to the long-term integration of the joint module in their curricula, thereby supporting continuous research activities in international comparative adult education.

In conclusion, the didactical structure of the COMPALL joint module promotes knowledge sharing and creation as well as mutual understanding in the field of adult education and lifelong learning on different levels. The involvement of students and teachers of various educational and cultural backgrounds in many ways provides opportunities for intercultural exchange. A cultural programme supports the interaction during the intensive phase. Throughout the project lifetime, the teaching and learning methods have been adjusted to participants' individual needs. External and internal evaluations monitored the development process and can outline the programme's impact on the individual level.

4 Learners' Voices

To measure the impact of the joint module, the German Institute of Adult Education—Leibniz Centre for Lifelong Learning (DIE) was asked to perform an external evaluation. A mix of qualitative and quantitative measures was used to evaluate the programme's short-term and mid-term effects. After each intensive phase during the project's three-year term, participants completed questionnaires. In addition, narratives of selective students were collected through qualitative interviews. The evaluation results mainly present the academic and personal outcomes of students' participation. In spring 2017 and 2018, an online questionnaire was sent to former students to survey the programme's medium-term effects and to identify the impact on participants' professional careers and/or further studies. The following outline is based on the evaluation reports of the external evaluation.

In all 3 years, students were highly satisfied with the programme, indicating increasing satisfaction over the years. By incorporating students' feedback on an ongoing basis, the project consortium could improve the organisational, academic, and didactical quality of all three didactical parts: preparation phase, first week, and second week of the intensive programme. There was some variation in the programme highlights identified by participants depending on their individual preferences, with group work, field visits, lectures/lessons, and role play mentioned most frequently. In terms of overarching issues, the international learning environment, learning atmosphere, and intercultural exchanges were prominent features of the joint module. Concerning content-related issues, participants highlighted their learning about adult education practices, new theoretical models, or doing research. Social- and content-related aspects were interlinked in many cases (e.g. discussing and exchanging ideas on adult education with other participants). Moreover, participants mentioned aspects such as skill development, learning atmosphere, organisational issues, and networking. In the collected feedback, students particularly emphasised the programme's didactical concept, its connection of theory and practice, its methodological variety, and the interactive approach (COMPALL, n.d.-a, "Evaluation Results"). The following statements illustrate these experiences: "The interaction of different countries grasping of cultural knowledge and exchanging of ideas for education and educational ideas and learning different languages with so many opportunities." (Student's quote from the 2017 evaluation questionnaire). "Opportunities for: social learning; comparisons on various levels in and out of the class; comparisons of several aspects of ALE/LLL at different levels; meeting new people and expanding my network." (Student's quote from the 2018 evaluation questionnaire).

Complaints and concerns, which were expressed in all three short-term evaluations, were used to improve the programme. Single critical issues were related to the intense schedule, the final group work presentation, lack of clarity/guidance during the comparative group work, and some participants' English language proficiency. By the end of the project, the joint module's finalised concept, resulting from intense discussions of each single aspect, could minimise the criticism (e.g. by extending the programme from 10 to 14 days). In the final stage, issues raised by participants merely reflected individual preferences and tastes. No substantial problems were stated that might affect the overall quality of the programme.

The results of the short-term and mid-term surveys indicate that the programme contributed to students' professional and personal development as adult education researchers or experts. On a 5-point scale ($1 =$ not at all, $5 =$ very much), participants rated their competence outcomes very positively. In 2018, mean values were 4.09 for academic and 4.22 for personal outcomes. This is an increase compared to 2017 (3.86 and 4.16, respectively) (Lattke & Egetenmeyer, 2018, p. 14). Participants developed subject-related competences as well as transversal competences and personal soft skills. Related to the academic outcomes, they gained knowledge related to adult learning and enhanced their analytical and research skills, particularly concerning comparative research methods. Furthermore, they developed intercultural competences, English language competences, critical thinking skills, time management skills, knowledge of new teaching methods, and communication skills, amongst others (COMPALL, n.d.-a, "Evaluation Results").

Besides taking part in an enjoyable experience, students also had the opportunity to create personal and professional networks. The skills and competences they developed are highly relevant to their professional careers. The mid-term results suggest that the joint module enhanced students' competitive advantage on the labour market, especially if the job includes international aspects. The joint module has increased master's students' motivation to earn a doctoral degree and improved PhD students' methodological and analytical quality. In the long run, students mentioned that the programme influenced their master's or PhD thesis. Many included international perspectives in their research or said they intended to do so. In summary, it can be stated that the structure of the joint module facilitates opportunities for participants' professional and personal development. Regardless of their academic, national, or cultural background, students can develop highly relevant skills and competences for an increasingly globalised world (COMPALL n.d.-a, "Evaluation Results").

5 Academic Results

The academic outcomes of the Strategic Partnership COMPALL cannot only be measured on the students' level, they are also visible to the scientific community, with two book publications on comparative analysis released during the project term. These publications include selected papers by PhD students who jointly wrote on the comparative studies they performed in the intensive programme. Following the principle "From Studies to Research" (Egetenmeyer, 2017, p. 166), students were supported with writing a scientific paper by international experts involved in the programme. An established supervision model ensured adequate service, providing newcomers in the field of comparative studies with the opportunity to take a first (visible) step in the academic field. The international volumes focus on professionalisation in adult education and lifelong learning in an international context (Egetenmeyer, Schmidt-Lauff, & Boffo, 2017) and adult education and work contexts (Egetenmeyer & Fedeli, 2017).

The third volume *Joint Modules and Internationalisation in Higher Education. Reflections on the Joint Module "Comparatives Studies in Adult Education and Lifelong Learning"* (Egetenmeyer, Guimarães, & Németh, 2017) was published by the partner consortium and selected experts in adult education and lifelong learning. The book explores issues in internationalisation and internationality in higher education with regard to the aim and structure of the COMPALL joint module. It provides means for the implementation of (parts of) the joint module at other higher education institutions to sustain the impact and usefulness of the developed teaching and learning strategies. The Strategic Partnership pursued the goal to implement the joint module over the long term and to reach continuous comparative research activities in the field. This is why all developed products are accessible on the project website and can be fully or partially used by interested students and experts. This can contribute to the internationalisation of theory and practice in the field. The joint module was also named a best practice example by the German Rectors' Conference (HRK) in the project "nexus—Forming Transitions, Promoting Student Success" (2014–2020). Several published project descriptions and analyses as well as book reviews indicate the ongoing interest from the scientific society even beyond the partnership.

6 Lessons Learnt

In conclusion, several lessons learnt can be derived from the COMPALL experience. The joint module presents a completely new approach to comparative studies in adult education and lifelong learning. The blended learning module features (1) a self-directed preparatory phase with online tutorials, online discussions, supervised transnational essays, and (optional) local lesson preparation; (2) a joint intensive phase featuring intercultural lessons, role plays, field visits, guest lectures, and supervised comparative group work; (3) a professional online network; and (4) the (optional) supervised preparation of a comparative research paper. The module allows master's and doctoral students in adult education and lifelong learning to get mobile and experience Europe first hand. Accompanied by their professors in the preparatory phase and during the intensive programme, both students and teachers can benefit from the international learning environment. Students can develop analytical and comparative competences to create systematic links between inter- and transnational issues, as well as national and local issues in adult education and lifelong learning. Moreover, they can enhance their transversal competences (e.g. professional language and professional networking skills). In contrast, professors and teaching staff can gather international experiences and reflect on teaching methods for their own teaching at home. By having the comparative groups guided by a young co-moderator, the teaching of the professors does not happen in isolation. Mutual learning can emerge from the constant interactions between teacher and co-moderator. The consortium partners observed that the intergenerational teaching setting supported the use of ICT in the classroom and contributed to the professional development of the participating teaching staff.

Continuing evaluation activities improved the quality of the joint module. By reviewing teaching and learning methods on an ongoing basis, the programme's didactical structure could be adapted to students' and partners' individual needs and interests. Taking account of the diverse target group, the personalised pathway model successfully involved students from different academic levels, study programmes, partner institutions, and cultural and national backgrounds. Students are recognised as representatives of their home countries and can experience themselves as relevant actors in the teaching and learning process. The evaluation results suggest that the diversity of the programme, instead of being an obstacle, helps enrich learning outcomes. The intercultural exchanges taking place inside and outside the lessons promote mutual understanding and the sharing and creation of (new) knowledge on the individual and academic level. Social activities and networking opportunities foster long-lasting partnerships among students and professionals in the field. The didactical concept of the joint module combines content-related topics with social aspects while taking account of the diverse needs and interests of participating students, experts, and partner institutions. The Strategic Partnership demonstrates that diversity offers ways for innovative teaching methods:

> The success of the COMPALL consortium can be identified in the possibility to mitigate the differences between the various teaching, didactical, and cultural perspectives by bridging them through the Joint Module COMPALL while at the same time respecting personal and local traditions and being aware of the constraints of contexts and policies. (Tino et al., 2017, p. 170).

Moreover, the evaluation results strongly suggest that the joint module raised participants' interest in international topics and promoted intercultural competences, such as an intercultural mindset. This means being open to and appreciative of other cultures and being ready to embrace and value different perspectives. On the one hand, COMPALL resulted in sustainable international networks among students, professors, and experts in the field. On the other hand, the cross-border relations advanced the participants' future careers and led to more degree theses with an international focus. In the 2018 medium-term evaluation, a mean of 3.97 students were encouraged to include international (-comparative) perspectives in their thesis. Especially respondents who were in a "crucial" phase of their studies when deciding on a possible follow-up PhD study highlighted the influence of COMPALL (n.d.-a, "Evaluation results"). As the programme recognises students as valuable contributors in the field of international adult education and lifelong learning, the opportunity for PhD students to publish their findings promoted the academic careers of these young researchers. They were assisted with co-authoring their first publication activity on an international level. Besides, the joint volumes increased the related research activities on comparative studies in adult education and lifelong learning.

Reflecting on the outcomes of the programme, the partner consortium mentioned that the Strategic Partnership fostered mutual collaboration and learning among the different universities. The joint module noticeably enhanced the quality of students' learning at all partner institutions. It can be assumed that co-teaching courses have strong academic value and that teachers can benefit from not teaching on their own. As one partner pointed out, the evolved learning community supported the successful development and implementation of the joint module:

> Compall project has not only widely achieved its main goals, but it has created the roots and the development plan of an effective Faculty Learning Community powered by the familiar and friendly atmosphere that has always characterized the meetings and the recognition of the competences of all professionals involved that has allowed each person to be recognized and to take part in the decision making processes. The active listening to all the voices involved was an ongoing process that empowered people makes the project stronger and meaningful. (COMPALL partner from University of Padua, Italy, personal communication, 2018)

The good and extensive collaboration and willingness of the partners has also led to a complementary ERASMUS+ Strategic Partnership "International and Comparative Studies for Students and Practitioners in Adult Education and Lifelong

Learning" (INTALL 2018–2021). The recently launched project involves six of the seven COMPALL universities together with four new partners and aims to bring university and practice in international and comparative studies in adult education and lifelong learning together for the first time.

In summary, the COMPALL Strategic Partnership developed a joint module on adult education and lifelong learning that was successfully implemented at all partner universities. Through the ongoing evaluation process, the partner consortium could improve the module's didactical structure and raise the quality of the programme. Mutual understanding and joint learning accompanied the COMPALL process, which fostered organisational learning and change. The partner consortium could reach satisfying results, which have had an impact on the individual, institutional, and disciplinary levels. The joint module can be considered an important contribution to improving learning and teaching in study programmes related to adult education and lifelong learning. The academic results and learning outcomes will play a role in the improvement of quality in theory and practice in adult education and promote international comparative research in the field.

References

Bray, M. (2008). The multifaceted field of comparative education: Evolution, themes, actors, and applications. In J. Reischmann & M. Bron Jr. (Eds.), *Comparative adult education* (pp. 33–44). Frankfurt a. M: Peter Lang.

Charters, A. N. (1999). Standards for comparative adult education research. In J. Reischmann, M. Bron Jr., & J. Zoran (Eds.), *Comparative adult education 1998. The contribution of ISCAE to an emerging field of study* (pp. 51–64). Ljubljana: Slovenian Institute for Adult Education.

Charters, A. N., & Hilton, R. J. (1989). Introduction. In A. N. Charters & R. J. Hilton (Eds.), *Landmarks in international adult education. A comparative analysis* (pp. 1–14). London: Routledge.

COMPALL. (n.d.-a). *Evaluation results. Evaluation on the impact of the joint module – outcomes of the Winter School.* Retrieved May 10, 2019, from https://www.hw.uni-wuerzburg.de/compall/results/evaluation-results/

COMPALL. (n.d.-b). *Joint module in comparative studies in adult education and lifelong learning.* Retrieved May, 10, 2019 from https://www.hw.uni-wuerzburg.de/compall/joint-module/

Egetenmeyer, R. (2016). What to compare? Comparative issues in adult education. In M. Slowey (Ed.), *Comparative adult education and learning. Authors and texts* (pp. 79–116). Florence: Firenze University Press.

Egetenmeyer, R. (2017). Zwischen Erwachsenenbildung und Lebenslangem Lernen. Zusammenarbeit von Hochschulen und Akteuren der Erwachsenenbildung/Weiterbildung in Erasmus+. In DAAD – Deutscher Akademischer Austauschdienst (Ed.), *Europa in Bewegung – das europäische Erfolgsprogramm. ERASMUS feiert sein 30-jähriges Jubiläum* (pp. 164–167). Bonn: DAAD. Retrieved November 11, 2018, from https://www.daad.de/medien/na_jubilaeumsbrosch_fin_web.pdf

Egetenmeyer, R., & Fedeli, M. (2017). *Adult education and work contexts: International perspectives and challenges. Comparative perspectives from the 2017 Würzburg Winter School.* Frankfurt a. M: Peter Lang.

Egetenmeyer, R., Guimarães, P., & Németh, B. (Eds.). (2017). *Joint modules and internationalisation in higher education. Reflections on the joint module "Comparative studies in adult education and lifelong learning"*. Frankfurt a. M: Peter Lang.

Egetenmeyer, R., Schmidt-Lauff, S., & Boffo, V. (2017). *Adult learning and education in international contexts. Future challenges for it professionalisation. Comparative perspectives from the 2016 Würzburg Winter School*. Frankfurt a. M: Peter Lang.

European Commission. (2011). *Council resolution on a renewed European agenda for adult learning*. Brussels: European Commission. Retrieved November 26, 2018, from https://eur-lex.europa.eu/legal-content/EN/TXT/PDF/?uri=CELEX:32011G1220(01)&from=EN

Lattke, S., & Egetenmeyer, R. (2018). *External evaluation COMPALL*. Report on the Evaluation of the International Winter School Würzburg, Würzburg, 5–16 February 2018. Unpublished manuscript.

Reischmann, J. (2008). Comparative adult education: Arguments, typology, difficulties. In J. Reischmann & M. j. Bron (Eds.), *Comparative adult education* (pp. 19–32). Frankfurt a. M: Peter Lang.

Research voor Beleid. (2008). *ALPINE – Adult learning professions in Europe. A study of the current situation, trends and issues*. Final report, Zoetermeer. Retrieved from https://www.nemo.org/fileadmin/Dateien/public/MumAE/adultprofreport_en.pdf

Schmidt-Lauff, S., & Egetenmeyer, R. (2015). Internationalisierung. In J. Dinkelaker & A. von Hippel (Eds.), *Erwachsenenbildung in Grundbegriffen* (pp. 272–279). Stuttgart: Verlag W. Kohlhammer.

Singh, S. (2017). Transnational comparative studies as sources for research: How scientific, how relevant? *International Journal of Multidisciplinary Educational Research, 6*(8(1)), 113–133.

Tino, C., Guimarães, P., Frison, D., & Fedeli, M. (2017). COMPALL-joint module: Diversity of participants and models of curricular and local implementation. In R. Egetenmeyer, P. Guimarães, & B. Németh (Eds.), *Joint modules and internationalisation in higher education. Reflections on the joint module "Comparative studies in adult education and lifelong learning"* (pp. 159–171). Frankfurt a. M: Peter Lang.

Fostering Knowledge Sharing Via Technology: A Case Study of Collaborative Learning Using *Padlet*

Daniela Frison and Concetta Tino

Abstract The chapter describes a collaborative learning experience in higher education carried out through the use of the Additional Collaborative Tool *Padlet.* The study refers to a master course focused on Organizational Development and based on the *EMI—English as a Medium of Instruction* methodology. Starting from a focus on collaborative learning strategies literature and the proposal of Additional Collaborative Tool in Higher Education, the chapter presents the design process of an online activity based on the use of Padlet, an online whiteboard that offers space for multiple participants to collaborate in real time. Students' feedback about the Padlet experience has been collected and analyzed (*The Organizational development. Teaching and learning methods* course was jointly conducted by Prof. Monica Fedeli, University of Padua, and Prof. Laura Bierema, Georgia State University. The authors, Daniela Frison and Concetta Tino, jointly led the online activities and conceived of the presented idea. Daniela Frison led the design of the study and edited Sects. 4 and 5. Concetta Tino edited Sect. 1. The authors jointly discussed the results and edited Sects. 2, 3, and 6.).

1 The Role of Additional Collaborative Tools in Collaborative Learning Processes

Collaboration, social networking, as well as the construction and sharing of knowledge are key categories that characterize the learning process mediated by technological tools (Brown & Adler, 2008). Their aim is to make over the educational and training methods according to a constructivist approach. With the increase of online learning environments, collaborative tools and strategies have taken a decisive role

---

D. Frison (✉)
University of Firenze, Firenze, FI, Italy
e-mail: daniela.frison@unifi.it

C. Tino
University of Padova, Padova, PD, Italy
e-mail: concetta.tino@unipd.it

© Springer Nature Switzerland AG 2019
M. Fedeli, L. L. Bierema (eds.), *Connecting Adult Learning and Knowledge Management*, Knowledge Management and Organizational Learning 8,
https://doi.org/10.1007/978-3-030-29872-2_13

in generating student involvement. Such involvement is defined by Trowler (2010) as "the interaction between the time, effort and other relevant resources invested by both students and their institutions intended to optimize the student experience and enhance the learning outcomes and development of students and the performance, and reputation of the institution" (p. 5). Furthermore, as Alavi and Leidner (2001) state: "the role of IT in [organizational] knowledge management ought to receive considerable scholarly attention and become a focal point of inquiry" because advanced information technologies and online learning environments can be used to systematize, enhance, and expedite knowledge management.

In general, collaborative activities that can be implemented using technologies include the use of tools that make it possible to perform a set of functions ranging from synchronous and asynchronous communication, to video-chat as an online space to facilitate brainstorming activities, from the construction and continuous updating of documents, to the presentation of content and learning themes from remote. Tools such as Padlet, Google drive, MindMeister, and Skype can be used as a brainstorming space to carry out collaborative activities in real time. In addition, they offer the opportunity of writing, drawing, sharing images, chatting or talking with collaborators, building and sharing knowledge in a common environment (Mallon & Bernsten, 2015). Chickering and Ehrmann (1996) consider these active learning strategies useful to promote student involvement in online environments, where the collaborative activity and participation create bonds that allow students to learn and share their opinions, and where the quality of these interactions directly affects teaching and learning success (Nandi, Hamilton, & Harland, 2012). The attention given to collaborative environments as a way to support learning has promoted their constant evolution. The most important features that identify them as collaborative environments are class organizing, virtual environments, open/free environment, cloud computing, communication, and additional collaborative tools (Seralidou & Douligeris, 2015).

More specifically, Additional Collaborative Tools, like Padlet, make it possible to create a group whiteboard to encourage collaborative editing and posting activities that support students' collaboration, participation, and engagement. There are studies that show how the use of Padlet supports the construction of new knowledge (Dewitt, Alias, & Siraj, 2015). Indeed, this collaborative tool can be used both as a space for debating and for generating new ideas and as a tool for supporting the learning of content. In addition, it can be used to promote the development of skills, to facilitate the acquisition, internalization, application, and creation of new knowledge (Pasher & Ronen, 2011). The advantage of the use of collaborative tools and cooperative learning is based on two important aspects: (a) the improvement of students' memory and motivation (Bligh, 2000), and (b) the creation of a learning community with the common goal of building new knowledge (Kuo, Hwang, Chen, & Chen, 2012), through discussions aimed at solving problems collaboratively. Therefore, in this perspective, Padlet can be used as a "wall where students can hang their thoughts," where they can reflect on together and from which they can start to generate knowledge, thanks also to the support of links, videos, articles, and images. Indeed, this tool and the way the research group proposed it to the class supported knowledge management processes (i.e., knowledge capture, sharing, and apply) involving both individual learning and collective learning (King, 2009; King, Chung, & Haney, 2008; Zhang et al., 2015).

2 The Use of Padlet: The Case of Using a Collaborative Tool in an Academic Course

During the second year of a master course in management and education delivered in English, the research group designed a Padlet-supported collaborative activity (Dewitt et al., 2014, 2015) in order to help students, to learn contents in English. The *English as a Medium of Instruction* (EMI) methodology is increasingly widespread in the educational programs of the European states, as suggested by the recommendations of the European Commission that highlight the ability to speak foreign languages as one of the factors of competitiveness and modernization of the European Higher Education system (European Commission, 2012; European Union, 2013; Eurydice, 2012).

As it is well known, the term EMI refers to the use of the English language to convey knowledge of the subject matter not within the context of foreign language courses, but within the framework of non-curricula languages courses (Brusasco, 2015). The design and delivery of teaching using a vehicular language can be really challenging for teachers, because the process requires some additional tasks and commitment to the management of traditional teaching, obviously. This aspect, in fact, has been highlighted by a comparative interpretative research conducted by Coryell, Fedeli, Frison, and Tyner (2015) with two groups of American and Italian instructors who teach international classes in English. Specifically, Italian teachers, who teach international students in their own universities or abroad, show a personal sense of responsibility about the necessity to improve both teaching in the English language, mainly by acquiring greater mastery of the language, and active and interactive teaching and learning methods (Coryell et al., 2015). They do their best to take part in English language acquisition seminars and courses in order to learn more about classroom interactions with diverse student groups. The majority wished for additional support on teaching in English, recognizing that teaching domestic or international students according to an EMI methodology constitutes a great challenge, for both teachers and students.

3 Teaching Context and Learning Objectives of the Experience

The experience described in this paper developed according to a blended approach that requires teachers to deliver 2/3 of the teaching in the classroom and 1/3 online. The activity was proposed to 17 second year students (15 attending and 2 not attending) during the academic year 2016–2017, and to 13 students (11 attending and 2 not attending) during the academic year 2017–2018, enrolled in the *Adult and Continuing Education* master's degree course. The design of the teaching and learning experience for the next academic year is currently in progress. The chapter presents the academic year 2017–2018 experience.

According to the remarks on the usefulness of Additional Collaborative Tools and the EMI methodology, the use of the Padlet tool was proposed in order to pursue the following objectives:

- To support students taking part in a course delivered in English
- To encourage the active participation of students and the interaction among attending and non-attending students.

Next to these general goals, the online activities (including the use of the Padlet described herein) pursued the following specific learning objectives:

- To learn strategies and tools that promote reflection on the content and processes of learning
- To encourage critical thinking about adult training and teaching contexts in which to promote the reflective processes
- To test strategies and tools to support adult learning process

4 The Design of the Padlet Walls

The 2017–2018 class group ($N = 13$) was split into three subgroups of four-four-five members. The activity named *Reflection on content: connecting knowledge and sharing learning with Padlet* was linked to three Padlet Walls, each one dedicated to a specific topic related to a book chapter that was part of the course program. The three chapters, in English, were proposed one at a time, according to the same chronological order in which they were developed in the classroom. Each Padlet Wall activity lasted 5 days, between the lesson concerned and the following one. Students had to conclude and deliver the results of the activity by the fifth day, followed by the instructor's assessment phase.

Using Discussion Methods The first Padlet Wall, on *Using discussion methods,* was especially conceived to encourage discussion among group members and, at the same time, to explore the use of the Padlet tool and its functionalities.

The first wall was set up according to the "columns" format for categorization tasks. Reflection on the use of group discussion methods was encouraged, inviting students to focus on opportunities offered by the adoption of discussion methods, both from the teachers' and students' perspective, and challenges related to the proposal of such methods, again from both points of view (Fig. 1).

Teaching for Critical Thinking The second wall was devoted to the topic *Teaching for critical thinking* and was set up following the "canvas" format, a sort of mind-

Fig. 1 The first Padlet Wall focused on using discussion methods

map showing the interrelationships and connections among group members' postings. Consistent with the subject matter, the following statement was offered to the students for discussion: "Critical thinking is an individual process." This opened the discussion on the topic and the students were invited:

1. To link their postings to the statement
2. To formulate postings that provided colleagues with a reflective input (questions, provocations, audio/video stimuli, etc.),
3. To link their postings to colleagues' comments

The development of the Wall does not therefore refer exclusively to a chronological succession, but also to a sort of "hierarchical graduation," allowing to visualize the pre- and post-reflections and idea development.

Fostering Self-directed Learning The third wall was structured according to a "blog" format, which optimizes the contents in a feed ordered from top to bottom, one item at a time. This last Padlet Wall asked students to elaborate a set of guidelines, a series of principles to follow in order to encourage *self-directed learning* in adult education (Brookfield, 2013; Knowles, 1975), deepening and reworking again the contents of the related chapter.

5 Students' Feedback About Padlet

At the end of each Padlet session, as a part of the "reflection on content activity, connecting knowledge and sharing learning with Padlet," a personal and timely feedback was sent to each student. It was focused on his or her contribution to the Padlet wall. Feedback allowed students to fine-tune their contribution toward the next Padlet session. Indeed, as underscored in the literature, feedback acquires centrality in the teaching and learning process when it is timely, adequately designed, and closely anchored to the contents of the activity to which it refers, providing students with evidence of the performance expected and the gap to be filled (Fedeli, 2016; Grion, 2016; Hattie & Timperley, 2007). Feedback was collected from students as well, to get their reactions about the use of Padlet. With this aim, a feedback tool inspired by the Brookfield's critical incident questionnaire (2013) was administered.

The first stimulus provided was the following: "If you look back to the Padlet experience what moments were meaningful for you? And why?" Two main foci emerged. The first, reported by the totality of the participants, was linked to the possibility of collaboration and connection among group members, according to the Padlet objectives:

- "I learned to stimulate my companions with reflective questions based on concrete examples."
- "Through Padlet you can learn together with your colleagues and understand new points of view."

The second focus was related to linguistic support:

- "It was useful for improving my English language, because I did my best to write in a clear way."

The second stimulus invited participants to reflect on the potential of Padlet as a tool to support the reflection on content: "What is your opinion about Padlet as a tool to encourage reflection on content?" In this case, the students highlighted that working with Padlet provided them with a more direct connection with contents developed in the classroom: "The experience with Padlet was very informative and strongly linked to what I learned in the classroom."

Furthermore, as planned, Padlet promoted the connection between attending and non-attending students:

- "I am a not attending student and I very often feel that I have some gaps. Through this tool, I felt really involved in the activities, but above all I connected myself with my colleagues."

The last stimulus was intended to identify strengths and weaknesses in the use of Padlet in view of the redesign of activities for the following year: "Please, identify at least one strength and one weakness related to the use of Padlet for the online activities."

Concerning strengths, students said:

- "To write down ideas and opinions on a virtual blackboard and the visual impact as well can help to understand the different ideas."
- "One strength is the possibility to create connections with the comments of my colleagues."
- "It's a funny and different way of discussion."
- "Collaboration with non-attending students."

On the contrary, about the challenges, students highlighted the complexity concerning the use of the tool when postings are numerous:

- "It is not suitable for large group work."
- "It can be chaotic when there are many comments on the wall."

Fostering Knowledge Sharing Via Technology: A Case Study of... 233

Feedback collected from students allowed the research group to deeply reflect on the Padlet learning environment and to connect the learning experience, as described by students, to the focus on collaborative learning and knowledge management.

6 Conclusion and Future Development

This paper was meant to present the use of the Padlet tool as part of a course conducted according to the EMI methodology. This Additional Collaborative Tool was proposed first to support students facing critical issues related to the studying of contents in English and second to stimulate reflection on the offered disciplinary contents. The experience presented here and the collection and analysis of students' feedback show three main attention foci, as follows.

Additional Collaborative Tool and Flipped Classroom As mentioned before, the Padlet was proposed within a blended course in order to encourage a *flipped* approach (Abeysekera & Dawson, 2015; Bergmann & Sams, 2012; Roehl, Reddy, & Shannon, 2013). As Abeysekera and Dawson (2015) state, under the *flipped* or *inverted classroom* approach "the information-transmission component of a traditional face-to-face lecture is moved out of class time. In its place are active, collaborative tasks. Students prepare for class by engaging with resources that cover what would have been in a traditional lecture" (p. 1). As a tool for collaborative learning, Padlet offers a space for multiple participants to collaborate in real time, drawing, sharing images, chatting, and recording work to submit to the instructor for assessment (Mallon & Bernsten, 2015). As students underlined, Padlet allows the design of *active and collaborative tasks* (Abeysekera & Dawson, 2015), flipping the teaching and learning process, engaging students under an *active learning* framework.

Collaborative Learning for Attending and Non-attending Students Furthermore, this *active* approach, by means of the proposed Additional Collaborative Tool, was addressed to the whole group of students, both attending and non-attending ones. The involvement of non-attending students is always a critical issue for instructors. The use of Padlet made the "collaboration with non-attending students" possible, as a student underlined. Despite this enhancement of collaboration, students also highlighted that Padlet is not so suitable for large groups. From the students' perspective, the number of postings on the wall strongly affects the development of the final output.

The interrelationships and connections among group members' postings are chaotic, and make it hard to identify the *common thread*, when there is the participation of a large group. This "chaos" also requires continuous attention on the part of the student, and timely postings: to be away from Padlet for long increases the difficulty of reconnecting and understanding the cognitive passages carried out by colleagues, even if the application records the date and the time of publication. This issue could affect, in particular, the contribution of non-attending students who engage in the activities according to a schedule that is notoriously different from traditional students (for example, in the evening or early night or morning). This weakness could be faced with an accurate design of the activity that takes into account the target group and its peculiarities.

Collaborative Learning and Peer Learning From the EMI perspective, the use of an Additional Collaborative Tool offers the instructor the opportunity of monitoring the learning process and the language issue as well. Also, peers have a crucial role in offering linguistic support, becoming a sort of "helper" to support each other in facing the challenges of their joint activities (Topping, 2005). In this regard, a further consideration concerns precisely the *peer-learning process* encouraged by the application with reference to the acquisition of "knowledge and skills through active helping and supporting among status equals or matched companions" (Topping, 2005, p. 631). This process of mutual support is crucial in order to deal with the language difficulties encountered by students.

Collaborative Learning and Knowledge Management Finally, from a knowledge management point of view, Additional Collaborative Tools can support knowledge capture and sharing and apply three subprocesses of knowledge management recognized by Zhang et al. (2015). Precisely, collaborative learning enhanced by the Padlet walls can play an important role for capturing and sharing knowledge among students, and these processes are strictly connected with the peer-learning one mentioned above. And concerning application, Padlet, integrated by the Moodle forum, offers students the opportunity to "manipulate" the disciplinary content, also on the linguistic side, thus revealing itself as an interesting application to support knowledge management processes in addition to *active* and *peer-learning* ones.

References

Abeysekera, L., & Dawson, P. (2015). Motivation and cognitive load in the flipped classroom: Definition, rationale and a call for research. *Higher Education Research & Development, 34*(1), 1–14.

Alavi, M., & Leidner, D. (2001). Knowledge management and knowledge management systems: Conceptual foundations and research issues. *MIS Quarterly, 25*(1), 107–136.

Bergmann, J., & Sams, A. (2012). *Flip your classroom: Reach every student in every class every day.* Eugente, Oregon/Arlington, Virginia: International Society for Technology in Education.

Bligh, D. (2000). *What's the point in discussion?* Exeter, UK: Intellect Books.

Brookfield, S. D. (2013). *Powerful techniques for teaching adults.* San Francisco, US: John Wiley & Sons.

Brown, J. S., & Adler, R. P. (2008). Minds on fire: Open education, the long tail, and learning 2.0. *Educause Review, 43*(1), 17–32.

Brusasco, P. (2015). English as a medium of instruction: An introduction. RiCOGNIZIONI. *Rivista di Lingue e Letterature straniere e Culture moderne, 2*(4), 109–110.

Chickering, A., & Ehrmann, S. (1996, October). Implementing the seven principles: Technology as lever. *AAHE Bulletin, 3*, 3–6.

Coryell, J. E., Fedeli, M., Frison, D., & Tyner, J. (2015). Teaching internationally divers students: An international comparative study of faculty development during higher education internationalization. *ICERI 2015 Proceedings* (pp. 311–320).

Dewitt, D., Alias, N., & Siraj, S. (2015). Collaborative learning: Interactive debates using Padlet in a higher education institution. *Journal of Educational Technology & Society, 17*(1), 89–101.

Dewitt, D., Alias, A., Siraj, S., & Zakaria, A. R. (2014). Interactions in online forums: A case study among first-year undergraduate students. *Frontiers in Education, 2*(1), 6–13.

European Commission. (2012). *Rethinking education: Investing in skills for better socioeconomic outcomes*. Strasbourg: European Commission. Online: http://eur-lex.europa.eu/legalcontent/EN/TXT/?qid=1389776578033&uri=CELEX:52012DC0669

European Union. (2013). *Modernisation of higher education*. Luxembourg: European Union.

Eurydice. (2012). *Key data on teaching languages at school in Europe*. Online: http://eacea.ec.europa.eu/education/Eurydice/documents/key_data_series/143EN.pdf

Fedeli, M. (2016). Coinvolgere gli studenti nelle pratiche didattiche: potere, dialogo, partecipazione. In M. Fedeli, V. Grion, & D. Frison (Eds.), *Coinvolgere per apprendere. Metodi e tecniche partecipative per la formazione* (pp. 133–142). Lecce, IT: Pensa Multimedia.

Grion, V. (2016). Assessment for Learning all'università: uno strumento per modernizzare la formazione. In M. Fedeli, V. Grion, & D. Frison (Eds.), *Coinvolgere per apprendere. Metodi e tecniche partecipative per la formazione* (pp. 289–317). Lecce, IT: Pensa Multimedia.

Hattie, J., & Timperley, H. (2007). The power of feedback. *Review of Educational Research, 77*(1), 81–112.

King, W. R. (2009). *Knowledge management and organizational learning*. New York, NY: Springer.

King, W. R., Chung, T. R., & Haney, M. H. (2008). Knowledge management and organizational learning. *Omega, 36*(2), 167–172.

Knowles, M. S. (1975). *Self-directed learning*. New York: Association Press.

Kuo, F. R., Hwang, G. J., Chen, S. C., & Chen, S. Y. (2012). A cognitive apprenticeship approach to facilitating web-based collaborative problem solving. *Educational Technology & Society, 15*(4), 319–331.

Mallon, M., & Bernsten, S. (2015, Winter). *Collaborative learning technologies. Tips and trends*. Chicago, IL: ACRL American Library Association.

Nandi, D., Hamilton, M., & Harland, J. (2012). Evaluating the quality of interaction in asynchronous discussion forums in fully online courses. *Distance Education, 33*(1), 5–30.

Pasher, E., & Ronen, T. (2011). *The complete guide to knowledge management. A strategic plan to leverage your company's intellectual capital*. Hoboken, NJ: Wiley Online Library.

Roehl, A., Reddy, S. L., & Shannon, G. J. (2013). The flipped classroom: An opportunity to engage millennial students through active learning strategies. *Journal of Family & Consumer Sciences, 105*(2), 44–49.

Seralidou, E., & Douligeris, C. (2015). Identification and classification of educational collaborative learning environments. *Procedia Computer Science, 65*, 249–258.

Topping, K. J. (2005). Trends in peer learning. *Educational Psychology, 25*(6), 631–645.

Trowler, V. (2010). Student engagement literature review. *The higher education academy, 11*(1), 1–15.

Zhang, X., Gao, Y., Yan, X., Ordóñez de Pablos, P., Sun, Y., & Cao, X. (2015). From e-learning to social-learning: Mapping development of studies on social media-supported knowledge management. *Computers in Human Behavior, 51*(2015), 803–811.

The Peer Observation: "Mentore" Project at University of Palermo

Marcella Cannarozzo, Pierluigi Gallo, Alida Lo Coco, Bartolomeo Megna, Pasquale Musso, and Onofrio Scialdone

Abstract During the last 6 years at the University of Palermo, a group of academics has been involved in a project called "MENTORE" ("Modifying and ENhancing Teaching through peer Observation and Reflections with Experts.") The objectives of the project are to help teachers improve their teaching, through the help of two mentors; to experiment new approaches in pilot courses to extend, if useful, to other ones; and to change the traditional model of academic teaching based on one single teacher with the class to go toward a model where there is a group of teachers working together in search of improvements. All the participants of the MENTORE project attend to lectures/workshops on teaching and learning and participate in meetings where they share experiences and ideas. In the program, each participant has two mentors who help him or her to improve the quality of his or her teaching. The two mentors are other academics who participate in the program. Indeed, each participant is both mentor and mentee during the same year. Mentors follow some of the lectures of the mentee, meet the students in the final part of the course in order to collect their opinion, and, finally, meet the mentee in order to discuss the actions to carry out for improving the quality of his or her teaching. This chapter describes the aforementioned peer observation practice adopted at the University of Palermo and focuses on the role of mentors describing their activities during the peer observation process.

M. Cannarozzo · P. Gallo (✉) · A. L. Coco · B. Megna · O. Scialdone
Università degli Studi di Palermo, Palermo, PA, Italy
e-mail: marcella.cannarozzo@unipa.it; pierluigi.gallo@unipa.it; alida.lococo@unipa.it; bartolomeo.megna@unipa.it; onofrio.scialdone@unipa.it

P. Musso
Department of Educational Sciences, Psychology, Communication, University of Studies of Bari "Aldo Moro", Bari, Italy
e-mail: pasquale.musso@uniba.it

© Springer Nature Switzerland AG 2019
M. Fedeli, L. L. Bierema (eds.), *Connecting Adult Learning and Knowledge Management*, Knowledge Management and Organizational Learning 8,
https://doi.org/10.1007/978-3-030-29872-2_14

1 The Context of the Project "MENTORE"

For some professors, teaching may be quite easy while for others it is quite difficult. In either case, University teachers are often experts of their fields with little knowledge of teaching and learning methods and educational theories. According to Martinez, Taut, and Schaaf (2016), teacher development policies are in the midst of substantial reform in education system around the world. Particularly, in Italy, there are not general and systemic actions to improve the university teaching. In most universities, the training of lecturers is not carried out and there is no mentoring activity; the teacher is often alone with his or her students without sufficient tools to assess the quality of his or her teaching and to improve it. The MENTORE Project started up at the University of Palermo in 2013 from an idea of five engineers. The aim of the project is to help and support improving academics' teaching. In the first 2 years, the project involved about 20 academics, mainly from engineering courses. In 2018, the project involved about 85 teachers from all the disciplines and for the next year more than one hundred participants are expected.

The objectives of the project are (Felisatti, Cannarozzo, Pennisi, & Scialdone, 2020): (1) help teachers improve their teaching, through the help of two mentors; (2) experiment new approaches in pilot courses to extend, if useful, to other ones; (3) change the traditional model of academic teaching based on one single teacher with the class to go toward a model where there is a group of teachers working together in search of improvements. The MENTORE Project, in particular, is based on two main aspects:

- Two peer mentors help the mentee to improve the teaching quality using information acquired by attending to some lectures, by meeting the students and discussing with them about classes, and by collecting results of anonymous surveys filled out by the students.
- Lectures/workshops on teaching and learning and meetings to share experiences and ideas.

The MENTORE Project was synthetically described in its main elements in Felisatti et al. (2020); this chapter focuses on the role of mentors and provides more information on their activities, especially on the peer observation activity.

2 Goals, Role, and Activities of Mentors

The mentorship program in Palermo has some peculiar features that differentiates it from most of mentorship programs, in terms of goals and methodologies. The main goal in fact is improving teaching and learning as in the developmental model, i.e., a model that puts the improving in teaching and learning at the center by step by step mutual enhancing (Centre for Teaching Support & Innovation, 2017), by focusing on a methodology that uses peer observation and review. As reported by Lomas and Kinchin (2006), UK universities have introduced peer observation as a quality enhancement tool rather than a quality assurance mechanism. Similarly, our project aims to enhance quality of teaching and learning rather than evaluate it. Each participant to the project is both mentor and mentee. Unlike other programs that use self and mutual mentorship, each participant to the MENTORE project has two mentors. Mentors and mentee are peers.

Actually, the mentors are not (a) evaluators; (b) experts of teaching methods and models; (c) experts of contents; (d) psychologist consultants; on the other hand, mentors are peers who acquire various kinds of information (see the following paragraph for details) on the teaching of their mentee and provide indications to improve the quality of teaching. They do not give evaluations or marks but suggestions for possible improvements. In general, they help the mentee stimulating critical thinking on his or her teaching and how to improve it. In this frame, the presence of two mentors is essential to avoid not corrected relationships between mentors and mentees (e.g., between doctor and patient) and to benefit from the two mentors' different experiences and points of view. A friendly approach is favored by the fact that mentors and mentee are peers.

Mentors are not interested in the lessons' matter, but they observe the teaching and learning process. Hence, they may not be experts of the specific topic. Usually, mentors are associated with their mentee so that one with long experience joins the other with shorter experience in mentoring. Association criteria select, preferably, one mentor from the same disciplinary area of the mentee (e.g., engineering, humanities, medicine) to be aware of specific way of teaching of the area and the second from a different area with other experiences on teaching and learning approaches.

Mentors have to carry out the following activities:

1. Peer observation—Mentors attend few lectures given by the mentee, at least two or three. In general, mentees do not know when their mentors will attend their conferences. Mentors have to attend together at least one lecture. During the observation in the class, they use a specific observation grid prepared for the project (see the paragraph on observation grid).
2. Interactive observation—In the final part of the course, they meet the students without the mentee and discuss with them the strong points and the improvement areas of course. In the same occasion, they collect students' opinions through anonymous surveys.
3. Analysis/decision—After the end of the course, the two mentors discuss their observations, revise the information collected by the students, and decide on (a) strengths, (b) improvement areas, and (c) suggestions to give to the mentee.
4. Action—The two mentors meet the mentee. In this occasion, the mentors describe their opinions on strength points and improvement areas, and the mentee explains his or her doubts and his or her point of view on his or her teaching. Mentors and mentee discuss together the potential actions to improve the course and, in the end, they collectively define the steps that the mentee will carry out the next year in order to improve his/her teaching.

The year after, mentors continue to follow the mentee, and the process continues iteratively, in the circle reported in Fig. 1.

Fig. 1 Annual actions of the MENTORE project

Each couple of mentors is assigned to a senior mentor that has participated in the program for many years and that has developed competences on academic teaching. If mentors have some difficulties or doubts about their activities, they will contact their senior mentor asking for help.

3 Peer Observation

Mentors observe teaching attitude and methods (e.g., lecture and time management, students' involvement, the trade-off between speech pleasantness and amount of useful information, use of interactive learning methods). Mentors neglect course contents. A grid guides the observation, helping mentors focus on teaching methods; nevertheless, mentors have some degrees of freedom to contribute to the observation with their own opinions and expectations. Mentors' observation also includes different types of external factors; some can be invisible to the instructor and the students because the familiarity with the context can "mask" possible critical elements. The context includes light conditions, thermal and acoustical comfort, the available technical resources for education, and other environmental components which impact on the focus and can hinder the learning process.

Even during this passive phase, the peer observation has an impact on the trail; in fact, the presence of the mentor(s) inevitably influences the lecturer during the observed class. In a certain sense, it affects the lecturer also outside the observed classes, i.e., during the entire teaching period, as mentors' observations may randomly occur during the whole teaching period and the mentee needs to keep a high level of methodological preparedness.

The observation process is inevitably prone to few causes of uncertainty, as the observed teaching/learning process and the observation are both run by humans. First, the lecture quality and the effectiveness of the teaching strategies can change over time depending on the instructor and the context; second, the quality of the observation depends on the observed elements (e.g., the lecturer used an excellent teaching strategy with a poor timing); finally, the mentors' subjectivity may introduce a bias on the general evaluation of the lecture.

The MENTORE project aims at mitigating the effects of uncertainty listed above applying few countermeasures. First, mentors attend few lectures to average the observations over a (limited) number of samples; then they refer to a predefined grid of observable parameters, so they can all focus on the same elements. Finally, to mitigate subjectivity, even if the two mentors may singularly attend different lectures of the mentee, they need to visit at least one jointly. The presence of two mentors participating in the same lecture permits to smooth eventual biases on the observed process; this smoothing occurs during the discussion between the two observers.

The central role of peer observation becomes even more critical under the recent internationalization process that is sweeping the University of Palermo. Teaching methods have to be considered jointly with the linguistic element for courses taught in English and attended by international students. In facts, teaching in a foreign language requires special attention for both the lecturer and the students. Dedicated strategies should be considered to smooth the communication burden given by the foreign language, for example, making periodic recaps, explaining using different words, and providing new examples. The use of a foreign language for teaching has to be known in advance to the mentors of the course, who have to explicitly agree on this. Otherwise, a different mentor should be assigned. Furthermore, mentors will focus not only on the observable factors (e.g., the lecturer's ability to capture student's attention and curiosity) but also on the adopted strategies to involve students with various comprehension skills in the foreign language.

4 The Observation Grid

As mentioned, mentors' observation is guided by an observation grid appropriately designed and prepared for the MENTORE project. Previous studies suggested to consider four main critical reference areas: (a) management, organization, and coherence of the lesson; (b) teaching abilities and competencies; (c) interaction with students; (d) learning environment [see, for example, references Berk (2005), Berk et al. (2004), Fernandez and Yu (2007), Gosling (2002), Trujillo et al. (2008)]. These abstract (high-inference) dimensions were operationalized by using specific (low-inference) corresponding indicators. To create these indicators, an extensive literature search was conducted by two experts in the field. Several articles, selected chapters of books, and other web-based sources of information were selected and reviewed to obtain an initial list of 40 items (10 for each dimension). Then, each expert simultaneously met a distinct small group of instructors (eight on average) closely involved with the MENTORE project in several meetings to be provided with feedback on the organization, terminology, clarity, and face validity of the tool. After each meeting, the two experts met each other to discuss the received feedback. Once all the discrepancies were resolved, they proceeded in revising the observation grid by removing, combining, and clarifying items as well as reorganizing the general content.

In this way, the same revised instrument was presented again to each small group. The final version of the observation grid consists of 24 items reflecting the initial reference areas (see Fig. 2). All items can be scored using a 4-point Likert scale with responses ranging from 1 (*Not at all*) to 4 (*Very much*). In addition, space for notes is included in relation to each item. To obtain summary results for each reference area, mentors are suggested to use median or mode rather than the mean of the corresponding item scores as the measure of central tendency, due to the ordinal nature of the data. Furthermore, frequencies or percentages of responses in each area and for each item should be privileged as starting points for discussion between mentors in the analysis stage as well as between mentors and mentee in the action stage.

5 Mentors' Interaction with the Students

The interaction with the students occurs always in the last days of the course and it is always announced in advance to ensure a high number of students in the class and to let them prepare for it. This interaction is a central part of the project as mentors' viewpoint and feedback is different than students' one, and because mentors can verify the meaningfulness and relevance of their observations by comparing that with the feedbacks of the students. The first part of the meeting is focused on the description of the goals of the project. Mentors usually start the interview asking for teacher's strength points moving to weakness or improvement area in a second moment.

Sometimes students are shy and trust their lecturers more than the external mentors, so that they often claim that teachers involved in MENTORE project are "the good ones." This is a critical element to overcome which is useful to point out first the strengths and to explain that the mentees are firmly committed to identifying the improvement areas.

At the end of the meeting, students are invited to fill out an anonymous survey, to give the possibility to each student, even the shyest, to express their opinions anonymously, and to collect data that can be analyzed with statistical tools. The survey contains both open-ended and multiple-choice questions on many points,

The Peer Observation: "Mentore" Project at University of Palermo

MENTORE Project

- Teaching Observation Grid -

Teaching of: _____

Professor: _____

Lesson time schedule: _____

Number of students: _____

Classroom type: ☐ Ordinary classroom ☐ Amphitheatre ☐ Auditorium ☐ Lecture hall

Reference area	Tick one number *from a minimum of 1 to a maximum of 4*				*Report any personal comments*
	Not at all	Just a little	Pretty much	Very much	
Management, organization, and coherence of the lesson					
1. Punctuality entry	1	2	3	4	
2. Classification of the lesson in the program of the course (she/he proposes, at the beginning of the lesson, an overview of the activities and match with the last lesson made)	1	2	3	4	
3. Definition of outline / lesson's objectives	1	2	3	4	
4. Good articulation of the lesson	1	2	3	4	
5. Adequacy of useful information provided during the lesson	1	2	3	4	
6. Skilful use of available resources (storytelling, blackboard, presentations and others)	1	2	3	4	
7. Use of a final summary to fix the focal points of the lesson	1	2	3	4	
8. Outgoing punctuality	1	2	3	4	
Teaching abilities and competencies					
9. Explanatory clarity of the covered topics	1	2	3	4	
10. Communicative efficacy (for example, use of rhythm and pauses, diction, etc.)	1	2	3	4	
11. Tendency to stay focused	1	2	3	4	
12. Presence of enthusiasm and passion for what is teaching	1	2	3	4	
13. Ability to capture students' attention and curiosity	1	2	3	4	
14. Ability to stimulate students' critical thinking	1	2	3	4	
15. Clear and direct answers to the questions	1	2	3	4	
Interaction with students					
16. Inter-action with most of the class group	1	2	3	4	
17. Movement across the class and approach to the students	1	2	3	4	
18. Active involvement of students during the phases of the lesson	1	2	3	4	
19. Assessment of students' level of understanding	1	2	3	4	
20. Suitable space for students' questions	1	2	3	4	
Learning environment					
21. Presentation of examples and applications	1	2	3	4	
22. Presentation of summaries that support understanding (both verbally and written, for example in terms of educational material, graphics, slides, etc.)	1	2	3	4	
23. Short breaks to facilitate students' attention	1	2	3	4	
24. Use of a variety of teaching strategies to encourage learning	1	2	3	4	

Fig. 2 Observation grid used in the *MENTORE project*

including the organization of the course and of the lessons, the effectiveness of the teacher, and the interaction with the students.

Solicitation of students' feedback and dedicated time to it provides complementary results to the survey filled by students. The interaction with observers allows them to discuss the course and the teacher more than can be done with standardized questions, allowing the students to discuss topics not included in the survey; moreover, the mentors are strongly invited to accept and promote every student's suggestion.

6 The Final Meeting of Mentors and Mentee: Analysis and Decisions

After the observation in the class and the interaction with the students, the two mentors meet to share their observations and points of view, to discuss the comments of the students, and to analyze the results of the survey. The discussion between the two mentors represents a critical moment to share observations and experiences since they often belong to different cultural areas and they can focus on various and different aspects. The primary goal of the meeting is to reach a shared conclusion on the following points: (a) main strengths of the mentee teaching, (b) main improvement areas, and (c) main suggestions to give to the mentee.

The last phase of the process is one of the more relevant: the meeting between the mentee and the two mentors. The meeting takes place in a friendly and constructive atmosphere, often in the mentee's office or at the university canteen. Mentors give indications and advice in a friendly way avoiding any judgment or evaluation. The meeting is an important occasion for the mentee to share his or her point of view and doubts on his or her way of teaching. The mentee discusses with mentors also the actions that have been carried out in the past to improve his or her teaching and ideas on potential steps that could be carried out. Mentors are expected to describe the results of their observations and the opinion of the students. In particular, they represent the main strengths (since the mentee must be aware of them to be more effective) and the main improvement areas of the mentee's teaching.

The meeting is concluded with a shared definition of the actions that the mentee has to carry out in the future. Since it is tough to carry on too many changes in 1 year, usually mentors and mentee identify also a set of main actions that the mentee will try to adopt the next year.

After the meeting, the mentors prepare a "summary sheet" that resumes the main points discussed during the meeting. An example of part of this sheet is given in Fig. 3 for one teacher belonging to the humanities area.

The next year at least one of the two mentors will not change to ensure continuity in the observation, and the mentors will also evaluate the actions carried out by the mentee to improve his or her course as defined in the "summary sheet." As an example, Fig. 4 reports the second-year summary sheet of the case reported in Fig. 3. There is evidence that the teacher carried out with success various actions planned at the end of the first year and also that in the second-year mentors give some new indications, as for example:

The Peer Observation: "Mentore" Project at University of Palermo

---

Summary sheet

Academic year 2017/2018
Number of students in the class: 30-35
Cultural area: Humanistic.

Strength areas
The teacher for some topics is able to explain in a clear way.
The teacher is available, in time and communicate every novelty in an effective way.
The teacher well describes and comments the sources.

Improvement areas
For other topics, the explanation is less clear and it is not clear what are the most relevant points and the less relevant ones.
The objectives of the lesson and the relationship with the previous lesson and with the rest of the course could be better highlighted.
It would be possible to better define the main points of the lesson (as an example using the blackboard or some slides).
During the lesson, the explanation can he helped using more examples to clarify the concepts.
The interaction of the students is very small. Students do not make questions and the teacher does not interact with them. The interaction can be strongly improved by making questions, guiding the students to think and discuss the main points, etc.

Actions to carry out the next year
For each lesson, prepare a synthetic list of the main points to be explained and few interesting examples to better clarify the concepts.
To work on the interaction according to the indications received on the workshop performed in September 2018. The interaction can be strongly improved by making questions, guiding the students to critical think and discuss the main points, etc.
To better highlight the objectives of the lesson and the relationship with the previous lesson and with the rest of the course.

Fig. 3 Example of summary sheet

7 The MENTORE Control Loop in Academic Teaching

Academic teaching is a sequence of cognitive activities that can be measured and controlled for obtaining defined levels of quality in terms of learning achievements. Modeling controlled process commonly applies in several engineering fields and is also useful to describe the teaching and learning processes. In academic teaching, control actions can be used through (1) open-loop control mechanisms (without feedback), where the lecturer teaches and students passively receive information, and through (2) closed-loop control mechanisms, where the instructor gets feedback given by midterm exams and course evaluation forms, as described in Arbos and Ponsa (2011).

In such a vision, the controller monitors the process and generates a control action to bring it to the desired value. A model that implements these general concepts within the framework of the MENTORE proposal is reported in Fig. 5, where the

---

Summary sheet

Academic year 2018/2019
Number of students in the class: 30-35
Cultural area: Humanistic.

Strength areas
The teacher is able to explain in a clear way in most of cases.
The teacher is available, in time and communicate every novelty in an effective way.
The teacher well describes and comment the sources.
Interaction rich and appreciated. The teacher stimulates very fruitful and interesting discussions.
The teacher well describes the objectives of the lesson and well relates it with the previous ones.

Actions planned the previous year.
"To work on the interaction according to the indications received on the workshop performed in September 2018. The interaction can be strongly improved by making questions, guiding the students to critical think and discuss the main points, etc." A very good work was carried out. The next year the interactions could be still improved.
"To better highlight the objectives of the lesson and the relationship with the previous lesson and with the rest of the course." A very good work was carried out.
"For each lesson, prepare a synthetic list of the main points to be explained and few interesting examples to better clarify the concepts." It would be possible to continue to work on this point.

Improvement areas
Continue to work on the interaction by governing better it. It is relevant to give space to discussions and to questions, but without confusing students. It is important to govern the interaction; the students have to understand clearly the main points of the lesson and the different points of view. The teacher after the discussion can summarize it in order to make the main points more clear for the students.
It would be possible to better define the main points of the lesson (as an example using the blackboard or some slides).

Actions to carry out the next year
Continue to work on the interaction by governing better it.
Highlight the main points of the lesson (as an example using the blackboard or some slides).

Fig. 4 Example 2 of the summary sheet

learning process is depicted with a closed control loop that includes peer observation and the interaction with the students.

The four phases for mentors' activities, previously described in the paragraph Goals, Role, and Activities of Mentors, appear in Fig. 5. First, mentors observe the teaching actions, stimulate feedback from students, analyze data, and achieve consensus on their decisions; then they report their input and provide directions to the instructor. Finally, mentors edit a final report for statistical purposes.

All these phases are organized in a closed-loop mechanism to control the teaching and learning process. Actors and actions that are specific of the MENTORE program are reported in bold to distinguish them from standard teaching actions. The instructor acts as a controller that receives the learning objectives of the course in inputs and executes teaching actions upon students. Students provide both the results,

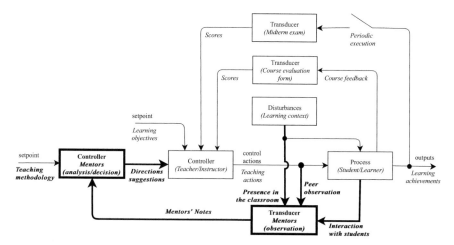

Fig. 5 Closed-loop instructional control system with peer observation of the MENTORE project

the learning achievements, and some feedbacks, i.e., the course evaluation forms and the results of the exams. These feedbacks are the only one for the teachers in courses that are not peer-reviewed, while MENTORE provides an extra interaction between mentors and students and then provide inputs to the instructor through suggestions on teaching methodology taking into account the observed teaching context. The goal of the MENTORE project is the teaching methodology, which is modeled as a set point. The MENTORE project proposes a teaching and learning process reported with the dual closed-loop control of Fig. 5. The extra control loop introduced by the MENTORE project has a different effect than the feedback given by students through the scores at midterm exams and their course evaluation forms. In fact, on the one hand, mentors' observation permits to understand better the biased feedback provided by students when filling the course evaluation form.

On the other hand, mentors are not interested in the teaching contents. Therefore, they do not analyze the learning achievements obtained by students and focus only on the used teaching methodology. The figure also shows that mentors take into account (jointly) the passive peer observations, the active interaction with students, and the disturbances coming from external factors (i.e., the learning context), having a privileged and holistic view of the whole process.

8 Conclusions

This chapter presents the characteristics of the MENTORE project, especially from the point of view of mentors. The phases that characterize the mentorship process, the tools used, and the reference system within which all the action is moving have been described. Although the project is at an advanced stage of its initial phase, a systematic collection of data on its effectiveness has been planned in the near future. However, the growing number of faculty who express their willingness to participate in the project can represent a first indication of the practical impact of the MENTORE project, which already promoted changes in the organizational and management models and teaching methods of the courses held at the University of Palermo. In addition, the results of an anonymous survey highlight that teachers involved in the project and their students consider the project very useful to improve the quality of the teaching. In particular, academics consider very useful in order to improve their teaching both the help of their mentors and their activity as mentors.

Acknowledgments All the participants (see https://www.unipa.it/progetti/progetto-mentore/) to the MENTORE project are gratefully acknowledged for their enthusiastic contribution to the development of the project.

References

Arbos, R. V., & Ponsa, P. (2011). Positive effect of increasing feedback for student self-adjustment of learning habits. *Journal of Technology and Science Education, 1*, 38–48.

Berk, R. (2005). A survey of 12 strategies to measure teaching effectiveness. *International Journal of Teaching and Learning in Higher Education, 17*, 48–62.

Berk, R. A., Naumann, P. L., & Appling, S. E. (2004). Beyond student ratings: Peer observation of classroom and clinical teaching. *International Journal of Nursing Education Scholarship, 1*(1), 1–26.

Centre for Teaching Support & Innovation. (2017). *Peer observation of teaching: Effective practices*. Toronto, ON: Centre for Teaching Support & Innovation, University of Toronto.

Felisatti, E., Cannarozzo, M., Pennisi, S., & Scialdone, O. (2020). Manuscript in preparation.

Fernandez, C. E., & Yu, J. (2007). Peer review of teaching. *Journal of Chiropractic Education, 21*, 154–161.

Gosling, D. (2002). Models of peer observation of teaching. *Generic Centre: Learning and Teaching Support Network. Retrieved, 8*, 08.

Lomas, L., & Kinchin, I. (2006). Developing a peer observation program with university teachers. *International Journal of Teaching and Learning in Higher Education, 18*, 204–214.

Martinez, F., Taut, S., & Schaaf, K. (2016). Classroom observation for evaluating and improving teaching: An international perspective. *Studies in Educational Evaluation, 49*, 15–29.

Trujillo, J. M., DiVall, M. V., Barr, J., Gonyeau, M., Van Amburgh, J. A., Matthews, S. J., & Qualters, D. (2008). Development of a peer teaching-assessment program and a peer observation and evaluation tool. *American Journal of Pharmaceutical Education, 72*, 147.

Printed in the United States
By Bookmasters